GOVERNMENT OFFICE
FOR THE NORTH WEST

# The North West of England Plan
# Regional Spatial Strategy to 2021

An accompanying
CD is enclosed
inside this book

Com
and

London: TSO

September 2008

Published by TSO (The Stationery Office) and available from:

**Online**
www.tsoshop.co.uk

**Mail, Telephone, Fax & E-mail**
TSO
PO Box 29, Norwich NR3 1GN
Telephone orders/General enquiries: 0870 600 5522
Fax orders: 0870 600 5533
E-mail: customer.services@tso.co.uk
Textphone 0870 240 3701

**TSO Shops**
16 Arthur Street, Belfast BT1 4GD
028 9023 8451 Fax 028 9023 5401
71 Lothian Road, Edinburgh EH3 9AZ
0870 606 5566 Fax 0870 606 5588

**TSO @ Blackwall and other Accredited Agents**

Communities and Local Government, Eland House, Bressenden Place, London SW1E 5DU
Telephone 020 7944 4400
Web site www.communities.gov.uk

Any queries relating to the content of this document should be referred to the Government Office for the North West or the Regional Planning Body at the following address:
Government Office for North West, City Tower, Piccadilly Plaza, Manchester M1 4BE.

ISBN 978 0 11 754000 2

Printed in Great Britain on material containing 75% post-consumer waste and 25% ECF pulp
N5920414 C10 09/08

# Introduction

# Chapters

# Appendices

# Index of Policies

# Contents

Our Vision for the North West by 2021...

## Our Vision for the North West by 2021...

By 2021 we will see a region that has acted to deliver sustainable development, leading to a higher quality of life for all, and reduced social, economic and environmental disparities. Development will be seen in a global context, and the region will contribute to the reduction of carbon dioxide and other greenhouse gas emissions.

By 2021 we aim to see Manchester and Liverpool firmly established as world class cities thanks to their international connections, highly developed service and knowledge sectors and flourishing culture, sport and leisure industries. The growth and development of the Central Lancashire City Region as a focus for economic growth will continue, building on the existing individual strengths of the urban centres around commerce, higher education, advanced manufacturing and resort tourism. The economy of Cumbria will be improved. The region's towns and cities will offer strong and distinctive centres for their hinterlands, with attractive, high quality living environments that meet the needs of their inhabitants. Our rural communities will enjoy increased prosperity and quality of life, whilst respecting the character of their surroundings and natural environment.

The Implementation Framework that accompanies this Regional Spatial Strategy establishes a set of indicators and targets to monitor performance against this vision, the objectives set out at the start of subsequent chapters, and the overarching spatial framework. Together these comprise the high level outcomes that this strategy seeks to achieve.

# 1 The Role and Purpose of RSS

**1.1** The Regional Spatial Strategy (RSS) for North West England provides a framework for development and investment in the region over the next fifteen to twenty years. It establishes a broad vision for the region and its sub-regions, priorities for growth and regeneration, and policies to achieve sustainable development across a wide range of topics – from jobs, housing and transport to climate change, waste and energy.

**1.2** RSS complements but does not repeat national policy as expressed, for example, in Planning Policy Statements (PPSs) circulars and White Papers. It brings an understanding of the North West region to target the delivery of such policy and address specific challenges and opportunities. The spatial dimension is very valuable in this respect, providing focus for developing, integrating and articulating policy in a way that acknowledges functional linkages and disparities.

**1.3** The RSS is required by the Planning and Compulsory Purchase Act 2004, and matters of process and content are prescribed in PPS11 [1]. It incorporates regional transport policies (RTS) which have both informed, and been informed by, the Spatial Principles, Regional and Sub-regional Spatial Frameworks and Policies of RSS. The regional transport policies aim to achieve the same shared vision of sustainable development and include the region's priorities for transport investment and management.

**1.4** This RSS replaces all of the saved structure plan policies of the Joint Lancashire Structure Plan (2005) which were extended under transitional provisions of schedule 8 of the Planning and Compulsory Purchase Act 2004. This RSS also replaces the policies of the Cheshire Structure Plan (2005) and the Cumbria and Lake District Joint Structure Plan (2006) with the exception of those outlined as extended for a further period until replaced by future RSS review as set out in Chapter 15.

**1.5** RSS is part of the statutory development plan for every local authority in the North West. Local Development Documents (LDDs), which are prepared by Local Planning Authorities, must be in general conformity with the RSS. Planning applications will be considered against the provisions of RSS and relevant Local Development Documents. However, RSS policies are not restricted to implementation through the grant or refusal of planning permission and a wide range of stakeholders in the public, private and voluntary sectors, many of them new to this process, will need to be engaged to deliver the strategy effectively.

**1.6** The "plans and strategies" referred to in this document include statutory Local Development Documents (LDDs) and other elements of the Local Development Framework (LDF); Local Transport Plans (LTPs); Community Strategies; local housing and economic strategies; and also various strategies and programmes produced by government departments, agencies and partnerships; the utility companies and transport providers; other private businesses and voluntary organisations. The "proposals and schemes" mentioned include, but are not limited to, development proposals subject to planning applications and other consents, infrastructure projects and environmental management schemes.

**1.7** RSS must be read as a whole. Cross referencing has been kept to a minimum and duplication avoided as far as possible. It is, therefore, important that policies across the whole RSS are read together when considering implementation - whether via land use planning

---

1    Planning Policy Statement 11: Regional Spatial Strategies, ODPM, 2004.

mechanisms or other tools. For example, policies DP1 to DP9 cut across the themes of the "living", "working", "transport, and "environment, minerals, waste and energy" and contain advice relevant to decision making in all these topic areas. The sub-regional policies amplify, and should be read together with, the broad regional priorities for growth and development in Chapter 5, notably RDF1.

1.8    Policies are highlighted in shaded boxes to distinguish them from supporting text which explains and justifies them. A Key Diagram and one for each of the sub-regions, illustrate the policies and draw out key themes.

1.9    A separate Implementation Framework is being prepared by the Regional Planning Body to provide more detail on methods for the delivery of RSS, the agencies that will carry it out, targets to be met and arrangements for monitoring progress. As a separate document this will enable it to be more readily updated and to provide a rolling programme of actions. The Regional Planning Body will prepare an Annual Monitoring Report to report progress on implementation and any issues arising.

1.10    The RSS for North West England is published by the Secretary of State for Communities and Local Government (CLG). The draft version [2] was prepared by North West Regional Assembly (NWRA), acting as the designated Regional Planning Body (RPB). The draft has been amended in response to a formal consultation process held between March and June 2006, and the Report of the independent Panel [3] that held an Examination in Public (EiP) between October 2006 and February 2007. The Final RSS replaces all earlier versions, including Regional Planning Guidance for the North West (RPG13) [4], which became the RSS on commencement of the Planning and Compulsory Purchase Act  2004.

1.11    Preparation of the RSS has been informed by Sustainability Appraisal incorporating Strategic Environmental Assessment at both Draft [5] and Proposed Changes [6] stages. A Habitats Regulations Assessment [7]. has also been carried out in line with the UK Conservation Regulations which give effect to the European Commission's Habitats Directive.

---

2    The North West Plan Submitted Draft Regional Spatial Strategy for the North West of England, NWRA, 2006.
3    North West Draft  Regional Spatial Strategy  Examination in Public October 2006 – February 2007 Report of the Panel, 2007.
4    RPG 13 Regional Planning Guidance for the North West, GONW, ODPM, 2003.
5    The North West Plan Submitted Draft Regional Spatial Strategy for the North West of England, NWRA, 2006.
6    Secretary of State's Proposed Changes to the North West of England's Submitted Draft Regional Spatial Strategy (RSS), 2008.
7    Habitats Regulations Assessment is required under Articles 6(3) and 6(4) of Directive 92/43/EEC on the Conservation of Natural Habitats and of Wild Fauna and Flora (known as the 'Habitats Directive')

# 2 Our Region

**2.1**    North West England comprises the counties of Cumbria, Lancashire and Cheshire; the metropolitan districts in Greater Manchester and Merseyside; the unitary authorities of Blackburn-with-Darwen, Blackpool, Halton and Warrington. This strategy covers all of these places. It covers the whole of the Lake District National Park but not those parts of the Yorkshire Dales and Peak District National Parks that fall within the North West Region. These are dealt with in the RSSs for Yorkshire and the Humber and the East Midlands, respectively, and these documents should be taken into account by the relevant planning and transport authorities in the North West.

**2.2**    A region of stark contrasts and striking landscapes, the North West is the scene of economic growth and urban renaissance to rival any in Europe. From the outstanding natural beauty of the Lake District, England's premier National Park, to the bustling, modern contemporary European City Region conurbations of Manchester and Liverpool, European Capital of Culture in 2008; from its extensive coastline and popular resorts like Blackpool and Southport, to great historic towns and cities such as Carlisle, Lancaster and Chester; with World Heritage Sites as wide ranging as Liverpool City Centre and Hadrian's Wall, and superb landscapes including many Areas of Outstanding Natural Beauty, the region is distinctive and diverse.

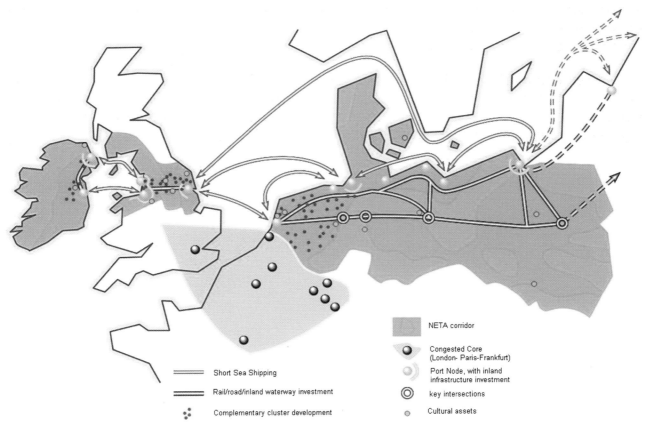

| | NETA corridor |
| | Congested Core (London- Paris-Frankfurt) |
| Short Sea Shipping | Port Node, with inland infrastructure investment |
| Rail/road/inland waterway investment | key intersections |
| Complementary cluster development | Cultural assets |

**Diagram 2.1 – North European Trade Axis (NETA) Corridor**

**2.3**    It is this diversity, along with its sheer scale that is the North West's defining characteristic. It is home to 6.8 million people - that's more than several European countries – and is the largest English region outside London and the South East.

# 2 Our Region

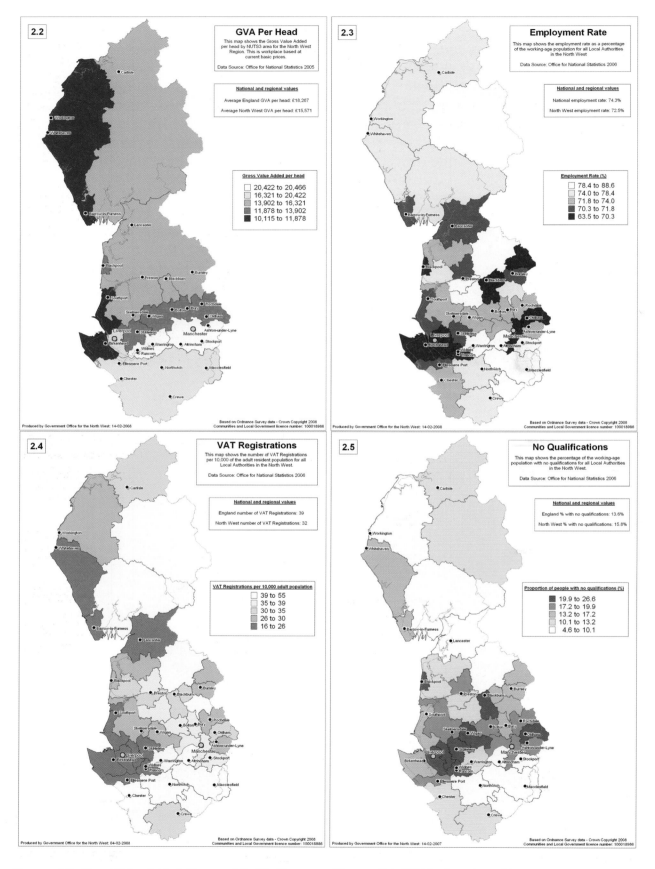

**Diagram 2.2 - Gross Value Added; Diagram 2.3 - Worklessness; Diagram 2.4 - VAT Registrations; Diagram 2.5 - Qualifications**

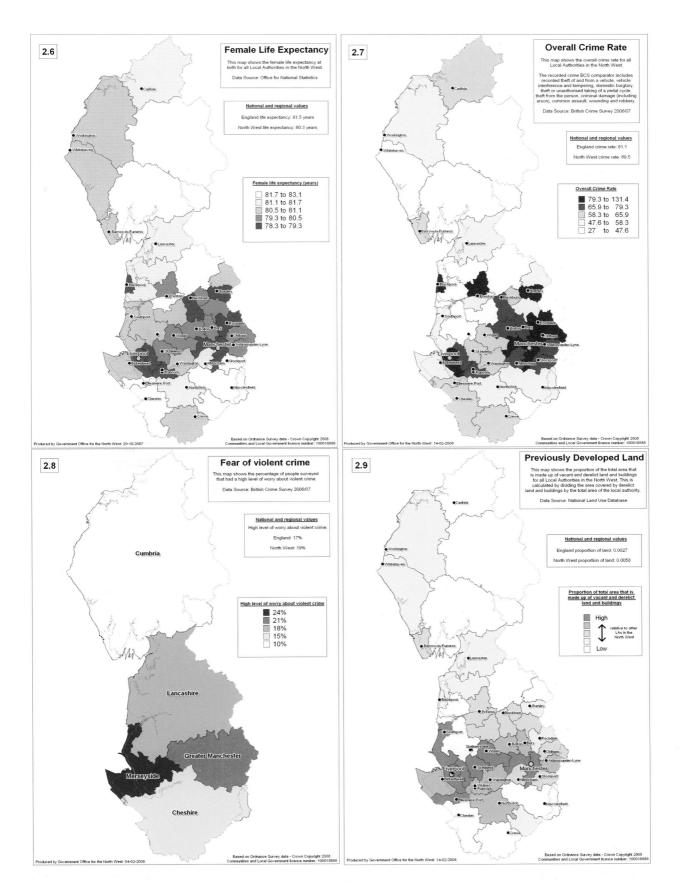

Diagram 2.6 - Life Expectancy; Diagram 2.7 - Crime; Diagram 2.8 - Fear of Crime; Diagram 2.9 - Derelict Land and Buildings

**2.4**    The North West lies at the intersection of two internationally important transport corridors running North-South (the M6 and West Coast Mainline link Scotland to Europe via the Channel Tunnel and ports in the East and South East) and West-East (from Ireland, through Liverpool and other Irish Sea ports across the Pennines to Europe via the North Sea and Baltic Sea ports in a route that has become known as the North European Trade Axis (NETA) and can be seen on Diagram 2.1).

**2.5**    The North West is a hub of learning, research and development, including 15 Universities. Its traditional manufacturing base may have declined, but the region still contains world-leading industries such as aerospace. An excellent transport network provides for the movement of people and goods within the North West and with other UK regions and, thanks to Manchester Airport and the historic port of Liverpool, links to the rest of the world to match any in the UK.

**2.6**    Despite these and other considerable assets, the North West is not without its challenges. The following maps highlight some of the spatial variations and disparities within the region.

**The economy**

**2.7**    During the 1980s and 1990s the North West economy went through a major period of restructuring and underperformance. Since 2000 the region's performance has improved, but it is still not contributing its full potential to the UK economy. The Regional Economic Strategy highlights the fact that Gross Value Added (GVA) per head is 12% lower than the England average, resulting in an output gap of £13 billion. £3billion of this is due to fewer people of working age and fewer people working than the England average, £10 billion is due to lower productivity. There are significant variations in GVA, skills, enterprise and worklessness across the region, as Diagrams 2.2 – 2.9 demonstrate.

**2.8**    The economic focus must now be on creating a more competitive region and developing the economic sectors with the highest growth potential. North West industry must be able to compete with its international rivals and this demands a first rate infrastructure, a highly skilled and adaptable workforce, and the best possible links to other parts of the UK, the rest of Europe and the world.

**2.9**    The Regional Funding Allocations (RFA) [8] advice of the North West region to Government suggests there are three main brakes on the region's ability to fulfil its economic and social development potential – weaknesses in the housing market; the effectiveness of key transport infrastructure; and high levels of worklessness together with concentrations of low productivity and enterprise levels. The RSS for the North West seeks to address these issues in a sustainable way.

**2.10**    To be sustainable future economic growth must support urban renaissance and greater levels of social inclusion. It must respect the environment. Increasingly sustainable economic growth will need to be decoupled from resource use, which indicates the need for different and more sustainable patterns of economic activity and movement.

---

8    HM Treasury Indicative allocations intended to enable regions to better align their strategies and provide an enhanced input into Government policy development and public spending decisions that affect the regions.

## Transport

**2.11** Substantial investment over the last 50 years, particularly in highway construction, has created a high quality network of transport links across much of the North West and with other regions. Following completion of the West Coast Main Line upgrade and the fleet replacement programme currently being progressed by First TransPennine Express, much of the region is now benefiting from significantly improved rail services to the rest of Great Britain. However, the quality of many local services and infrastructure leaves much to be desired, and congestion on some rail routes, both in terms of the number of trains and passengers, is now a serious concern. On parts of the motorway network, worsening journey time reliability is a major problem, particularly for business and industry, and in urban areas, congestion is reducing the reliability of road-based public transport. Elsewhere, the main issues relate to road safety and the environmental and social impact of traffic in towns, villages and the wider countryside.

## Social Inclusion

**2.12** Issues of deprivation, worklessness and social exclusion are concentrated in disadvantaged areas in and around the cores of Liverpool and Manchester, in the inner parts of other older industrialised towns, and in some of our coastal towns. They are frequently closely associated with health inequalities, crime and fear of crime, as Diagrams 2.2 – 2.9 demonstrate.

**2.13** These areas also contain most of the region's disused land and buildings (see Diagram 2.9) - a valuable resource that, if managed properly, can be reused to achieve an improved environment and more sustainable patterns of development, higher levels of economic activity, access to local facilities (including health and education) and better quality housing. All of these issues are also increasingly affecting our rural areas, especially the least settled parts. The restructuring of agriculture highlights the need for diversification, and in the more prosperous rural areas housing affordability is a growing problem, as it is in some of our urban areas.

**2.14** The population of the region is now rising – a positive outcome of an improving economy – but the population is also ageing, which will change the nature of demands on the region's services, infrastructure and buildings.
There are disadvantaged groups and communities within the region such as older people, black and minority ethnic groups, and remoter rural communities. Specific policy and implementation approaches at the local level may be necessary to ensure that disadvantaged and hard to reach groups are engaged in changes and benefit from improvements to the economy and provision of services.

**2.15** Our challenge is to tackle these issues and boost quality of life for North West people as a whole including for hard to reach groups – to create sustainable, cohesive communities that respect and promote equality and diversity. We must marry opportunity and need to make the best use of all the region's resources and talents.

## Environment

**2.16** The highly urbanised nature of large parts of the North West has created a significant 'ecological footprint' [9]. From an environmental point of view, it is important not only to develop the North West as a better place to live, but also to make a more substantial contribution to national and global environmental targets and initiatives. Particularly critical is the need to adapt

---

9     A system of measuring how much land and water a human population needs to produce the resources it consumes and absorb the resulting waste.

## 2 Our Region

to and, as far as possible, reduce, the effects of climate change; including by planning for the efficient use of energy and by developing renewable sources. We must also deal with dereliction; improve air and water quality; manage the fabric of towns and cities and sensitive coastal and rural landscapes; protect wildlife; increase tree cover; and find more sustainable ways of dealing with waste (see maps 2.10-2.11).

### 2.10 - Environmental Assets

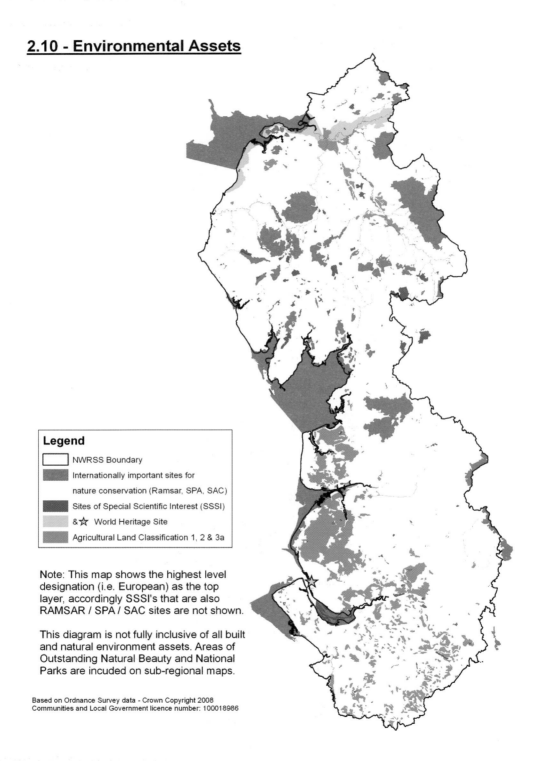

**Legend**

| | |
|---|---|
| ☐ | NWRSS Boundary |
| ■ | Internationally important sites for nature conservation (Ramsar, SPA, SAC) |
| ■ | Sites of Special Scientific Interest (SSSI) |
| ☆ | & ☆ World Heritage Site |
| ■ | Agricultural Land Classification 1, 2 & 3a |

Note: This map shows the highest level designation (i.e. European) as the top layer, accordingly SSSI's that are also RAMSAR / SPA / SAC sites are not shown.

This diagram is not fully inclusive of all built and natural environment assets. Areas of Outstanding Natural Beauty and National Parks are incuded on sub-regional maps.

Based on Ordnance Survey data - Crown Copyright 2008
Communities and Local Government licence number: 100018986

## 2.11 - Flood Risk

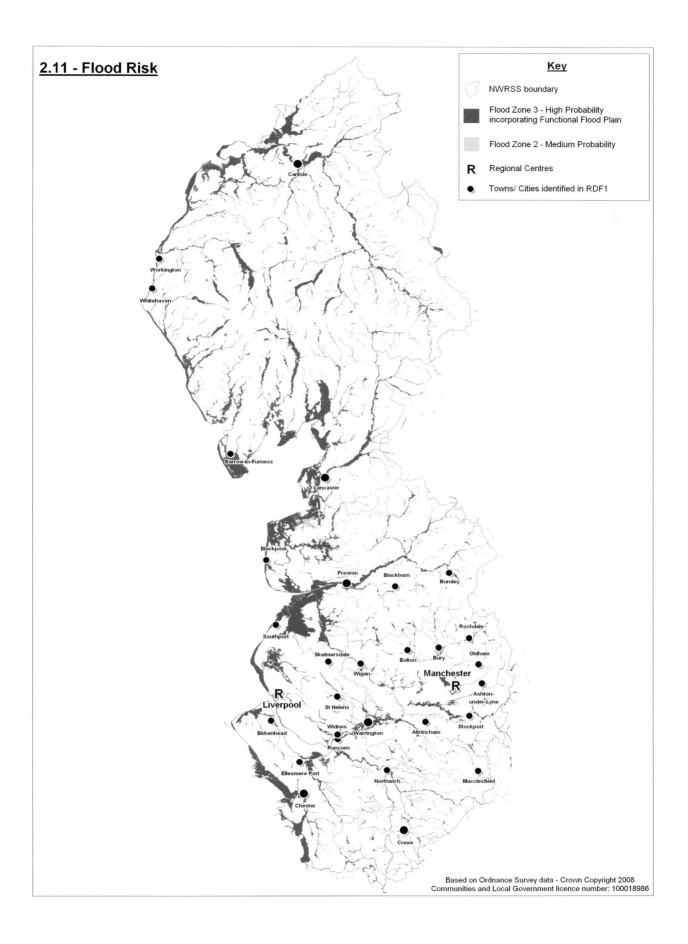

Based on Ordnance Survey data - Crown Copyright 2008
Communities and Local Government licence number: 100018986

## 2 Our Region

### Cities and City Regions

2.17    We must build on the strengths of the region and address the challenges. The cities have a very important role to play in this as drivers of economic growth. Economic theory suggests that economic success and failure are becoming increasingly concentrated – and the role of the cities is increasing – as the twin drivers of globalisation and the knowledge economy interact. They facilitate networking – business and social. Their critical mass enables sustainable transport modes to support this and give access to employment and services. The frequent proximity of opportunity (in the form of job growth and training) and need (manifest as high levels of worklessness) offers the chance to tackle deep seated problems of disadvantage.

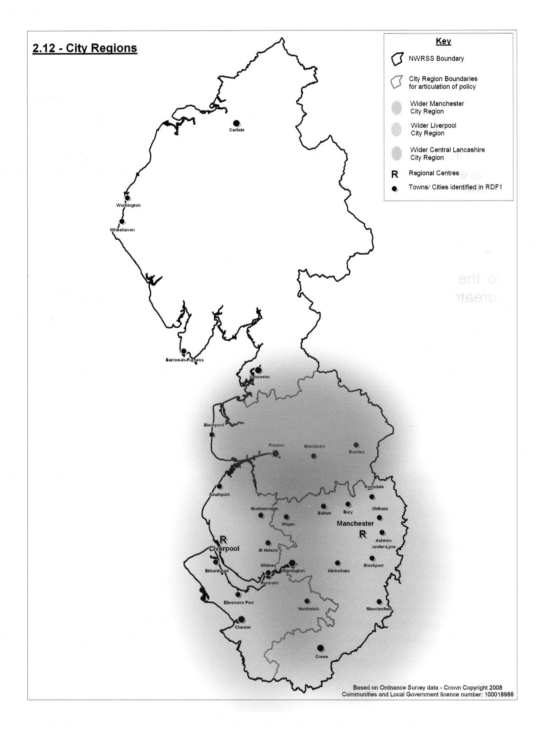

2.12 - City Regions

**Key**

NWRSS Boundary

City Region Boundaries for articulation of policy

Wider Manchester City Region

Wider Liverpool City Region

Wider Central Lancashire City Region

R    Regional Centres

Towns/ Cities identified in RDF1

Based on Ordnance Survey data - Crown Copyright 2008
Communities and Local Government licence number: 100018986

2.18    City regions are the economic footprint of a city – the area over which key economic markets, such as labour markets measured by travel-to-work areas, housing markets, and retail markets operate. The Northern Way Growth Strategy [10] formalised academic thinking on the city region concept, translating it into practical delivery. It identified eight city regions in the North of England, including those of Manchester, Liverpool and the polycentric city region of Central Lancashire. Their broad overlapping areas of influence, with their "fuzzy" boundaries, are shown in the City Regions Diagram 2.12.  Analysing the functional linkages within and between them, with other parts of the region, and with city regions in other English regions, will help us to understand the dynamics of policy and the requirements of critical infrastructure such as transport, water supply and energy. We need to look beyond administrative boundaries to do this. We also need to look beyond regional boundaries to consider, for example, the close relationships between West Cheshire and North Wales; and between Manchester and Leeds.

## Sub-regions

2.19    However, for the articulation and implementation of RSS policy we need to be more place-specific, and in this we need to be mindful of administrative boundaries. For this reason we have identified a set of discrete sub-regions shown in the sub-regional diagrams accompanied by specific sub-regional policies.  Although some places, such as Warrington, Vale Royal and West Lancashire are subject to influences from more than one city region, sub-regional policy for them is articulated in a single section. The paragraphs below summarise key features of each sub-region and our rural and coastal areas.

## Manchester City Region

2.20    Home to the North West's largest sub regional economy, Manchester City Region represents the greatest potential for boosting economic performance in both the North West and North of England as a whole, and for closing the gap that exists with regions in southern England. While it boasts world-class assets like the vibrant city centre and Manchester Airport, and many prosperous areas within its southern part, it is also the scene of marked social and economic inequality and faces the challenge of regenerating communities within its inner areas and northern parts.

## South Cheshire

2.21    In South Cheshire, Crewe acts as a key gateway to the North West. Its economic and transport links feed the city regions, and selective regeneration and development would support this role. A future review of RSS will need to consider Crewe's relationship to the North Staffordshire conurbation in the West Midlands.

## Liverpool City Region

2.22    The focus for increased economic prosperity within the Liverpool City Region will be in the Regional Centre where the opportunity exists to maximise retail and cultural opportunities – including its status as European Capital of Culture 2008 – while further regeneration is carried out. However, a balanced approach to spatial development matches accessible jobs and other facilities to local needs and this is unlikely to be achieved without significant levels of economic

---

10    The Northern Way is a unique collaboration between the three Northern Regional Development Agencies: Yorkshire Forward, Northwest Regional Development Agency and One NorthEast. This is a 20 year strategy to transform the economy of the North of England. Success will be determined by the bridging of a £30 billion output gap between the North and the average for England.

## 2 Our Region

development and allied regeneration in other parts of the city region, building on the opportunities provided not just by the Regional Centre, but also by the Mersey Ports and the Airport (in line with RT5 and 6).

2.23    Liverpool City Region includes West Cheshire and Vale Royal where the historic city of Chester is a world-class tourist asset with a prosperous, compact retail and business centre, and the town of Ellesmere Port which has a strong manufacturing base with scope for expansion. Both have close links with North Wales with real opportunities for establishing more sustainable patterns of cross-border development and movement.

### Central Lancashire City Region

2.24    The Central Lancashire City Region has a rather different profile to the major conurbations of Manchester and Liverpool. Here the City of Preston and the towns of Blackpool, Blackburn and Burnley present the greatest potential for delivering sustainable economic growth, building on the existing individual strengths of these urban centres around commerce, higher education, advanced manufacturing and resort tourism. The City Region's regeneration requirements, and its looser, multi-centred geography, provide the need and opportunity respectively for a future approach to development that emphasises green infrastructure (multi-purpose open space networks).

### Cumbria and North Lancashire

2.25    To the north of the city regions lies a particularly extensive and distinctive part of the region, encompassing the county of Cumbria, the major cities of Lancaster and Carlisle and their surrounding areas, the town of Barrow-in-Furness and the Lake District National Park. Here in Cumbria and North Lancashire, the numbers of people leaving the area exacerbate problems of economic decline and structural weakness; local communities are unbalanced and regeneration becomes more difficult to achieve. Over recent years Cumbria has experienced the slowest growth rate of all UK sub-regions.

2.26    West Cumbria and Furness both face major industrial restructuring, with large-scale nuclear decommissioning and the decline of employment in shipbuilding. These communities are relatively isolated and in need of improved communications with the rest of Cumbria and the North West.  On the positive side, outstanding natural and cultural assets, like the Lake District National Park and the historic cities of Carlisle and Lancaster, offer a potential for sustainable growth that benefits both this sub-region and the wider North West.

2.27    The functional relationships between the Lake District National Park and adjoining areas in Cumbria provide sound opportunities for development in areas outside the National Park boundary – for example, in Cockermouth, Kendal, Penrith and Ulverston – that benefits not only local communities, but also those within the National Park itself.  While the overriding concern is to protect its valuable landscapes, the National Park must also meet its own, locally generated needs.

### Rural and coastal areas

2.28    The North West's glorious countryside is both an environmental and economic asset in its own right. Tourism and agriculture remain important to many rural areas and economic diversification of rural areas must continue to be encouraged. Housing affordability issues must be tackled. Key service centres, which will range in size from large villages with a few thousand inhabitants to bustling market towns, offer focal points for development that serve the needs of smaller villages and hamlets. In the least-settled parts of Cumbria and North Lancashire (also referred to as "sparse rural areas") access to housing, jobs, shops and services such as education and health must be addressed.

2.29    Our long coastline is mostly low-lying, with estuaries internationally renowned, and protected, for their bird life. Considerable areas of the coastline particularly estuaries are protected as area of international importance  for nature conservation. For internationally important sites proposals must be assessed under the Habitats Regulations (see Environmental constraints map).The cities, towns, fishing ports and resorts that line it face their own, individual challenges. Some serve mainly local communities and would benefit from improved access; others have potential as freight or passenger gateways into the North West; and resorts need to respond to changing leisure patterns. Because of their coastal location, however, all must deal with the implications of climate change and ensure that plans for growth and development take account of their vulnerable environments.

3 Policy Context

# 3 Policy Context

## Sustainable Development

3.1    A key test of how successful RSS – and the North West itself – is in achieving its ambitions will be the extent to which spatial development in the region adopts the principles of sustainable development.  These are set out, in the UK Sustainable Development Strategy [11], as being to achieve the twin goals of living within environmental limits, and ensuring a strong, healthy and just society, by means of achieving a sustainable economy, promoting good governance, and using sound science responsibly. Four shared priorities for UK action flow from this:

- sustainable production and consumption;
- climate change and energy;
- natural resource protection and environmental enhancement; and
- sustainable communities.

3.2    These are reflected and developed in the ten regional priorities set out in "Action for Sustainability" [12], the region's sustainable development framework, revised in 2004 and supported by an Integrated Appraisal Toolkit [13].

## Aligning Key Strategies in the North West

3.3    A number of strategies exist to guide development in the North West, the most important of which are the Regional Economic Strategy (RES) [14], Regional Housing Strategy (RHS) [15] and RSS itself.  All deal with different, but related, aspects of public policy and must therefore complement each other.  They also now serve the crucial purpose of advising government ministers on the degree of funding necessary to secure appropriate economic, housing and transport development.

3.4    In 2004/2005, the three key regional bodies – The North West Regional Assembly (NWRA), Government Office North West (GONW) and North West Regional Development Agency (NWDA) – worked together to find a ways of aligning these three strategies, including:  the joint commissioning of research; shared representation on working and steering groups; and the use of shared evidence on economic scenarios, housing markets, transport priorities and other relevant issues.  Preparation of RSS has taken the content of its fellow strategies into full account .

## Regional Economic Strategy

3.5    The RES provides a regional framework for economic development, skills and regeneration in a bid to ensure that activity in the region is more clearly focused. It identifies five priority areas – business; skills and employment; regeneration; infrastructure; and quality of life – sets out key aims and objectives for each, and highlights the activities that the NWDA believes will promote the change necessary to transform the North West economy.

---

11    "Securing the future - delivering UK Sustainable Development Strategy" Defra, March 2005.
12    Action for Sustainability (AfS) is the North West's Regional Sustainable Development Framework and is used to inform sustainability appraisals of regional plans and strategies, NWRA, 2004.
13    The broad aim of the IAT is to highlight the economic, social and environmental impacts of policies, projects, plans and strategies and to provide useful information to support decision making, as well as a flexible approach to assessment, that will help to enhance the delivery of public benefits whilst according with the principles of sustainable development.
14    Regional Economic Strategy 2006, NWDA.
15    Regional Housing Strategy, North West Regional Housing Board, 2005.

## Regional Housing Strategy

3.6    The updated Regional Housing Strategy was submitted to the Government in July 2005. The Regional Housing Board has developed detailed priorities to guide housing investment in the region, based on a better understanding of local markets. These are to deliver urban renaissance, affordable homes that support balanced communities, decent homes in thriving neighbourhoods, and to meet the needs of local communities and provide support for those who require it.

## Other Regional Strategies

3.7    Other strategies which have influenced this document include the Regional Rural Delivery Framework [16], the North West Waste [17] and Sustainable Energy [18] Strategies and the North West Climate Change Action Plan [19]. Also, the Freight Strategy [20], Regional Health Investment Plan [21] North West Tourism Strategy [22] and Vision for Coastal Resorts [23].

## Europe and Spatial Development

3.8    The European Spatial Development Perspective, drawn up at European Commission level, establishes principles for achieving balanced and sustainable development in Europe. This has been developed further by research conducted by the European Spatial Planning Observatory Network (ESPON) [24] and work to develop a spatial framework for North West Europe carried out under the EC's INTERREG IIIB initiative [25]. The importance of Northern English cities pooling their economic power to act as a counterweight to the core of Europe based around London, Paris and Frankfurt is therefore recognised (see Diagram 2.1).

## Sustainable Communities

3.9    Launched by Government in February 2003 "Sustainable Communities: Building for the Future" [26] sets out a long-term action programme for the development of sustainable communities in both urban and rural areas. It aims to tackle issues of housing supply in the South East, low demand in other parts of the country (the North West contains four of the nine English Housing Market Renewal Pathfinders), and the quality of public spaces. It was followed up with a Five Year Plan [27] which has been a key influence on the RSS and is specifically reflected in policy DP2.

## The Northern Way

3.10    In September 2004, Northern England's three RDAs and their partners published the Northern Way Growth Strategy to address the prospect of continuing economic inequality among the regions.  An estimated £29 billion gap in economic output, measured as Gross Value Added

16      Regional Rural Delivery Framework, GONW and partners, 2006.
17      Regional Waste Strategy for the North West, NWRA, 2004.
18      North West Sustainable Energy Strategy, NWRA and partners, 2006.
19      'Rising to the Challenge: A Climate Change Action Plan for England's Northwest', NWDA, 2006.
20      North West Freight Advisory Group, 2003.
21      Investment for Health , A Plan for North West England 2003, Dept for Health and partners.
22      The Strategy for Tourism in England's Northwest 2003 – 2010, NWDA, revised 2007.
23      A New Vision for North West Coastal Resorts, NWDA, 2003.
24      see http://www.espon.org.uk/
25      see http://www.interregiii.org.uk/
26      Sustainable Communities: Building for the Future, ODPM, 2003.
27      Five Year Plan – Sustainable Communities:People, Places and Prosperity, ODPM, 2005.

# 3 Policy Context

(GVA), currently exists between the North and the rest of the UK. The Northern Way raises the question of what the North should do differently in order to significantly accelerate its economic growth rate.

3.11 It aims to exploit the North of England's particular strengths, such as its world class universities, outstanding countryside and coastal areas and its unique heritage. It contains clear messages about what government can and should do to help; complements the three Regional Economic Strategies and Regional Spatial Strategies and defines actions at the most appropriate scale. It focuses principally on eight City Regions that harbour the majority of assets and growth potential, including those in the North West: Manchester, Liverpool and Central Lancashire. However, it also recognises the national significance of assets outside these areas, such as the nuclear industry in West Cumbria, its supply chains and labour markets. It highlights the importance of linkages and connectivity between City Regions, notably Manchester and Leeds. City Region Development Programmes have now been prepared as informal documents by each of the eight – broadly drawn - city regions to support the Growth Strategy, and have informed RSS.

## Other influences

3.12 RSS reflects national policy, for example as set out in Planning Policy Statements [28], and the Ports [29] and Air Transport [30] White Papers. RSS has also been informed by the results of a number of studies commissioned by the NWRA and other bodies, and has been the subject of wide public discussion and consultation, as well as more focused work with government agencies, local authorities, and representatives from the business sector, local communities and environmental groups.

3.13 In line with PPS 11, first detailed proposals for the sub-regional dimension of RSS were drawn up by the region's section 4(4) authorities (i.e. County Councils, Metropolitan District Councils, National Park Authorities, and District Councils for area where there is no County Council), working in partnership. These variously reflected existing statutory plans, the City Region Development Programmes, and emerging non-statutory sub-regional spatial plans. Of particular note, as an example of cross-border co-operation, is the work undertaken for West Cheshire / North East Wales by a partnership involving local authorities, NWRA and the Welsh Assembly Government.

28    PPSs are prepared by Government to explain statutory provisions and provide guidance to local authorities and others on planning policy and the planning system.
29    Ports policy review interim report, DfT, 2007.
30    The Future of Air Transport White Paper, DfT, 2004.

# 4 Spatial Principles

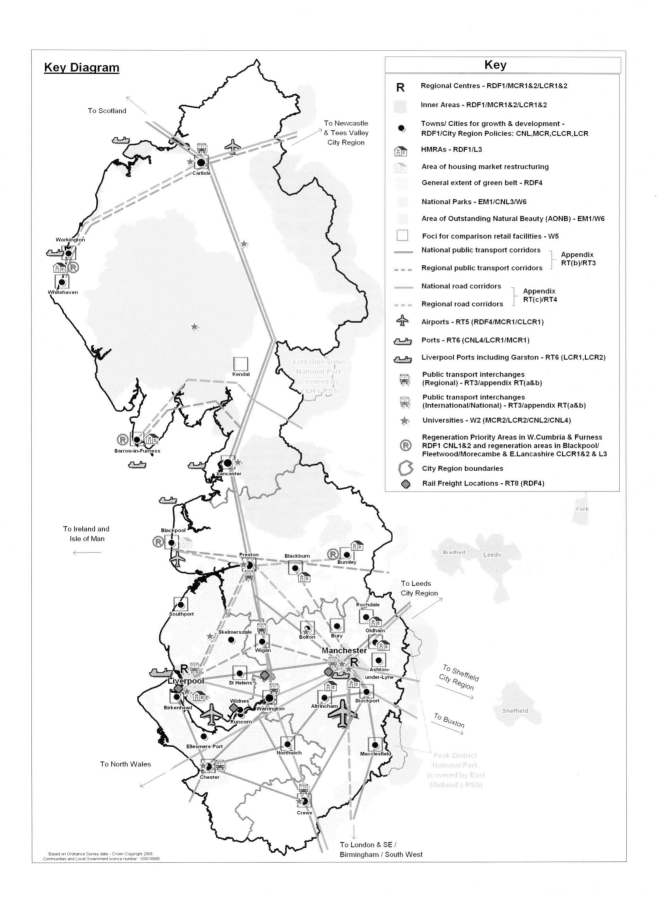

**Key Diagram**

**Key**

| | |
|---|---|
| R | Regional Centres - RDF1/MCR1&2/LCR1&2 |
| | Inner Areas - RDF1/MCR1&2/LCR1&2 |
| ● | Towns/ Cities for growth & development - RDF1/City Region Policies: CNL,MCR,CLCR,LCR |
| | HMRAs - RDF1/L3 |
| | Area of housing market restructuring |
| | General extent of green belt - RDF4 |
| | National Parks - EM1/CNL3/W6 |
| | Area of Outstanding Natural Beauty (AONB) - EM1/W6 |
| | Foci for comparison retail facilities - W5 |
| | National public transport corridors |
| | Regional public transport corridors — Appendix RT(b)/RT3 |
| | National road corridors |
| | Regional road corridors — Appendix RT(c)/RT4 |
| ✈ | Airports - RT5 (RDF4/MCR1/CLCR1) |
| | Ports - RT6 (CNL4/LCR1/MCR1) |
| | Liverpool Ports including Garston - RT6 (LCR1,LCR2) |
| | Public transport interchanges (Regional) - RT3/appendix RT(a&b) |
| | Public transport interchanges (International/National) - RT3/appendix RT(a&b) |
| ★ | Universities - W2 (MCR2/LCR2/CNL2/CNL4) |
| ® | Regeneration Priority Areas in W.Cumbria & Furness RDF1 CNL1&2 and regeneration areas in Blackpool/ Fleetwood/Morecambe & E.Lancashire CLCR1&2 & L3 |
| | City Region boundaries |
| ◆ | Rail Freight Locations - RT8 (RDF4) |

Based on Ordnance Survey data - Crown Copyright 2008
Communities and Local Government licence number  100018986

# 4 Spatial Principles

## Policy DP 1

**Spatial Principles**

The following principles underpin RSS (incorporating RTS)

Other regional, sub-regional and local plans and strategies and all individual proposals, schemes and investment decisions should adhere to these principles. All may be applicable to development management in particular circumstances:

- promote sustainable communities;
- promote sustainable economic development;
- make the best use of existing resources and infrastructure;
- manage travel demand, reduce the need to travel, and increase accessibility;
- marry opportunity and need;
- promote environmental quality;
- mainstreaming rural issues;
- reduce emissions and adapt to climate change.

The 8 Policies DP 2 -9 amplify these principles and should be taken together as the spatial principles underlying the Strategy. They are not in order of priority.

The whole of the RSS should be read together and these principles should be applied alongside the other policies which follow.

4.1    These are the principles which have shaped this RSS. Applying them to all plans and strategies in the North West that affect the development and management of different land uses, as well as to individual proposals, will help to ensure an effective cascade of policy from regional to sub-regional and local levels, promoting sustainability and subsidiarity.

## Policy DP 2

### Promote Sustainable Communities

Building sustainable communities – places where people want to live and work - is a regional priority in both urban and rural areas. Sustainable Communities should meet the diverse needs of existing and future residents, promote community cohesion and equality and diversity, be sensitive to the environment, and contribute to a high quality of life, particularly by:

- fostering sustainable relationships between homes, workplaces and other concentrations of regularly used services and facilities;
- taking into account the economic, environmental, social and cultural implications of development and spatial investment decisions on communities;
- improving the built and natural environment, and conserving the region's heritage;
- improving the health and educational attainment of the region's population, reducing present inequalities;
- promoting community safety and security, including flood risk (see map 2.11);
- encouraging leadership, joint working practices, community consultation and engagement;
- reviving local economies, especially in the Housing Market Renewal Areas and other areas in need of regeneration and housing restructuring such as Blackpool, Fleetwood and Morecambe;
- integrating and phasing the provision public services (including lifelong learning) and facilities to meet the current and future needs of the whole community, ensuring that those services are conveniently located, close to the people they serve, and genuinely accessible by public transport;
- promoting physical exercise through opportunities for sport and formal / informal recreation, walking and cycling.

The guiding principles of the UK Sustainable Development Strategy 2005 [31] or its successors and the basic elements of sustainable communities as set out in 'Sustainable Communities: People, Places and Prosperity (A Five Year Plan) should be followed.

4.2    The Sustainable Communities Five Year Plan defines the components of sustainable communities. In short they are: active, inclusive and safe; well run; environmentally sensitive; well designed and built; well connected; thriving; well served; and fair for everyone. Investing in housing is an important part of achieving this vision, but creating sustainable communities is about more than this. It is about addressing disparities and improving quality of life; increasing jobs and economic growth; encouraging people to get involved in the decisions that affect their community; building schools and hospitals as an integral part of development, not an afterthought; and improving the natural and built environment.

---

31    Securing the future delivering UK sustainable development strategy, UK Govt, 2005.

## 4 Spatial Principles

---

### Policy DP 3

**Promote Sustainable Economic Development**

It is a fundamental principle of this Strategy to seek to improve productivity, and to close the gap in economic performance between the North West and other parts of the UK. Sustainable economic growth should be supported and promoted, and so should reductions of economic, environmental, education, health and other social inequalities between different parts of the North West, within the sub-regions, and at local level.

---

4.3    Building a strong, stable and sustainable economy is a key factor in improving quality of life and one of the UK Guiding Principles for Sustainable Development. After years of deep-rooted industrial decline, the NW economy has performed well in recent years, but there is still much to do. Overall GVA per head in the NW is 12% lower than the England average, but there are considerable variations across the region, with Cheshire having the highest GVA per head and Manchester City Region experiencing the highest growth rates and Cumbria the lowest. We need to strengthen regional economic performance, to continue the transformation of the economy in a sustainable way, enabling the sub-regions to achieve their potential in light of a clear understanding of their distinctive roles and visions for the future as set out in the sub regional policies in chapters 10-13 of this document.

4.4    There are also other disparities – not just in economic growth – between the NW and the rest of the UK; between the NW sub-regions; and within them. The maps at Diagrams 2.2- 2.9 illustrate just some of them. In addition to spatial disparities, there can also be concentrations of disadvantage within specific groups such as older people, Black and Minority and Ethnic groups and people with disabilities. Plans and strategies should seek to better understand these disparities and concentrations of disadvantage, devise policies and focus investment to address them. The new spatial approach in planning will facilitate this, integrating different policy themes and delivery mechanisms (horizontal) and between different geographic levels (vertical) in knowledge of the needs and priorities of specific places. At the local level these priorities will be articulated in Sustainable Community Strategies and reflected in Local Area Agreements (LAAs) and Multi Area Agreements (MAAs).

## Policy DP 4

### Make the Best Use of Existing Resources and Infrastructure

Priority should be given to developments in locations consistent with the regional and sub-regional spatial frameworks as set out in Chapter 5 (notably policy RDF1) and sub regional policies in Chapters 10-13 which:

- build upon existing concentrations of activities and existing infrastructure;
- do not require major investment in new infrastructure, including transport, water supply and sewerage. Where this is unavoidable development should be appropriately phased to coincide with new infrastructure provision.

Development should accord with the following sequential approach:

- first, using existing buildings (including conversion) within settlements, and previously developed land within settlements;
- second, using other suitable infill opportunities within settlements, where compatible with other RSS policies;
- third, the development of other land where this is well-located in relation to housing, jobs, other services and infrastructure and which complies with the other principles in DP1-9.

Natural and man-made resources should be managed prudently and efficiently. Sustainable construction and efficiency in resource use (including reuse and recycling of materials) should be promoted.

4.5     The competitiveness of the region's economy is important and its growth must be facilitated but, increasingly, demands for houses, workplaces and services will need to be met in a more sustainable fashion, making the best use of land and existing infrastructure, and managing resources prudently and efficiently. There will be many opportunities to encourage the re-use of disused land and buildings. This is critical to improving the Region's image. The Region contains a very large extent of dereliction and a large number of old industrial buildings of historic interest and great character in need of new uses, especially in the urban areas. Greater use of land that has been previously developed, and lies within settlements, is required for all forms of development across the Region. Not all areas of previously developed land, however, will be suitable or appropriate for built development. For example, former military bases in rural areas could be relatively remote, may have returned to open land uses or be supporting valuable habitats. Other policies, particularly those on the wider countryside (RDF2), and on derelict land and contamination (EM2), provide further guidance on this issue, and Table 7.1 sets out indicative District targets for the proportion of housing to use brownfield land and buildings.

## 4 Spatial Principles

### Policy DP 5

**Manage Travel Demand; Reduce the Need to Travel, and Increase Accessibility**

Development should be located so as to reduce the need to travel, especially by car, and to enable people as far as possible to meet their needs locally. A shift to more sustainable modes of transport for both people and freight should be secured, an integrated approach to managing travel demand should be encouraged, and road safety improved.

Safe and sustainable access for all, particularly by public transport, between homes and employment and a range of services and facilities (such as retail, health, education, and leisure) should be promoted, and should influence locational choices and investment decisions.

Major growth should, as far as possible, be located in urban areas where strategic networks connect and public transport is well provided.

All new development should be genuinely accessible by public transport, walking and cycling, and priority will be given to locations where such access is already available.

In rural areas accessibility by public transport should also be a key consideration in providing services and locating new development, emphasising the role of Key Service Centres (Policy RDF2).

4.6    This principle is clearly reflected in the transport objectives and policies of RSS. But its impact is much wider than this. It has helped shape the broad spatial priorities in the RSS, which have in turn influenced the distribution of housing in table 7.1. It has influenced the locational criteria for regionally significant economic development, with accessibility by public transport highlighted as a key consideration in policy W2. It underpins retail policy and the emphasis on development in town centres and KSCs. These considerations are equally applicable at local and sub-regional levels when preparing plans and strategies such as LDFs and LTPs, or deciding on individual schemes and proposals. RDF2 sets out the policy for developments in more remote rural locations where innovative solutions will be needed to address the need to manage travel demand and reduce the need to travel.

### Policy DP 6

**Marry Opportunity and Need**

Priority should be given, in locational choices and investment decisions, to linking areas of economic opportunity with areas in greatest need of economic, social and physical restructuring and regeneration. Proximity to, and access via public transport from, such areas will be important considerations in the choice of employment locations and sites.

**4.7** This principle is closely related to the previous one encouraging accessibility. It has implications for both the linkages between areas, notably by public transport, and for locational decisions in respect of employment, housing, services and facilities. It brings together two important spatial concepts – proximity and connectivity – to address social inclusion in its widest sense and regeneration.

**4.8** It is an important feature of society today, notably in our cities, that some of the poorest, most deprived areas are frequently close to areas of growth and opportunity. For example, concentrations of worklessness (see Diagram 2.3) - 40% of unemployment in the region is in the ten Districts with the best record for recent economic growth. We need to understand these geographies and the needs of different communities living within them and promote policies to marry opportunity and need through land use and physical infrastructure decisions, including transport, and through skills and employability initiatives. The RES and Northern Way Growth Strategy provide a context for this at regional level. Sub-regional and local plans and strategies should also address these issues.

## Policy DP 7

### Promote Environmental Quality

Environmental quality (including air, coastal and inland waters), should be protected and enhanced, especially by:

- understanding and respecting the character and distinctiveness of places and landscapes;
- the protection and enhancement of the historic environment;
- promoting good quality design in new development and ensuring that development respects its setting taking into account relevant design requirements, the NW Design Guide and other best practice;
- reclaiming derelict land and remediating contaminated land for end-uses to improve the image of the region and use land resources efficiently;
- maximising opportunities for the regeneration of derelict or dilapidated areas;
- assessing the potential impacts of managing traffic growth and mitigating the impacts of road traffic on air quality, noise and health;
- promoting policies relating to green infrastructure and the greening of towns and cities;
- maintaining and enhancing the tranquillity of open countryside and rural areas;
- maintaining and enhancing the quantity and quality of biodiversity and habitat;
- ensuring that plans, strategies and proposals which alone or in combination could have a significant effect on the integrity and conservation objectives of sites of international importance for nature conservation are subject to assessment, this includes assessment and amelioration of the potential impacts of development (and associated traffic) on air quality, water quality and water levels.

**4.9** The pursuit of sustainable development demands that we live within environmental limits, respecting the environment, natural resources and biodiversity. It is a fundamental tenet that has not only influenced RSS polices on the environment, waste and energy, but cross-cuts the thematic policies on jobs, housing and transport. Work currently in hand to assess the environmental capacity of the region will provide a vital evidence base to monitor performance and underpin future policy development in this respect.

**4.10** This principle highlights specific aspects of protecting and enhancing rural and urban, built and natural environments. As we have seen with other topics, environmental quality varies significantly across the region encompassing landscapes of great beauty and areas degraded by the legacy of our industrial past. Plans and strategies should respond to the different challenges these present and recognise the distinctiveness of different places. Good design, creativity and innovation, are essential to improve the built environment and make better use of land to support sustainable patterns, for example promoting energy efficiency or car-free neighbourhoods. An imaginative mix of land uses can improve the character of both urban and suburban areas, strengthening social integration and civic life and support new approaches to neighbourhood structure.

**4.11** The North West has significant areas which are internationally important for nature conservation (see map 2.10) this includes significant areas of the coastline of the region. Development and policies which seek to deliver RSS at a local level could have the potential to have significant adverse effects on sites of international importance for nature conservation such as Ramsars (designated by the UK Government under the Ramsar Convention to protect and conserve wetland areas that are of international importance, particularly as waterfowl habitats) and 'Natura 2000' sites (a network of internationally significant wildlife sites within the EU, comprising Special Areas of Conservation (SACs) and Special Protection Areas (SPAs) including proposed and candidate sites pSACs and cSPAs). Consideration of effects of development on sites of international importance for nature conservation will also include, where relevant, the potential effects on sites outside the region e.g. effects of development in the region on coastal and inland waters in Wales. Lower tier plans, strategies and proposals may need to be assessed under the Habitats Regulations for likely significant effects alone or in combination. Where it is indicated that plans and proposals are likely to have negative impacts which cannot be avoided, alternatives will need to be sought or imperative reasons of overriding public interest established and compensatory measures will be necessary. This is an onerous route and accordingly whilst this is a possible approach, development likely to have an adverse effect on the integrity and conservation objectives of sites of international importance for nature conservation is unlikely to meet the requirements of Habitats Directive and would be unlikely to be in accordance with the development plan. Many 'Natura 2000' and Ramsar sites are highly sensitive to existing levels of air pollution and water pollution, not withstanding the potential impacts of future development. Local authorities will need to ensure appropriate monitoring regimes are in place and consider amelioration measures where appropriate to ensure that development does not have adverse effects. Many of the 'Natura 2000' and Ramsar sites extend well beyond individual local authority boundaries and Local Authorities and Partnership organisations will need to work together to prepare plans and strategies which minimise, avoid and manage potential negative impacts on valuable sites.

## Policy DP 8

### Mainstreaming Rural Issues

The rural areas of the North West should be considered in a way which is integrated with other decision making, and not seen as a separate topic.

The problems of rural communities (such as housing affordability, economic diversification, and access to jobs and services), especially in Cumbria, have particular causes and require particular solutions – different in sparsely populated areas from those closer to large settlements. Plans and strategies should acknowledge this and respond to spatial variations in rural need and opportunities. The positive interaction between rural and urban areas should be promoted when appropriate.

4.12    Rural areas comprise 81% of the land area of the NW, 22% of the population and 25% of the GVA. Their importance should not be underestimated but they vary significantly in role and character. There is a spatial dimension to this – not least the distinctions between "sparse" and "less sparse" [32] and between rural areas closely related to the conurbations and those more remote, isolated areas. Sometimes they face similar problems, such as housing affordability or access to services and facilities, but often the underlying causes are very different. These need to be carefully thought through. There is no one-size-fits-all solution. Plans and strategies must recognise this spatial dimension, the disparities and the different opportunities and needs, drivers and constraints. They must also recognise the important linkages and potential for positive interaction between rural and urban areas.

4.13    We believe that the best way of tackling these issues is by mainstreaming rural considerations and not tackling them as a separate silo of activity. It is an approach sometimes referred to as "rural-proofing". There is no separate rural chapter in this strategy, although there is a specific policy, RDF2, in the regional spatial framework which deals with the broad priorities and focus for development in rural areas. Rather, rural matters are dealt with as an integral part of each spatial principle and each thematic chapter.

---

32    As defined in The State of the Countryside, Commission for Rural Communities, 2007.

## 4 Spatial Principles

### Policy DP 9

**Reduce Emissions and Adapt to Climate Change**

As an urgent regional priority, plans, strategies, proposals, schemes and investment decisions should:

- contribute to reductions in the Region's carbon dioxide emissions from all sources, including energy generation and supply, buildings and transport in line with national targets to reduce emissions to 60% below 1990 levels by 2050; in particular, for residential and commercial development, by developing trajectories or other yardsticks for identifying trends in carbon performance;
- take into account future changes to national targets for carbon dioxide and other greenhouse gas emissions;
- identify, assess and apply measures to ensure effective adaptation to likely environmental, social and economic impacts of climate change.

Measures to reduce emissions might include as examples:

- increasing urban density;
- encouraging better built homes and energy efficiency, eco-friendly and adaptable buildings, with good thermal insulation, green roofs and microgeneration;
- reducing traffic growth, promoting walking, cycling and public transport;
- facilitating effective waste management;
- increasing renewable energy capacity;
- focusing substantial new development on locations where energy can be gained from decentralised supply systems;
- the improved management and rewetting of the regions blanket and raised bog resource.

Adaptation measures might include, for example:

- minimising threats from, and the impact of, increased coastal erosion, increased storminess and flood risk, habitat disturbance, fragmentation and increased pressure on water supply and drainage systems;
- protection of the most versatile agricultural land;
- Sustainable Urban Drainage.

Policy makers should use the North West Integrated Appraisal Toolkit as a basis to assess and strengthen the climate change mitigation and adaptation elements of their plans and strategies. Exceptionally, other comparable and robust methodologies might be used.

Applicants and local planning authorities should ensure that all developments meet at least the minimum standards set out in the North West Sustainability Checklist for Developments [33], and should apply 'good' or 'best practice' standards wherever practicable.

---

33    North West Sustainability Checklist for Developments, NWRA, 2007.

**4.14**    The Government believes that climate change is the greatest long-term challenge facing the world today.  In the North West, we face the risk of more extreme weather events, including drier summers, sea level rises and flooding.  In turn, this creates dangers to our health, prosperity, infrastructure and environment.  Actions to mitigate the damage we are causing, and adapt to any unavoidable change, should therefore be embedded in all plans for our sustainable development.  On a national level, policies and priorities for action are set out in the Climate Change Programme [34] and the Energy Bill 2007-8 [35], Planning and Climate Change PPS (PPS1 Supplement)  and the North West Climate Change Action Plan [36] sets out the regional response. The Climate Change Bill is expected to set legally binding targets for the reduction of carbon emissions [37].

**4.15**    If used positively, spatial planning can play a significant role in reducing our carbon emissions, promoting the use of renewable energy and shaping sustainable communities that are resilient to future climate change.

---

34    Climate Change, The UK Programme March 2006 CM6764.
35    Meeting the Energy Challenge May 2007 CM7124.
36    Rising to the Challenge, A Climate Change Action Plan for England's Northwest, http://www.climatechangenorthwest.co.uk.
37    Draft Climate Change Bill March 2007 CM7040.

# 5 Regional Spatial Framework

## Policy RDF 1

### Spatial Priorities

In making provision for development, plans and strategies should accord with the following priorities, taking into account specific considerations set out in Sub Regional Chapters 10-13:

- the first priority for growth and development should be the regional centres of Manchester and Liverpool;
- the second priority should be the inner areas surrounding these regional centres. Emphasis should be placed on areas in need of regeneration and Housing Market Renewal Areas in particular;
- the third priority should be the towns / cities in the 3 city regions: Altrincham, Ashton-under-Lyne, Blackburn, Blackpool, Bolton, Burnley, Bury, Chester, Crewe, Ellesmere Port, Macclesfield, Northwich, Oldham, Preston, Rochdale, Runcorn, St Helens, Skelmersdale, Southport, Stockport, Warrington, Widnes, Wigan. Development in larger suburban centres within the city regions would be compatible with this policy provided the development is of an appropriate scale and at points where transport networks connect and where public transport accessibility is good;
- the fourth priority should be the towns and cities outside the City Regions of Carlisle and Lancaster, with investment encouraged in Barrow- in -Furness and Workington and Whitehaven to address regeneration and workessness in Furness Peninsula and West Cumbria.

In the third and fourth priorities development should be focused in and around the centres of the towns and cities. Development elsewhere may be acceptable if it satisfies other policies, notably DP1 to 9. Emphasis should be placed on addressing regeneration and housing market renewal and restructuring.

5.1     This policy is the cornerstone of the RSS. Much of what comes later flows from this clear statement of spatial priorities for growth and development, investment and regeneration in the region. For example, it has influenced the distribution of housing numbers, retail policy and the public transport framework. Increasingly it will guide decision making and the targeting of resources, for example, in connection with transport investment priorities, the location of growth points and ecotowns [38], and employment land. It will help guide business planning and funding decisions in a wide range of public, private and voluntary organisations such as NWDA, Strategic Health Authorities, economic partnerships and utility companies.

5.2     RDF1 should be read together with the sub-regional policies in Chapters 10-13 which amplify this regional framework. For example, policies MCR2 and LCR2 broadly define the regional centres and surrounding inner areas, and go on to explain the approach to specific

---

38     Defined by UK Govt as exemplar green developments meeting the highest standards of sustainability, including low and zero carbon technologies and quality public transport systems.

sorts of development there, such as housing which will only be acceptable in certain circumstances. CLCR1 and 2 and supporting text set the specific priorities and visions for Preston, Blackpool, Blackburn and Burnley.

5.3 RDF1 has itself been influenced by the spatial principles in DP1 to 9. It builds on the concepts of the city region, of public transport accessibility and making the best use of existing resources. It reflects the vision set out in the RES and the RFA. The focus is on the cores of the Manchester and Liverpool City Regions. The approach is balanced, spreading development across a large number of towns/cities. In this it follows through the approach in RPG13.

5.4 The approach in RDF1 also allows for development in accessible suburban/urban centres, this is particularly necessary where these sit within areas with deprivation and regeneration issues. It will be for Local Development Documents to identify such centres and indicate their role. The Land Use Consultants (LUC) study could provide some useful insight into the roles and characteristics of different types of suburban centres, but it is not considered that such centres are Key Service Centres as set out in RDF 2.

5.5 Unlike RPG13, this RSS does not specifically define Regeneration Priority Areas (RPAs), with the exception of those in West Cumbria and Furness. It is clear where the emphasis should be in terms of the overall priorities for investment and regeneration activity, it is in the regional centres and inner areas (frequently the location of Urban Regeneration Companies); in the HMRAs (including Pathfinder Areas) of Manchester/Salford, Liverpool/Sefton, Wirral, Oldham/Rochdale, East Lancashire; in Furness RPA and Housing Market Renewal Area, particularly in Barrow in Furness and in West Cumbria RPA and Housing Market Renewal Area, particularly in Workington/Whitehaven; as well as the areas of Housing Market restructuring of Blackpool, Fleetwood and Morecambe.

# 5 Regional Spatial Framework

## Policy RDF 2

### Rural Areas

Plans and strategies for the Region's rural areas should support the priorities of the Regional Rural Delivery Framework and:

- maximise the economic potential of the Region's rural areas;
- support sustainable farming and food;
- improve access to affordable rural housing;
- ensure fair access to services for rural communities;
- empower rural communities and address rural social exclusion;
- enhance the value of our rural environmental inheritance.

### Key Service Centres

Plans and Strategies should identify a subset of towns and villages as Key Service Centres which:

- act as service centres for surrounding areas, providing a range of services including retail, leisure, community, civic, health and education facilities and financial and professional services; and
- have good public transport links to surrounding towns and villages, or the potential for their development and enhancement.

Development in rural areas should be concentrated in these Key Service Centres and should be of a scale and nature appropriate to fulfil the needs of local communities for housing, employment and services, and to enhance the quality of rural life.

### Local Service Centres

Small scale development to help sustain local services, meet local needs, or support local businesses will be permitted in towns and villages defined as Local Service Centres in Local Development Documents which already provide a more limited range of services to the local community.

### Outside Key and Local Service Centres

In remoter rural areas particularly the 'sparse' rural areas of the region, more innovative and flexible solutions to meet their particular development needs should be implemented and targeted towards achieving:

- more equitable access to housing, services, education, healthcare and employment; and
- a more diverse economic base, whilst maintaining support for agriculture and tourism.

Exceptionally, new development will be permitted in the open countryside where it:

- has an essential requirement for a rural location, which cannot be accommodated elsewhere (such as mineral extraction);

- is needed to sustain existing businesses;
- provides for exceptional needs for affordable housing;
- is an extension of an existing building; or
- involves the appropriate change of use of an existing building.

LDDs should set out criteria for permitting the re use of buildings in the countryside in line with PPS7.

5.6     Government's Rural Strategy 2004 [39] identifies the need to target resources at rural areas that are 'lagging', i.e. falling behind their counterparts. The targeting of resources must be backed by sound evidence of need and is best undertaken at sub-regional level, where it can be tailored to the widely differing nature of the regions lagging areas.

5.7     This Strategy is being taken forward in the North West through the Regional Rural Delivery Framework (RRDF) for the region [40]. The RRDF was agreed by partners and is a driver for change across a range of issues that critically affect people who live in, work and visit the rural North West.

5.8     Good access to services is essential if rural communities are to survive and prosper [41]. By concentrating rural development in Key Service Centres, we can support sustainable development and social inclusion, providing focus for the economic regeneration of the wider rural area and housing to meet local needs, including affordable housing.  In some areas, cities and towns will also play a role in providing access to employment and services for the surrounding rural areas. This will need to be considered in formulating rural policy and will tie in with the sub regional policy frameworks in Chapter 10-13.

5.9     Key Service Centres should be defined in LDFs on the basis of their current role in serving the needs of their rural hinterland and their potential to act as hubs for the provision of services, facilities and public transport. Factors such as their location, size, and the range of services already provided will be important in this. However, just because a centre currently operates at a particular level in the hierarchy does not in itself justify its designation as a Key Service Centre. Key Service Centres may be market towns or large villages and may be freestanding or operate as part of a network. The Land Use Consultants study provides further guidance.

5.10    It will also be important to maintain services in smaller villages. For this reason, LDFs should also define Local Service Centres and less accessible areas particularly sparse rural areas where they will encourage innovative approaches to service and transport provision involving, for example, ICT, the shared use of buildings and participatory budgeting (See also Policy L1 and para 7.2).

5.11    Local planning authorities will need to take a balanced view on proposals for development outside Key Service Centres and development in open countryside will be permitted in the exceptional circumstances listed. The open countryside does not include the Green Belt where policy is provided by national guidance in PPG2 and RDF4 in RSS.  Proposals that seek to

---

39     Rural Strategy, DEFRA, 2004.
40     Regional Rural Delivery Framework, GONW and partners, 2006.
41     "State of the Countryside 2005", Commission for Rural Communities / Countryside Agency, 2005.

## 5 Regional Spatial Framework

diversify and expand existing rural businesses in areas that are lagging economically should be regarded positively, as long as they demonstrate the potential to help build and maintain sustainable communities and are sensitive towards the local environment.

5.12    RSS policy for rural areas builds upon a new system of classification for urban and rural areas introduced by Defra in 2004 [42], which is based on the size of the settlements they contain. Areas are classified, from 'sparse to dense'. Sparse rural areas in the North West (found within Cumbria & North Lancashire) require particular attention because their remote nature and physical geography tend to make them less accessible and economically active. These areas are more dependent on agriculture and farm based tourism, this renders them more vulnerable to any decline in the agricultural economy and to the potential physical impacts of climate change on agriculture. Therefore there is a particular need to support agriculture whilst diversifying the economy in these areas.  A flexible approach to the reuse of existing buildings for non agricultural use may be needed in some areas.

5.13    Recent reform of the EU Common Agricultural Policy represents a shift in support away from production subsidies and towards agri-environment and wider rural development measures. This may provide positive opportunities for sustainable farming and rural economic diversification. However, the decoupling of support payments from agricultural production may also have an adverse impact on the viability of upland farms.  This means economic diversification, and support for alternative, sustainable forms of land management will be particularly important in these areas. Tourism is an important factor in diversifying and strengthening the rural economy but needs to be sustainably developed (see W6 and W7).

5.14    Whilst much of policy RDF2 concerns the requirements for built development, it must be remembered that the majority of the rural land area in the region is used for agriculture, forestry and various other land based industries and activities such as fisheries, nature reserves, inland waterways and MOD training areas. These should be supported where they are sustainable in nature and contribute to the rural environment and economy.

---

42    See DEFRA's Rural Strategy 2004, Annex A  "A new Rural Definition".

## Policy RDF 3

### The Coast

Plans and strategies should:

- enhance the economic importance of the coast and the regeneration of coastal communities in ways that safeguard, restore or enhance and make sustainable use of the natural, built and cultural heritage assets of the North West Coast and address issues of environmental decline and socio-economic decline, through support for:
  - the protection, development and diversification of the North West's maritime economy;
  - regeneration based around opportunities for sustainable growth in coastal tourism and recreation;
  - regeneration opportunities associated with reuse of developed or under-used developed coast, former docks and other adjacent industrial areas;
  - improving the image of coastal resorts to attract inward investment and tourism;
  - the diversification of economic activity in coastal communities and rural coastal areas;
- define the undeveloped, developed (including despoiled), and remote coast at a strategic and local level using the criteria set out in paragraph 5.22;
- direct development requiring a coastal location, in all but exceptional circumstances, to the developed coast and safeguard the undeveloped and remote coast;
- protect the functional integrity of bays, estuaries and the inter-tidal areas immediately offshore;
- promote the conservation and enhancement of cultural, historical and natural environmental assets, including land and seascapes;
- promote the integrated planning and management of the coast (and adjacent sea areas and neighbouring coastal regions) and marine spatial planning of the Irish Sea;
- facilitate co-ordination and harmonisation between Local Development Frameworks and the wide range of plans, strategies and schemes which apply to the coastal zone.

5.15    This policy should be read in conjunction with Policy EM6, which provides further guidance on sustainable shoreline management policy and Policy RT6 (Ports).

5.16    Stretching from the Welsh border on the Dee Estuary to the Scottish border on the Solway Firth, the region's coastal area is complex and constantly changing, both in terms of the physical processes it is subject to and the broad mix of assets, uses and economic activity it encompasses. The majority of the North West population live no more than one hour's travel time from the coast, and large urban populations, notably in Merseyside, actually live within the coastal zone.

5.17    The North West coast is chiefly low-lying and sedimentary in nature, characterised by large estuaries and bays with vast inter-tidal mud flats and salt marshes, extensive sand dune systems and other habitats of national and international importance (Ramsars, SPAs, SACs, cSACs, pSPAs and SSSIs). Collectively estuaries and bays such as Morecambe Bay and the Dee, Ribble and Mersey Estuaries are home to many protected species and are an important point on a global migration route for birds. The coastal zone contains a wide range of cultural,

## 5 Regional Spatial Framework

heritage, economic and environmental assets including Heritage Coast, two Areas of Outstanding Natural Beauty, World Heritage Sites, part of the Lake District National Park, and many sites of international and national importance for nature conservation. Areas outside these designations may provide supporting habitat for species of importance.

5.18    The low lying nature of the coast makes it particularly vulnerable to the effects of climate change, including rising sea levels and increasingly stormy conditions.

5.19    Traditionally, the region's tourism industry is a major employer, thanks to large resorts like Blackpool and Southport, and smaller ones such as West Kirby, Fleetwood, Morecambe and Lytham and St Annes. Changes in tourism patterns have led the region [43] to take a fresh look at its own tourism offering and to encourage the economic diversification of many of its resorts to combat declining tourist revenue and associated social deprivation. At the same time, an increased interest in ecological ("green") issues and recreation ("activity") holidays is giving rise to new opportunities for themed short breaks that help to extend the tourist season. Tourism activity will need to be appropriately managed to ensure that national and internationally important sites for nature conservation are not adversely affected.

5.20    Initiatives such as the Mersey Waterfront [44] and Blackpool Master Plan [45] aim to capitalise on the strengths of the North West coast, as do proposals to develop parts of the Ribble Estuary and Morecambe Bay as Regional Parks and the North West Coastal Trail. The availability of high quality water for swimming, clean beaches and convenient facilities are increasingly important factors in maintaining tourist numbers and attracting new visitors to the coast.

5.21    Historically, the region's coastal areas – its ports and fisheries, major resort towns and clusters of industry like that around Widnes - have been instrumental in driving its economy. The North West maintains a thriving maritime economy. Liverpool is a port of national significance and the region's other active ports: Barrow, Fleetwood, Garston Dock, Glasson Dock, Heysham, The Port of Manchester (Manchester Ship Canal), Silloth, and Workington continue to provide employment. All provide important landfall sites for servicing offshore operations such as oil and gas, fisheries and newer industries like offshore wind farms. Disused areas of dockland, for example in Liverpool, Barrow, Bootle, Maryport, Preston, and Whitehaven, are now providing significant opportunities for regeneration, bringing new employment to previously derelict and economically depressed areas.

5.22    There are considerable lengths of the coast that remain undeveloped or even remote, and which require planning and managing sensitively to retain their character. The following factors should be taken into account to classify the coastal zone:

- settlement size;
- areas of tidal flood risk and coastal erosion or land instability, reflecting Shoreline Management Plan assessments;
- biological criteria relating to the influence of maritime conditions on habitats and species;
- landscape criteria including local landscape character assessments (set in the context of the North West Joint Character Area map) and the extent of visibility between land and sea;

43    " A New Vision for Northwest Coastal Resorts - Summary Report", Northwest Regional Development Agency, March 2003.
44    See http://www.merseywaterfront.com
45    "Blackpool Master Plan – Executive Summary", Blackpool Borough Council 2003. "Blackpool Master Plan – Update Brochure", Blackpool Borough Council 2005.

- patterns of economic activity and the extent of the maritime influence on the built environment;
- distinctive boundaries such as coastal roads, railways and field boundaries;
- the broader maritime zone to the three-mile seaward limit.

5.23    The coast is unique in the North West in its combination of exceptionally high economic, social, environmental importance and potential. Integrated Coastal Zone Management (Integrated Coastal Zone Management in Europe (2002/413/EC) includes full definitions and guidance) is critical to minimise conflict and maximise cooperation, to sustain and realise this value. This includes integration across the land – sea interface and country/international borders, including Isle of Man, Northern Ireland, Republic of Ireland, Scotland and Wales. The North West Coastal Forum and a network of regional and local coastal and estuary partnerships has developed in response to this need, with support of coastal communities, local authorities, agencies and others. These partnerships make important contributions to promoting sustainable development and use of the coast.

## Policy RDF 4

### Green Belts

Overall the general extent of the Region's Green Belt will be maintained.

There is no need for any exceptional substantial strategic change to Green Belt and its boundaries in the North West within the timescales set out below:

- within Cheshire, Greater Manchester, Lancashire or Merseyside before 2011; and
- within Warrington before 2021.

After 2011 the presumption will be against exceptional substantial strategic change to the Green Belt in Cheshire, Greater Manchester, Lancashire or Merseyside. Strategic studies, undertaken by The Regional Planning Body, together with relevant stakeholders should investigate both the need for change and options for implementation.  The findings will inform future reviews of RSS and subsequent reviews of plans and strategies.

Local Development Frameworks may provide for detailed changes in Green Belt boundaries to accommodate the expansion of Manchester Airport and Liverpool John Lennon Airport; and to provide for an inter-modal freight terminal at Newton-Le-Willows.  Subject to the agreement of The Regional Planning Body, any other local detailed boundary changes should be examined through the LDF process.

5.24    The North West has four major, linked areas of Green Belt - in Greater Manchester, Merseyside, North Cheshire and Lancashire - plus one in South Cheshire, which is, in effect, part of the North Staffordshire Green Belt.  Small but significant patches of green belt also exist on the Fylde Peninsula and in North Lancashire. The reasons for their designation vary but all fulfil to some extent the five main purposes of Green Belt set out in PPG2 [46] and their contribution to urban regeneration, whether directly or indirectly, will be of prime importance for the foreseeable future.

---

46    Planning Policy Guidance Note 2(PPG2) "Green Belts", DoE 1995.

## 5 Regional Spatial Framework

**5.25** It is anticipated that future development in the North West, as set out in this RSS, can generally be accommodated without the need for strategic reviews of the Green Belt. Where new evidence or the monitoring of RSS indicates the need for review, this should be investigated and informed by strategic studies carried out by the Regional Planning Body together with relevant stakeholders. Any subsequent changes to Green Belt boundaries should be carried forward through a future review of RSS and subsequent reviews of Local Development Frameworks. Local authorities should bear in mind that any proposal to adjust Green Belt boundaries would need to meet the Government's commitment to maintaining or increasing the amount of Green Belt in every UK region.

**5.26** Although no exceptional substantial change to the Green Belt is envisaged at this time, other more location specific detailed boundary changes may be required to meet exceptional purposes. Where such changes would not require a reconsideration of wider green belt boundaries through a strategic study and would comply with guidance in PPG2, they should be dealt with through the LDF process, subject to early consultation with, and the agreement of, the Regional Planning Body. Policy RDF4 confers that agreement in respect of specific changes to meet operational infrastructure requirements at Liverpool John Lennon and Manchester Airports, and to provide for an inter-modal freight terminal at Newton-le-Willows. Consideration of such schemes should be in the context of policies RT5 on Airports and RT8 on Inter modal freight facilities.

# 6 Working in the North West – Achieving a Sustainable Economy

## Economic Objectives

The RSS supports the economic programme put forward in the Regional Economic Strategy. It seeks generally to strengthen and regenerate the regional economy and address problems of worklessness in line with the overarching spatial principles set out in Policies DP1-9. Specifically it will:

- support the business sectors identified in the RES;
- make provision for a supply of employment land to ensure that sustainable economic development is not constrained;
- establish criteria for the location of regionally significant economic development;
- promote strong and viable centres, as locations for the concentration of retail, office and recreational development;
- support the sustainable diversification of the rural economy; and
- harness the economic development potential of tourism in preferred locations.

6.1     This chapter focuses on the spatial implications of economic development in the North West.  It sets out the spatial policy framework that local planning authorities and other agencies should follow in order to accommodate the scale and type of business facilities needed to sustain our vision for economic growth.

## Policy W 1

### Strengthening the Regional Economy

Plans and strategies should promote opportunities for economic development (including the provision of appropriate sites and premises, infrastructure, and clustering where appropriate) which will strengthen the economy of the North West by:

- building on the region's strengths, particularly the three City Regions of Manchester, Liverpool and Central Lancashire. This should reflect the following growth opportunities:
  - Manchester City Region – advanced manufacturing and engineering (includes chemicals, aerospace, automotive and flexible materials), financial and professional services, media, creative and cultural industries, biomedical (biotechnology, pharmaceuticals and medical devices), ICT / digital, and communications;
  - Liverpool City Region – advanced manufacturing and engineering, financial and professional services, media, creative and cultural industries, biomedical, high value added knowledge based industries, ICT / digital, tourism, maritime and communications;
  - Central Lancashire City Region – advanced manufacturing and engineering, environmental technologies and biomedical, tourism and conferencing;
- realising the opportunities for sustainable development to increase the prosperity of Carlisle and Lancaster, and to regenerate the economies of the Furness Peninsula in Barrow, and in West Cumbria in Workington and Whitehaven;
- giving positive support to the sustainable diversification and development of the rural economy through the growth of existing businesses and the creation of new enterprise, particularly within Cumbria where there is a need to both develop high value business activities and sustain traditional economic activities. Prospects for growth in tourism, food and energy sectors should be developed, including promoting links between regional agriculture and production and retail facilities to reduce food miles and support local businesses;
- ensuring the safe, reliable and effective operation of the region's transport networks and infrastructure in accordance with the regional transport policies and priorities as set out in Chapter 8;
- supporting growth in service sectors, which will continue to act as significant employers within the region, and in which the greatest improvements in productivity can be made;
- improving the skills base of the region, including tackling skills deficiencies and concentrations of unemployment;
- providing sufficient and appropriate housing to support economic growth (Policies L2 – L5);
- linking areas of opportunity and need.

6.2    The region will require a range of sites with influences at different spatial levels to support the growth potential identified above:

- **Regionally significant** – a limited number of sites which will have a significant role to play in the growth of the regional economy, as a result of the type of development accommodated and the location of the site e.g. sites to meet the needs of the region's key growth sectors, knowledge nuclei, inward investment and headquarters functions. The sectoral focus, location and supply of these sites is dealt with in policies W1, W2 and W3. Intermodal freight terminals are also of regional significance, but are dealt with in policy RT8.

- **Sub-regional** – sites which sit below, and play a complementary role to, regionally significant economic development sites and have the potential to make a significant contribution to the growth of the sub-regional economy, particularly focused on the growth opportunities identified in Policy W1. Although a number of policies are relevant (such as RDF1, DP1 – 9 and sub regional policies in chapter 10-13) the RSS does not specifically address the location of these sites, but the amount of land required is set out in policy W3.
- **Local** – provision of a wide range of sites for a variety of uses which will support the development of a diversified local economy, ensuring that there is access to a range of job opportunities for the local population. Policy W3 also covers the requirement for local employment land.

6.3    Other sectors beyond those identified in Policy W1 will continue to provide significant employment opportunities across the region, particularly education and health sectors.  The potential for further public sector growth through the opportunities presented by the Gershon [47] and Lyons [48] Reviews should be maximised.

6.4    A lack of basic skills and qualifications has been identified as a barrier to the growth of the regional economy.  In particular the following districts have the highest rates of working age population without qualifications: Liverpool, Manchester, Oldham, Knowsley, Tameside, St Helens, Salford, Halton and Blackpool, which all fall within the City Regions.  In addition Liverpool, Manchester, Salford, Halton, Knowsley, Wirral and Barrow have particularly high unemployment rates. Within and outside of these geographic areas there are also concentrations of low skills and unemployment within specific groups within the community. Localised policies and initiatives will need to focus on how best to enable the participation of such hard to reach groups in education and training initiatives in order that skills and participation in employment can be improved resulting in improved health and quality of life.

---

47    Releasing resources to the front line: Independent Review of Public Sector Efficiency, Sir Peter Gershon, July 2004.
48    Well Placed to Deliver?  Shaping the Pattern of Government Services, Sir Michael Lyons, March 2004.

## 6 Working in the North West – Achieving a Sustainable Economy

### Policy W 2

**Locations for Regionally Significant Economic Development**

Regionally significant economic development will be located close to sustainable transport nodes within the urban areas of Manchester, Liverpool and Central Lancashire City Regions and Lancaster, Carlisle, Barrow-in-Furness and Workington and Whitehaven.

Sites will be identified in Local Development Documents, having regard to the priorities in RDF1; spatial principles in Policies DP 1- 9 and relevant sub regional policies in Chapters 10-13. They should be:

- capable of development within the plan period, having regard to the condition and availability of the land, infrastructure capacity, market considerations and environmental capacity;
- highly accessible, especially by adequate public transport services, walking and cycling;
- well-related to areas with high levels of worklessness and/or areas in need of regeneration;
- well related to neighbouring uses, particularly in terms of access, traffic generation, noise and pollution.

They should not be used for development that could equally well be accommodated elsewhere and should not be developed in a piecemeal manner.

Sites for regionally significant office development should be located in accordance with the sequential approach in PPS6, focusing on the regional centres and the town/cities listed in RDF1.

Sites for regionally significant knowledge-based services may also be clustered close to universities, major hospitals or other research establishments. Sites for regionally significant knowledge-based manufacturing should be well connected to these facilities by transport and ICT links.

Sites for regionally significant logistics and high-volume manufacturing should be well connected to the primary freight transport networks.

6.5    If the vision and objectives of The Northern Way Growth Strategy, the RES and this RSS are to be achieved, the region must have a ready supply of land for employment use that is of sufficient quality and quantity to support economic growth.  The supply must also reflect the implications of creating a more productive economy, with a focus on improving the productivity of workers in the business and services sectors, increasing employment in knowledge-based industries and tackling unemployment and skills deficiencies across the region.

6.6    The Regional Planning Body will work with NWDA, GONW and partners to identify sites within these broad locations and monitor their progress.  Some will be new. Others may be the Strategic Regional Sites identified by NWDA as being critical to the delivery of the RES, especially where they already have planning permission or are allocated in adopted plans.

**6.7** The region currently has around 5,475 hectares of land committed to employment use. Based on the current average annual take up rate of approximately 313 hectares per annum across the region, this equates to a sixteen year supply. 70% of this land is allocated for general B1/B2/B8 use.

# 6 Working in the North West – Achieving a Sustainable Economy

## Policy W 3

### Supply of Employment Land

Provision should be made for a supply of employment land as outlined in Table 6.1. Local planning authorities should undertake a comprehensive review of commitments, to secure a portfolio of sites that complies with the spatial development principles outlined in Policies DP1 – 9, and RDF1 and sub regional policies (Chapters 10-13), and to ensure:

- the most appropriate range of sites, in terms of market attractiveness and social, environmental and economic sustainability, are safeguarded for employment use;
- these sites can meet the full range of needs and are actively marketed;
- at least 30% of sites are available at any one time so that all new and existing businesses have the ability to grow successfully;
- the amount of brownfield land used for employment purposes is maximised, reflecting the likely increases in the amount available as a result of economic restructuring;
- full consideration is given to the scope for mixed-use development particularly within centres, and on larger sites;
- appropriate provision is made in Key Service Centres and full consideration given to the innovative re-use of agricultural buildings to facilitate the growth and diversification of the rural economy;
- the implications of home working on the scale and location of future employment land requirements are considered.

Office development should, as far as possible, be focused in the regional centres, in or adjacent to town / city centres listed in RDF1 and in Key Service Centres, consistent with RDF2 and the sequential approach in PPS6 .

The portfolio must be kept under regular review to ensure that the region does not over- or under- allocate land in relation to the actual scale of economic growth.  Local Authorities should review their employment land portfolio every three years.

### Table 6.1 Provision of Employment Land 2005-2021 (hectares)

|  | Greater Manchester | Merseyside and Halton | Lancashire | Cumbria | Cheshire and Warrington | North West |
|---|---|---|---|---|---|---|
| 2005 Supply | 1368 | 1234 | 1069 | 633 | 1171 | 5475 |
| Current take up per annum | 112 | 76 | 68 | 16 | 41 | 313 |
| Projected inc in take up | 6% | 18.5% | 4.25% | 17.5% | 6.00% | 9.22% |
| Projected take up per annum | 119 | 90 | 71 | 19 | 43 | 342 |
| Need 2005 – 21 | 1904 | 1440 | 1136 | 304 | 688 | 5472 |

| | Greater Manchester | Merseyside and Halton | Lancashire | Cumbria | Cheshire and Warrington | North West |
|---|---|---|---|---|---|---|
| Extra allocation required | 536 | 206 | 67 | -329 | -483 | -3 |
| Flexibility factor | 20% | 20% | 20% | 33% | 27% | - |
| Need 2005-21 (incorporating flexibility factor) | 2285 | 1728 | 1363 | 404 | 874 | 6654 |
| Extra allocation required (incorporating flexibility factor) | 917 | 494 | 294 | -229 | -297 | 1179 |

6.8    Policy W3 focuses on allocations for B1, B2 and B8 land use. It includes regionally significant economic development (but not inter-modal freight terminals), sub-regional and local sites as described in paragraph 6.2. A wide range of other types of land use provide significant employment opportunities, particularly in retail, tourism, hotel, catering and education and in some parts of the region these sectors account for a large proportion of total employment. In respect of bullet three "available "is defined as fully serviced and actively marketed or likely to be fully serviced and actively marketed in the next three years.

6.9    As the economy of the North West continues to restructure, the demand for different land uses will change significantly.  This is likely to result in a decline in the requirement of land suitable for B2 uses and a significant increased demand for land suitable for B1 uses. Local Authorities need to reflect this within their own portfolio of sites.

6.10    In rural areas, employment opportunities are not necessarily associated with the allocation of new development land.  Agriculture will continue to play an important role in the rural economy, and is also important in relation to landscape management and ecological protection and enhancement, but the need for agricultural diversification [49] (particularly in sparsely settled rural areas) is pressing. This will mean finding new and sometimes imaginative uses for land and buildings previously used for farming purposes. Priority should be given to economic activity that has strong links with the area in question, for example food and drink processing, tourism and leisure; the conservation of natural, cultural and historic resources; and businesses that are ancillary to farming and forestry.

6.11    Table 6.1 quantifies the amount of the employment land needed in each sub region. However, it is acknowledged that there is a degree of uncertainty in establishing employment land requirements. It is also recognised that there may, exceptionally, be a need to provide additional land to take account of special circumstances, such as the expansion requirements of a particular business or the realisation of significant inward investment potential. Accordingly,

49    see "Farm Diversification in the North West – a Guide to Planning", North West Regional Assembly, 2003.

an allowance for flexibility has been factored into the table through the incorporation of a flexibility factor, which has the effect of adding between 20% and 33% to the employment land requirement for each sub-region.

6.12    The provision of figures by sub-region will require Local Authorities and other partners to work together to agree the distribution of land within each sub-region.  The Regional Planning Body will facilitate this approach.  Where possible, figures should be distributed in accordance with local labour market areas, broadly indicated by Travel to Work areas identified in the 2001 Census.  Further details regarding implementation of this policy will be set out in the RSS Implementation Framework.

6.13    In December 2004 Government published guidance [50] to Local Authorities to assist them in identifying an up to date and balanced portfolio of employment sites in Local Development Frameworks.  In particular, the guidance 'Employment Land Reviews: Guidance Note' suggests that Planning Authorities should undertake employment land reviews where possible alongside reviews of housing capacity (para 2.8–2.11 of Guidance Note) and quantitative assessments should be updated regularly at no more than five yearly intervals (para 5.49 of Guidance Note). In this context it is important to note that policy W3 requires Local Authorities to review their employment land portfolio every three years.

6.14    There is currently an oversupply of land in Cheshire and Warrington, and Cumbria which results in the requirement to de-allocate land over the RSS plan period. Where allocated employment sites are of a poor quality, poorly located, or unlikely to become available for development within the foreseeable future, local planning authorities should remove the allocations in question in the relevant Local Development Documents. This does not mean that new sites cannot and should not be brought forward in these areas.  Where they are of better quality and more suited to the demands of the changing economy this is supported.  However, the overall scale of provision should be reduced to avoid sterilising land for other desirable purposes, and to ensure that the legacy of unsatisfactory committed sites does not frustrate attempts to secure a more sustainable pattern of development.

6.15    In Cheshire and Warrington the average site size is over 20 hectares, far greater than in any other part of the region. Sites over 5 hectares make up 88% of committed employment land in this area.  Reducing the supply may be achieved by the de-allocation of a small number of larger sites.  Cumbria has dispersed settlement patterns, which coupled with the county's geographical isolation from regional, national and international markets, create discrete labour market areas.   It is necessary to offer a greater degree of choice and flexibility to prevent businesses locating outside Cumbria, and this is reflected in Table 6.1.

6.16    The impact of home working and other flexible working patterns, have not been fully considered in the preparation of this RSS and further work will need to be undertaken. However, ensuring that the figures identified in Table 6.1 are kept under regular review will enable this issue to be properly considered as its scale of influence become more fully understood.  This will also ensure that the figures can be revised in light of changes to the wider national, international and global economy which will impact on the appropriateness of the figures presented in Table 6.1.

6.17    The Regional Planning Body will develop more regionally-specific guidance on office (B1(a)) development in town Centres, as required by PPS6, as part of a future review.

---

50    Employment Land Reviews: Guidance Note, Office of the Deputy Prime Minister, December 2004.

## Policy W 4

### Release of Allocated Employment Land

Where sites are to be de-allocated in plans and strategies (following a comprehensive review of commitments outlined in Policy W3) consideration should be given to a range of alternative uses and determined as appropriate to the location and nature of each site. Alternative uses considered should include housing, and soft end uses, particularly where this will contribute to the delivery of Green Infrastructure networks (Policy EM3). Appropriate remediation may also be required to address issues of land contamination before sites can be effectively re-used (Policy EM2). In de-allocating sites Local Authorities should be mindful of the need to create and sustain mixed-used communities where there is access to a wide range of services and facilities.

Outside of a comprehensive review of commitments (Policy W3) when preparing plans and strategies and considering proposals and schemes there should be a presumption against the release of allocated employment sites for other uses. Sites should not be released where they provide, or have the potential to provide, an important contribution to the economy of the local area. If Local Authorities are minded to release sites they should be satisfied, before so doing, that:

- an appropriate supply of sites is available for employment uses. The de-allocation or re-allocation of a site should not result in a deficient supply of employment land, in either quantitative or qualitative terms, matched against the demand and supply requirements of the local economy;
- if required, there are replacement sites available, of equal or better quality, or that alternative means of incorporating employment land needs have been identified. This might mean considering mixed-use developments, greater intensity of land use or the availability of sites in adjacent authorities.

In both cases consideration should be given to the implications of releasing / retaining employment land in relation to the spatial principles in DP1-9, in particular the promotion of social and economic inclusion, sustainable travel choices and access to services, particularly within Housing Market Renewal Areas and rural areas.

6.18    In many areas there is a demand for allocated employment sites to be released for other uses, in particular housing and retail developments, and a stringent review of commitments will be necessary to justify the decision to either release or safeguard individual sites (Policy W3). However, where the demand for the reallocation of sites is to be dealt with outside such a review, a consistent approach should be applied across the region. Soft end uses are defined as those designed primarily to improve the environment, often by providing a cover of vegetation. Examples include public open spaces, nature conservation and playing fields.

6.19    The demand for employment land to be released for other uses is particularly strong in Eastern Cumbria (Carlisle, Eden, South Lakeland), South and Western parts of the Manchester City Region (Macclesfield, Stockport, Salford), Eastern parts of the Liverpool City Region (St

Helens and Knowsley) and parts of the Central Lancashire City Region (Wyre, South Ribble, Preston and Pendle) [51]. These areas, particularly those within the City Regions, have an important role to play in driving forward the regional economy.

6.20    In the Lake District National Park, employment land is in particularly short supply and subject to competition from other uses that command higher land values.   Demand for sites must be carefully managed to ensure that the National Park retains an adequate supply of employment sites to support improvements to the local economy.

## Policy W 5

### Retail Development

Plans and strategies should promote retail investment where it assists in the regeneration and economic growth of the North West's town and city centres. In considering proposals and schemes any investment made should be consistent with the scale and function of the centre, should not undermine the vitality and viability of any other centre or result in the creation of unsustainable shopping patterns.

Manchester/Salford and Liverpool City Centres will continue to function as the North West's primary retail centres.

Comparison retailing facilities should be enhanced and encouraged in the following centres to ensure a sustainable distribution of high quality retail facilities.

| | | |
|---|---|---|
| Altrincham | Ashton-under-Lyne | Barrow-in-Furness |
| Birkenhead | Blackburn | Blackpool |
| Bolton | Burnley | Bury |
| Carlisle | Chester | Crewe |
| Kendal | Lancaster | Macclesfield |
| Northwich | Oldham | Preston |
| Rochdale | Southport | St Helens |
| Stockport | Warrington | Wigan |
| Workington / Whitehaven | | |

Investment, of an appropriate scale, in centres not identified above will be encouraged in order to maintain and enhance their vitality and viability, including investment to underpin wider regeneration initiatives, to ensure that centres meet the needs of the local community, as identified by Local Authorities.

Retail development that supports entrepreneurship, particularly increasing the number of independent retailers, should be supported.

There will be a presumption against new out-of-centre regional or sub-regional comparison retailing facilities requiring Local Authorities to be pro-active in identifying and creating opportunities for development within town centres. There should also be a presumption against large-scale extensions to such facilities unless they are fully justified in line with the sequential approach established in PPS6. There is no justification for such facilities to be designated as town centres within plans and strategies.

6.21    For the avoidance of doubt, comparison retailing is the provision of items not purchased on a frequent basis (e.g. clothing, footwear, household goods) [52] and convenience retailing is the provision of everyday essential items (e.g. food, drinks, newspapers). Large-scale extensions are defined as being over 2,500m² net floorspace.

6.22    The centres identified in Policy W5 are well developed as vibrant retail centres, particularly for comparison goods retailing which has traditionally been concentrated in town centres, and should continue in this role.  Recent research [53] points to a significant growth in retail spending in the North West, which will in turn require the provision of additional retail floorspace across the region. The network of centres identified in Policy W5 will be the primary focus for this future growth and development, although they are not the only centres that should receive development through to 2021.  The policy does not preclude the investment of resources in other centres, particularly where this will assist in the regeneration of the centre and the wider area.  Future reviews of RSS may need to consider the impact of changes to retail formats on the pattern of both convenience and comparison retailing.

6.23    The flow of expenditure between sub-regions generally reflects the proximity of population to centres in adjoining sub-regions.  New investment should promote sustainable shopping patterns, which result in a reduced need to travel, especially by private car, to access retail facilities of an appropriate type and nature.

6.24    Local planning authorities will have to prepare retail need assessments for their local development frameworks, in line with the advice in PPS6. Specific retail development schemes will also require the preparation of detailed need assessments.

6.25    There are a significant number of outstanding comparison goods retailing planning commitments within the region, totalling over half a million m² net.  This would account for 89% of the growth identified to 2010.  Whilst some commitments are historic and may not necessarily be implemented, and some permissions may not support the 'town centres first' objectives of PPS6 and this RSS, it will be important for local planning authorities, as part of their own needs assessments, to monitor the scale of retail development permitted and how this can contribute to meeting identified needs.

6.26    The Trafford Centre is recognised as an important retail facility in the North West, but, within the context of Policy W5, it will not be appropriate to encourage the expansion of its floorspace in the future.

6.27    The Regional Planning Body will develop more regionally specific guidance on leisure development in town centres as part of a future review to address regionally specific issues for the wider range of Town Centre uses identified in PPS6.

52    PPS6, ODPM, March 2005.
53    Town Centre Assessment Study, White Young Green Planning for North West Regional Assembly, June 2005.

## Policy W 6

### Tourism and the Visitor Economy

Plans, strategies, proposals and schemes should seek to deliver improved economic growth and quality of life, through sustainable tourism activity in the North West. This should be in line with the principles outlined in Policy W7 and focused on:

- the regeneration of Blackpool as an International Tourism Destination, and the North West's other coastal resorts as priority locations for major footloose tourism development, where tourism is a critical component of the economy;
- the regional centres of Manchester, Liverpool (European Capital of Culture 2008), and Preston, where tourism is a contributory component of the economy;
- Chester as a heritage city of international renown where tourism is a significant component of the economy;
- Carlisle, Bolton, Birkenhead, Lancaster and Kendal as destinations with emerging potential for heritage related tourism development, where tourism supports and compliments their status as historic towns and cities;
- promoting business tourism through the development of high quality conference and exhibition facilities, particularly of European significance in Manchester and national significance in Liverpool and Blackpool;
- opportunities for diversifying the rural economy and regenerating rural areas should align with Policy RDF2. Development should be of an appropriate scale and be located where the environment and infrastructure can accommodate the visitor impact. Coastal sites of international importance for nature conservation, The Lake District National Park and Areas of Outstanding Natural Beauty are important tourist attractors in their own right. Sustainable tourism activity which will strengthen and diversify the economic base within these areas will be supported but the statutory purposes of these designations must not be adversely affected. Wherever possible, tourism development opportunities should be sought which take place in locations adjacent to the National Park and Areas of Outstanding Natural Beauty, thus spreading the economic benefit of tourism;
- opportunities related to Regional Parks, Hadrian's Wall and Liverpool World Heritage Sites. Tourism activity in these locations should be promoted within the context of the relevant Strategic Frameworks and Management Plans [54].

6.28 In respect of the first bullet, "footloose development" is defined as that which is not fundamentally connected to a specific location, e.g. hotels, conference and exhibition facilities, non site specific museums. Examples of "non-footloose development" include heritage sites, historic properties and gardens and natural features.

---

54 Hadrian's Wall Management Plan 2002 – 2007, Hadrian's Wall Company; Liverpool – Maritime Mercantile City Management Plan, 2003, Liverpool World Heritage Site Steering Group and Liverpool City Council.

6 Working in the North West – Achieving a Sustainable Economy

## Policy W 7

### Principles for Tourism Development

Plans and strategies should ensure (particularly to implement Policy W6) high quality, environmentally sensitive, well-designed tourist attractions, infrastructure and hospitality services, which:

- improve the region's overall tourism offer, increasing the market share of attractions;
- meet the needs of a diverse range of people and are easily accessible by sustainable means;
- support the provision of distinct tourism resources that harness the potential of sites and their natural attributes, including built heritage and cultural facilities;
- encourage and facilitate regeneration;
- promote facilities which will extend the existing visitor season;
- harness the potential of sport and recreation, particularly the role of major sporting events;
- improve the public realm;
- are viable in market and financial terms;
- help to relieve pressure on locations vulnerable to the impacts of climate change;
- respect the environmental sensitivity of the coast, particularly the undeveloped coast along with other sensitive areas, and ensure that the integrity of sites of international importance for nature conservation are maintained through assessment of proposals and through careful visitor management and restrictions on visitor access where necessary;
- promote eco-tourism in areas of high natural value in a way that minimises any adverse effect on the natural assets that visitors seek to experience.

The maintenance and enhancement of existing tourism development will be supported, providing that improvement, intensification and expansion proposals meet environmental and other development control criteria.

6.29    Improving the tourism offer in the North West is not simply about increasing the quantity of visitor attractions.   The region must improve the overall quality of its offer to compete effectively, not just with other parts of the UK, but increasingly with international resorts and attractions.  The region's coastal resorts (see Policy RDF3 and para 5.19), particularly Blackpool (see Policies CLCR1-2), have a very significant role to play in this along with the Lake District National Park.  However, the role of cities is increasing with the growing concepts of 'business tourism' and city breaks.  Manchester and Liverpool in particular have the potential to capture growth generated by these trends, while Chester will continue as a heritage city of international renown [55].

6.30    Whilst the benefits of tourism and the 'visitor economy' are numerous (the visitor economy is worth £7 billion per annum to the region and supports an estimated 40,000 jobs [56]) there are potential impacts which must be managed successfully if tourism is to have a positive benefit.

55    Historic Towns and Cities in England's Northwest, Northwest Regional Development Agency, October 2005.
56    Draft Northwest Regional Economic Strategy 2006 - 2009, Northwest Regional Development Agency, December 2005.

The impact of visitors on the environment, on transport infrastructure and on access to local services and facilities could be significant if left unmanaged. Ensuring environmental conservation and the long-term sustainability of both attractions and a tourism-dominated economy must be a priority.

6.31    In developing the region's business tourism offer the vision is for Manchester to become one of the most important convention and exhibition centres in Europe with Liverpool and Blackpool having the potential to become centres of national significance. Chester, Carlisle, Preston and Southport also have strong conference and exhibition potential which will be important in attracting 'business tourists' to the region [57].

6.32    Sport and recreation also have a key role to play. The British Open Golf Championship was hosted at Royal Liverpool in 2006 and at Royal Birkdale in 2008 and attracted a significant amount of tourism to the region. The legacy of success left by the Commonwealth Games in Manchester in 2002, provides the opportunity for further events in the region. The Major Events Strategy [58] provides a framework in which the value of sporting, and other events, to the region's economy can be developed.

6.33    The development of new tourism opportunities, including eco-tourism associated with the North West's rich and diverse wildlife, will be important in extending the existing visitor season.

6.34    Climate change will affect the visitor economy of the region. Of particular importance, some of the key natural attractions in the region are vulnerable to impacts of climate change (see DP9/EM5/EM6). It is crucial that these impacts are assessed to allow for early action to be taken to ensure the continued sustainable use of these resources. In addition, new developments will need to consider the provision of adequate infrastructure to take account of likely changes in climate.

6.35    The opportunity exists to capitalise upon links between tourist attractions in the North West and its surrounding regions, particularly in the Yorkshire Dales and Peak District National Parks, North Pennines Area of Outstanding Natural Beauty, with the North East through joint work being undertaken on Hadrian's Wall, and coastal resorts in North East Wales.

57    The Strategy for Tourism in England's Northwest, Northwest Regional Development Agency, June 2003.
58    Major Event Strategy, Northwest Regional Development Agency, March 2004.

# 7 Living in the North West – Ensuring a Strong, Healthy and Just Society

## Social Objectives

**7.1**   The RSS seeks to promote cohesive, mixed and thriving communities, where people will want to live, now and in the future.  It aims to deliver the objective of ensuring that everyone can have a decent home, which they can afford, in a secure environment, with reasonable access to health care, educational provision and recreational facilities.

It specifically seeks to:

- Build on current knowledge of housing markets in the region, so as to deliver a better balance between housing demand and supply;
- Provide for additional housing, so as to meet changing needs, support economic development, address the requirement for affordable accommodation, and ensure a choice in housing types;
- Improve the quality of the housing stock and its environment.

**7.2**   Local Authorities and other organisations should give a high priority to the development and improvement of infrastructure and services which are accessible to the whole community. Particular attention should be given to areas where social inclusion is being tackled by initiatives to address lack of employment opportunities (see Working chapter) and poor access to local services (including health [59], education and training opportunities). Many communities especially in rural areas, however prosperous, are experiencing a decline in local facilities and services [60] with disabled, younger or older people and those without access to a car being most affected. To maintain viable and sustainable rural communities it is essential to halt the continuing loss of commercial and public sector services, local employment, population, income and social and community services. Many of the problems associated with lack of access are often more acute within the sparse rural areas. Innovative ways of maintaining or re-introducing local services in centres of town and villages that are identified as being deficient or vulnerable to decline should be promoted (see Regional Development Framework chapter).

**7.3**   The National Offender Management Service (NOMS) have identified a potential need for the future development of prisons and other penal establishments in the region, there are currently 16 prison establishments in the North West provided in accordance with the provisions of the Prisons Act 1952. The identification of locations for these should be in accordance with guidance in Circular 3/98 [61].

---

59    "Technical Advisory Paper on NW Regional Spatial Strategy & Health" Pearl, Department of Civic Design, University of Liverpool, 2004.
60    The State of the Countryside in the North West 2003, Countryside Agency, 2003.
61    Circular 3/98: Planning for Future Prison Development.

## Policy L 1

### Health, Sport, Recreation, Cultural and Education Services Provision

Plans, strategies, proposals and schemes (including those of education, training and health service providers) should ensure that there is provision for all members of the community (including older people, disabled people and the black & minority ethnic population) for:

- the full spectrum of education, training and skills provision, ranging from childcare and pre-school facilities, through schools, to further and higher education and to continuing education facilities and work-related training;
- health facilities ranging from hospitals down to locally based community health facilities; and
- sport, recreation and cultural facilities.

In doing so they must take account of the views of the local community (including service users) and carry out an assessment of demographic, sporting, recreational, cultural, educational, skills & training and health needs in local communities. Furthermore, they should ensure that accessibility by public transport, walking and cycling is a central consideration.

Particular attention should be given to improving access to and addressing spatial disparities in service and facilities provision, in areas which have the greatest needs (in terms of poverty, deprivation, health and education inequalities, rural service provision), or where communities or the local economy are poorly served.

Proposals and schemes, for all major developments and regeneration schemes, and especially for housing, employment or mixed uses, should ensure appropriate health, cultural, recreational, sport, education and training provision from the outset including for example Children's Centres and SureStart Initiatives.

7.4    The spatial planning agenda stresses the need for local authorities to take issues beyond traditional land use into full account within their plans, strategies and programmes, making use of appraisal tools like health impact assessments. This policy does not seek to provide an exhaustive list of facilities or services which contribute to a healthy, sustainable community. Other strategies, for instance, address the promotion of participation in sport and physical activity for all groups.

7.5    RSS policy on wider service provision is concerned with the need to make these services accessible to everyone in the region. The quality of life of the region's population will be improved through good access to health facilities – one aspect of tackling inequalities. The health of the population is also enhanced by access to sport and recreational facilities. Good access to cultural, education and training provision will empower individuals and provide a more skilled workforce to meet the demands of local businesses (also see Policy W2). As well as helping to promote social inclusion, this policy aims to support North West educational institutions and encourage the retention of students and staff for the benefit of the regional economy. In addressing the implementation of this policy at local level, local authorities and their partners may need to consider issues including:

## 7 Living in the North West – Ensuring a Strong, Healthy and Just Society

- the location of specialist provision;
- the travel to work patterns of educational, health and other professionals;
- the location of student accommodation;
- provision of services for people in disadvantaged groups, including older people, black & minority ethnic (BME) communities, and rural communities;
- the demands of different economic sectors; and
- provision of services to serve areas of greatest need.

7.6    The Government's objectives for housing are set out in PPS3 [62] and the Housing Green Paper [63] and include the aims of providing sufficient housing, creating and sustaining mixed communities and improving affordability. Emphasis is placed on a 'plan, monitor and manage approach' to housing provision.   At the regional level future policies on housing are to be influenced by the Regional Housing Strategy [64], which sets out strategic regional priorities and linkages between RSS policies and the Regional Economic Strategy. In line with PPS3, there is a need to develop an understanding of housing markets at sub regional and local level in order to inform preparation of plans and strategies.

### Policy L 2

**Understanding Housing Markets**

Local Authorities should develop an understanding of local and sub-regional housing markets by undertaking Strategic Housing Market Assessments, in order to adopt a concerted and comprehensive approach to:

- influence housing supply across all types, sizes, tenures and values to achieve a better match between supply and need;
- improve the quality of the Region's housing stock;
- support housing market restructuring and renewal;
- overcome increasing issues of affordability; and
- ensure the needs of the wider population are met, including disabled people, students, older people, black & minority ethnic communities and families with children, including single headed households.

7.7    In line with PPS3, Strategic Housing Market Assessments should be undertaken regularly by groups of local authorities, working in partnership with the Regional Planning Body, the house building industry and other interested parties (such as rural housing enablers). These will integrate existing and new studies into all aspects of housing needs, housing market assessment, existing housing stock condition, the availability of land for development and related issues. It will allow the collection of detailed information which can be used to inform policy relating to the management, renewal and regeneration of the existing housing stock, its renewal and regeneration and the building of new homes, including affordable housing and stock that meets specific local needs. Where appropriate these assessments should include joint work with

---

62    Planning Policy Statement 3: Housing, DCLG, 2006.
63    Homes for the future: more affordable, more sustainable, DCLG, 2007.
64    North West Regional Housing Strategy 2005, North West Regional Housing Board, 2005.

adjoining Local Authorities and other stakeholders in other regions (e.g. North East Wales, North Staffordshire etc). In some circumstances, especially in rural areas, it may be necessary to undertake further more detailed local survey work to assess particular needs.

7.8     Regular Strategic Housing Market Assessments must be accompanied by a continuous process of monitoring housing market trends and drivers, as set out in PPS3 and accompanying guidance [65]. This should provide a basis for adjusting policy and management approaches at both local and regional level, as the impacts of current policies and changing market trends are understood.

7.9     Demographic trends will mean considerable increases in the proportion of older people by 2021. Coupled with the complexity associated with changing lifestyle and housing aspirations, this means that there is a need for:

- housing that more flexibly meets lifestyle changes;
- more variation in the housing offer to reflect the changing nature of household size and need; and
- specialist provision such as extra care homes.

7.10     There is also the requirement to assess the housing needs of gypsies and travellers in the Region. In this respect, the Regional Planning Body, in partnership with the Regional Housing Board has undertaken research on the future requirements of gypsies and travellers. This will inform a future review of both RSS and the Regional Housing Strategy.

---

65     Strategic Housing Market Assessments: Practice Guidance, DCLG, 2007.

## Policy L 3

**Existing Housing Stock and Housing Renewal**

Plans and strategies, across the North West, but particularly in:

a.   Housing Market Renewal Initiative Pathfinder Areas:

- New Heartlands (- Liverpool, Sefton and Wirral);
- Manchester and Salford;
- Oldham and Rochdale;
- Elevate (- Blackburn with Darwen, Burnley, Hyndburn, Pendle and Rossendale);

b.   West Cumbria and Furness Housing Market Renewal Areas;
c.   Lancashire Coastal Towns of Blackpool / Fleetwood and Morecambe;
d.   Other urban areas in the Manchester & Liverpool City Regions in need of housing regeneration \ market restructuring;

should:

- respond to any need to substantially restructure local housing markets;
- take account of and understand housing markets;
- manage the delivery of new build and its impacts on the existing housing stock;
- reduce vacancy rates to 3% in the existing dwelling stock, through the increased re-use of suitable vacant housing; and
- where appropriate make the best use of the existing stock.

Plans and strategies should designate areas, where necessary, for comprehensive regeneration as part of a broader course of action to regenerate local communities, reduce health inequalities, improve the sustainability and resource efficiency of the housing stock and its local environmental quality and increase numbers of and access to local jobs and services. The approach to be adopted, whether clearance, or renewal and refurbishment, or a mix of these, will depend on local circumstances.

Plans and strategies for comprehensive regeneration should:

- involve and engage the local community in determining the future of its area;
- include a prior evaluation of the environmental, economic, social and cultural impacts of the way any proposed clearance and after-uses will affect the surrounding area and the local community; and
- incorporate a clear and comprehensive action plan for implementing proposals, linked to the availability of resources.

**7.11**    One of the biggest problems facing the North West is the condition of some of its existing housing stock and the subsequent need to restructure housing markets in certain areas. Research in 2004 [66] concluded that the poor state of the region's housing stock should be recognised as one of the most significant factors detracting from the health of NW residents. This is now being tackled in line with the Sustainable Communities Plan, Northern Way Growth Strategy, the Regional Housing Strategy and the Housing Market Renewal Pathfinder Initiative.

**7.12**  The challenge in these areas, and elsewhere in the North West, is to ensure that the right mix of housing stock – in terms of type, size and tenure – is available to meet the needs and aspirations of residents (including BME communities), and to create the kind of communities and neighbourhoods where people actually want to live, while at the same time ensuring that the region's economic growth is supported in a sustainable way.

**7.13**  Whilst existing stock will be retained and refurbished wherever possible and appropriate, there may be a need for housing clearance in areas where it is:

- unfit to inhabit;
- beyond economic repair;
- life expired and unsuitable for modern living;
- in areas of extremely low demand; or
- where clearance is necessary to assist the local housing market or overall improvement or regeneration of the area.

**7.14**  In addressing clearance, local planning authorities will need to take account of local circumstances and distinctiveness.  The likely implications for the provision of future housing land should be assessed as part of the ongoing monitoring and review of RSS, regional and local housing strategies and Local Development Frameworks. It should also be considered whether properties need necessarily be replaced on a one-for-one basis.

**7.15**  In addition to new build and conversion activity, the opportunity exists to make better use of existing housing stock. Local authorities are encouraged to take a positive, coordinated approach towards dealing with under used housing stock, for example by identifying vacant and underused properties and introducing empty property strategies to help bring them back into full use. The domestic sector accounts for nearly 30% of greenhouse gas emissions resulting from energy use.  If this is to be reduced, then high standards of energy efficiency in new and existing housing is crucial, and other measures, such as microgeneration of energy from renewable sources on residential property should be encouraged (see policy EM16 and EM18). In addition, the predicted changing climatic conditions [67] mean that climate proofing of new and existing dwellings, using future climate change data will also be important to ensure that the provision of housing stock is fit for purpose. New housing development should incorporate sustainable drainage systems and water conservation and efficiency measures to the highest contemporary standard, and retrofitting of sustainable drainage systems and water efficiency within existing development should be encouraged (see policy EM5).

---

67  "Spatial Implications Of Climate Change For The North West": Centre for Urban & Regional Ecology, University of Manchester and Tyndall Centre North, UMIST 2003.

## Policy L 4

### Regional Housing Provision

Local Authorities should monitor and manage the availability of land identified in plans and strategies and through development control decisions on proposals and schemes, to achieve the housing provision (net of clearance replacement) set out in Table 7.1.

In doing so they should:

- work in partnership with developers and other housing providers to address the housing requirements (including local needs and affordable housing needs) of different groups, (for example disabled people, students, older people, black & minority ethnic communities and families with children including single headed households) to ensure the construction of a mix of appropriate house types, sizes, tenures and prices, in line with policies L2, L3 and L5;
- use the results of up-to-date Strategic Housing Market Assessments and Strategic Housing Land Availability Assessments [68] to inform the allocation of and development control decisions upon specific sites;
- encourage new homes to be built to Code for Sustainable Homes [69] standards and promote the use of the Lifetime Homes standard;
- ensure that new housing development does not have an adverse cumulative impact on the existing housing stock and market;
- ensure that new dwellings will be served by adequate water supply and sewage management facilities;
- allow for clearance replacement to reflect local circumstances, as a mechanism for the recreation of viable and sustainable neighbourhoods;
- introduce phasing policies which secure the orderly and managed release of housing land over the period of the plan in line with the sequential approach set out in Policy DP4, taking into account the need for co-ordinated provision of necessary infrastructure and the overall availability of land for housing;
- ensure that the transport networks (including public transport, pedestrian and cycle) can accommodate additional demand generated by new housing; and
- maximise the re-use of vacant and under-used brownfield land and buildings in line with Policy DP4 and indicative targets set out in Table 7.1.

For the purpose of producing Local Development Frameworks, local planning authorities should assume that the average annual requirement set out in Table 7.1 will continue for a limited period beyond 2021.

**7.16** The scale of housing provision and its distribution seeks to support the economic growth of the North West in line with the overall aspirations of the Regional Economic Strategy and the Regional Housing Strategy. In doing so, it seeks to focus development in those locations which are the key future economic drivers of the regions economy, whilst also taking account of [70]:

---

68    Strategic Housing Land Availability Assessments: Practice Guidance, DCLG, 2007.
69    "Proposals for Introducing a Code for Sustainable Homes - A Consultation Paper", ODPM, 2005.
70    Further details on how this approach has been derived are set out in the RSS Technical Appendix.

- regional development framework, sub regional policies and sustainable development principles embedded within RSS;
- impacts of economic growth scenarios on household growth and its distribution across the NW;
- need to address regional and sub regional disparities;
- future supply constraints;
- impact on existing housing markets and stock especially in those areas identified in Policy L3;
- need to support regeneration;
- need to provide affordable housing; and
- need to sustain rural communities.

In this respect the majority of new housing will be located in the three City Regions.

7.17    The Regional Flood Risk Appraisal provides a broad overview of flood risk issues in the North West, identifying higher risk areas including Salford, Manchester, Chorley, South Ribble and Lancaster.  Plans, strategies, proposals and schemes should appraise, manage and reduce risk, with early completion of Strategic Flood Risk Assessments a key objective to facilitate this.

7.18    The recommended distribution of housing provision between different parts of the North West (Table 7.1), reflects RSS and Regional Housing Strategy objectives, regional development framework and sub regional policies within RSS and takes account of the various strategic priorities and functional linkages, described below, that should be focused upon, in each area [71]. Clearly, housing market characteristics and conditions cannot be precisely or uniformly pinpointed to particular districts and these priorities are not necessarily the only issues that apply in each area.

a.    **Manchester / Salford and Liverpool / Knowsley** – provision of sufficient new residential development to support the role of the Regional Centres and inner city areas, including those parts involved in the Government's Housing Market Renewal Programme's Pathfinder Initiative (including replacement and renewal of housing stock), as priority areas for economic growth and regeneration.  Outside the inner city areas, development should be complementary to the regeneration of the inner core, and be focused on regenerating existing housing areas which suffer from high levels of deprivation.

b.    **Pennine Manchester, Central East Lancashire and East Lancashire** – support for potential economic growth and regeneration, particularly in Housing Market Renewal Pathfinder areas; including replacement and renewal of housing stock and, where appropriate, the development of a wider range of housing types (including high quality market housing). This should be achieved while ensuring that local and affordable housing needs can be met elsewhere.

c.    **Southern Manchester / North East Cheshire** – except in that part of Trafford lying within or adjacent to the Regional Centre, continued careful monitoring and management of housing provision will be necessary to ensure that new housing development does not result in an adverse cumulative impact on local and neighbouring housing markets.  Provision should focus on meeting local and affordable housing needs, and support agreed local regeneration strategies.  Within Macclesfield and Congleton, this development should take place within the context of the economic and social linkages with both the rest of the

---

71    They are not meant to represent distinct housing market areas. These will vary dependant upon different segments of the market and their functionality.

Manchester City Region and also the Potteries and the North Staffordshire Housing Market Renewal Pathfinder.

d.  **Northern Manchester, Mid Mersey and Greater Preston** – provision of sufficient new residential development to support the potential for economic growth and local regeneration strategies (including replacement and renewal of housing stock), a wider range of general and high quality market housing (in sustainable locations which are well served by public transport), while at the same time ensuring the ability to meet local needs and requirements for affordable housing. In Warrington the focus will be on housing provision which meets local and affordable housing needs, and development in support of agreed local regeneration strategies, with continued careful monitoring and management of housing provision, to ensure that new housing development does not result in an adverse cumulative impact on local and neighbouring housing markets.

e.  **South West Lancashire** – continued careful monitoring and management of housing provision will be necessary to ensure that new housing development does not result in an adverse cumulative impact on local and neighbouring housing markets.  Housing provision should focus on meeting local market and affordable housing needs, especially in Ormskirk, Burscough and the northern part of Sefton; and on development in sustainable locations well served by public transport to support agreed local regeneration strategies in Skelmersdale. In the southern part of Sefton the focus will be on providing sufficient new residential development to support inner areas as a priority area for economic growth and regeneration and Housing Market Renewal Initiative Pathfinder activity.

f.  **Wirral** – provision of sufficient new residential development in the eastern part of the district to support the inner areas as a priority for economic growth and regeneration, including via the Housing Market Renewal Pathfinder scheme (including replacement and renewal of housing stock). Elsewhere in the Wirral provision should focus on meeting local and affordable housing needs, with careful monitoring and management of housing provision, to ensure that new housing development does not result in an adverse cumulative impact on local and neighbouring housing markets.

g.  **Fylde Peninsula** – support for regeneration (including replacement and renewal of housing stock) and the potential for economic growth in Blackpool and Fleetwood, while ensuring that local and affordable housing needs can be met elsewhere in the Fylde Peninsula.

h.  **West Cumbria and Furness** – provision of sufficient new residential development to support housing market restructuring and regeneration (including replacement and renewal of housing stock), while ensuring that local and affordable housing needs of rural communities can be met elsewhere in West Cumbria and Furness.

i.  **Lakes & Morecambe Bay** – continued provision of housing to meet local and affordable housing needs of the area's communities, by delivering a choice of properties to suit the local population and workforce. General market housing should be focused in support of regeneration priorities and meeting agreed community priorities, especially within Morecambe and the Furness Peninsula part of South Lakeland, in and around Ulverston. Housing in the Lake District National Park must be developed in keeping with the scale and type that has been identified as appropriate to the area's strict requirements on meeting identified local and affordable needs of the locality.

j.  **North Cumbria** – provision of sufficient new residential development to support the economic growth and regeneration of Carlisle, while ensuring that the local and affordable housing needs of rural communities can be met elsewhere.

k.  **South Cheshire** – provision of housing to meet local and affordable needs, plus general market housing (in sustainable locations which are well served by public transport) to support agreed local regeneration strategies, and the role of Crewe as a key regional town and gateway to the North West. All development should take place within the context of the economic and social links with the rest of Manchester City Region, West Cheshire, the Potteries and the North Staffordshire Housing Market Renewal Pathfinder scheme.

I.  **West Cheshire** – provision of sufficient new residential development to support the economy of Chester and regeneration of Ellesmere Port, while ensuring that local and affordable housing needs can still be met. All this development should take place within the context of the significant economic and social links that exist with North East Wales and the Liverpool City Region. In Vale Royal sufficient housing development to support key local regeneration priorities particularly in Northwich town centre and to address affordable housing needs.

7.19   Detailed advice on managing the supply of housing land is given in PPS3 and in subsequent CLG advice [72]. Local authorities should manage their allocation of land and granting of planning permissions to maintain a minimum five year supply of deliverable housing land, and use their housing trajectory to help monitor and manage the achievement of the figures shown in Table 7.1, and the extent to which this meets local need and demand for housing. The requirement figures are expressed as 'net of clearance replacement', that is to say they are net dwelling gains or the increase over and above the replacement of any dwellings lost through conversion to non residential use or demolition. The overall housing requirement figures for the period covered by this RSS from 2003 to 2021 and the annual average figures are not absolute targets and may be exceeded where justified by evidence of need, demand, affordability and sustainability issues and fit with relevant local and sub-regional strategies. Policies DP1-9 and policy RDF1 should be considered in the application of this policy. Some areas will achieve lower levels in the early years, for example during major housing renewal, which will be compensated later. It is important to ensure that a range of house types, sizes, tenures and prices, which address the housing requirements (including local needs and affordable housing needs), of different groups in the community, whilst making the best use of available land. To achieve this it will be important to build housing at appropriate densities taking account of local circumstances.

7.20   The location of housing will be determined through the Local Development Framework process, using a sequential approach taken to development form in line with DP4. Land supply management should be developed in line with results of Strategic Housing Market Assessments, an assessment of existing housing provision and the potential of urban areas to accommodate more. Local Planning Authorities should take the following guiding principles into account when deciding how development should be phased:

- phasing will be based on the Local Development Framework process; housing land supply should be actively managed in line with PPS3;
- new housing should be located so as to prioritise the re-use of brownfield land and buildings within existing urban areas that are accessible by a choice of transport methods in line with DP4 and W4;
- sites should not be released unless sufficient capacity including water supply and waste-water treatment exists or can be provided ahead of the development without environmental harm in line with EM5.

Local authorities should be aware of the policy framework and potential provision of housing land that exists in adjoining areas taking a joint approach where possible. A consistent approach across the sub region will ensure that an early release of land in one district does not undermine urban renaissance in another.

---

72   Planning Policy Statement 3: Housing (PPS3), DCLG, 2006; and Demonstrating a 5 Year Supply of Deliverable Sites, CLG advice available at http://www.planning-inspectorate.gov.uk.

# 7 Living in the North West – Ensuring a Strong, Healthy and Just Society

**7.21** Where housing market areas cross administrative (and in some cases regional) boundaries, or where major disparities in levels of previously developed land exist between neighbouring authorities, cooperation and joint working will be necessary to ensure that sites are released in a way that supports sustainable patterns of development. The Local Planning Authorities involved should take care not to either pursue Local Development Framework allocations or else grant planning permissions that result in over provision and early release of land in one district to the detriment of urban renaissance either in the same district or in other Local Authority areas. Where a particular district has insufficient sustainable sites that match the above criteria to meet their target, they should consider working with their neighbours to find ways of meeting the balance elsewhere in the sub region.

**Table 7.1 Distribution of Regional Housing Provision 2003-2021**

| | Total Housing Provision 2003 – 2021 (Net of clearance replacement) | Annual Average rates of Housing Provision (Net of clearance replacement) | Indicative target proportion of housing provision to use brownfield land & buildings |
|---|---|---|---|
| **NORTH WEST** | 416,000 | 23,111 | At least 70% |
| **Manchester / Salford** | | | |
| Manchester | 63,000 | 3,500 | At least 90% |
| Salford | 28,800 | 1,600 | |
| **Pennine Manchester** | | | |
| Oldham | 5,200 | 289 | At least 80% |
| Rochdale | 7,200 | 400 | |
| Tameside | 13,500 | 750 | |
| **Southern Manchester / North East Cheshire** | | | |
| Stockport | 8,100 | 450 | At least 80% |
| Trafford | 10,400 | 578 | |
| Congleton | 5,400 | 300 | |
| Macclesfield | 7,200 | 400 | |
| **Northern Manchester** | | | |
| Bolton | 10,400 | 578 | At least 80% |
| Bury | 9,000 | 500 | |
| Wigan | 17,600 | 978 | |
| **Liverpool / Knowsley** | | | |
| Knowsley | 8,100 | 450 | At least 65% |
| Liverpool | 35,100 | 1,950 | At least 90% |
| **Mid Mersey** | | | |
| Halton | 9,000 | 500 | At least 65% |
| St Helens | 10,260 | 570 | |
| Warrington | 6,840 | 380 | At least 80% |
| **Wirral** | | | |
| Wirral | 9,000 | 500 | At least 80% |
| **South West Lancashire** | | | |
| Sefton | 9,000 | 500 | At least 65% |
| West Lancashire | 5,400 | 300 | |
| **Greater Preston** | | | |
| Chorley | 7,500 | 417 | At least 70% |
| Preston | 9,120 | 507 | |

| | Total Housing Provision 2003 – 2021 (Net of clearance replacement) | Annual Average rates of Housing Provision (Net of clearance replacement) | Indicative target proportion of housing provision to use brownfield land & buildings |
|---|---|---|---|
| South Ribble | 7,500 | 417 | |
| **Central East Lancashire** | | | |
| Blackburn with Darwen | 8,800 | 489 | At least 65% |
| Hyndburn | 3,400 | 189 | |
| RibbleValley | 2,900 | 161 | |
| **East Lancashire** | | | |
| Burnley | 2,340 | 130 | At least 65% |
| Pendle | 3,420 | 190 | |
| Rossendale | 4,000 | 222 | |
| **Fylde Peninsula** | | | |
| Wyre | 3,700 | 206 | At least 65% |
| Blackpool | 8,000 | 444 | |
| Fylde | 5,500 | 306 | |
| **West Cumbria and Furness** | | | |
| Allerdale (outside of National Park) | 4,800 | 267 | At least 50% |
| Barrow in Furness | 2,700 | 150 | At least 80% |
| Copeland (outside of National Park) | 4,140 | 230 | At least 50% |
| **Lakes & Morecambe Bay** | | | |
| Eden (outside of National Park) | 4,300 | 239 | At least 50% |
| South Lakeland (outside of National Park) | 7,200 | 400 | |
| Lake District National Park | 1,080 | 60 | |
| Lancaster | 7,200 | 400 | At least 70% |
| **North Cumbria** | | | |
| Carlisle | 8,100 | 450 | At least 50% |
| **South Cheshire** | | | |
| Crewe and Nantwich | 8,100 | 450 | At least 60% |
| **West Cheshire** | | | |
| Chester | 7,500 | 417 | At least 80% |
| Ellesmere Port and Neston | 7,200 | 400 | |
| Vale Royal | 9,000 | 500 | |

**7** Living in the North West – Ensuring a Strong, Healthy and Just Society

## Policy L 5

### Affordable Housing

Plans and strategies should set out requirements for affordable housing [73], and the location, size and types of development to which these requirements apply. Evidence, including from Strategic Housing Market Assessments, should be used to support the setting of quotas and thresholds for affordable housing provision along with an indication of the type, size and tenure of affordable housing required.

It is anticipated that the greatest need will be in areas of high demand where affordability issues are unbalancing local communities, due to high prices and low wages and/or the adverse effects of second homes, although affordability is an increasing concern in many parts of the region.

Plans and strategies should set out a range of delivery mechanisms to secure the provision of affordable housing. Local authorities should consider all or some of the following where appropriate:

- seeking a proportion of affordable housing on all development sites which are above the relevant thresholds;
- allocating the development of sites solely (or primarily) for affordable housing use (i.e. up to 100% affordable in rural areas), where necessary;
- using local occupancy criteria to support provision for local housing need so long as this need can be clearly demonstrated, to be implemented through the use of planning conditions and obligations;
- actively promoting the rural exception site policy;
- for all sites containing housing in rural settlements with populations of under 3,000 promote onsite affordable housing provision and where on site affordable housing provision is not possible, seeking developer contributions towards affordable housing;
- making the most of publicly owned land;
- making the most of existing housing stock;
- in line with Policy W4, permitting the conversion of buildings in sustainable locations to residential use (including as part of mixed use schemes), particularly where commercial premises which are vacant or under-used and offer no long term potential or viable contribution to the local economy;
- encouraging employers to provide housing for their key workers;
- ensuring that wherever possible (and subject to continuing evidence), that property remains affordable and available in perpetuity.

---

73    Affordable housing is defined in Annex B of Planning Policy Statement 3: Housing (PPS), DCLG, 2006.

**7.22** The affordability of housing is established by taking into account the ratio between income levels and house prices or rents (a more detailed and reliable picture can be obtained by mapping lower quartile incomes to lower quartile house prices). To a greater or lesser extent, there is a shortage of supply of affordable housing in all parts of the North West [74], and certain issues are relevant to both rural and urban areas, not least the need to maintain sustainable, balanced communities. Additionally in some locations affordability needs are compounded by low wage levels, which inhibit access to the housing market. The holistic approach necessary to address the problems caused by this shortage is considered in more detail in the Regional Housing Strategy [75], whilst action to tackle the low wage economy of some areas is tackled by both the economic policies of this RSS and the Regional Economic Strategy.

**7.23** Using the results of up to date Strategic Housing Market Assessments and local studies where appropriate, local authorities must address the need for more affordable housing and identify the methods by which they will aim to introduce an element of affordable housing into residential and mixed use development schemes, ensuring long term provision and availability in perpetuity, which may include the need to set conditions relating to occupancy. Such assessments should identify the specific needs of particular groups within the community.

**7.24** For monitoring purposes, in line with current practice, all affordable housing constructed (including that built on 'rural exceptions sites') will count towards an individual districts housing provision figures set out in Table 7.1.

---

74    Table 4.11 Appendix 4 – "North West Household Growth Estimates Study" prepared by Nathaniel Lichfield & Partners for North West Regional Assembly, 2005.

75    Priority 2 of "The North West Regional Housing Strategy 2005" North West Regional Housing Board, 2005.

8 Transport in the North West – Connecting People and Places

# 8 Transport in the North West – Connecting People and Places

## Transport Objectives

The Regional Transport Strategy embraces the spatial principles (DP1-9) and the regional and sub-regional spatial frameworks (policy RDF1) and sub regional policies. In particular it seeks to:

- maintain existing transport infrastructure in good order;
- improve journey time reliability, tackle congestion and overcrowding in the region's main transport corridors shown on the Key Diagram, particularly within and between City Regions;
- secure a shift towards the use of more sustainable modes of transport;
- secure safe and efficient access between residential areas and key destinations, including centres of employment, schools, shops and other services;
- improve surface access and interchange arrangements at the international, national and regional gateways (as defined in Appendix RT(b));
- reduce the adverse impacts of transport, in terms of safety hazards, climate change, environmental degradation, residential amenity and social exclusion;
- integrate the management and planning of transport systems.

8.1 The RSS transport policies (RTS) support the vision and objectives of RSS by concentrating on the development of better transport links within the region, and between the North West and other parts of the UK, Ireland, mainland Europe and beyond. They aim to do this by significantly improving the quality and provision of public transport and by promoting a more structured approach to managing and selectively improving the region's highway network. In doing so, the policies align with the RES objective to develop the North West's strategic transport, communications and economic infrastructure, and with the policy priorities of the Northern Way Growth Strategy, particularly in terms of improving road and rail access to the North of England's main ports and airports and creating better integrated public transport services within and between City Regions. This chapter of RSS also advocates policies and proposals which should contribute to reducing greenhouse gas emissions from the transport sector.

## Policy RT 1

### Integrated Transport Networks

Transport problems and issues in the region should be examined on a multi-modal basis to develop sustainable, integrated and accessible solutions for all users. The management of routes in the Regional Highway Network should be closely co-ordinated with relevant Route Utilisation Strategies on the rail network where available.

Plans and strategies should seek to make best use of existing infrastructure and to capitalise on developments in intelligent transport systems and information and communications technology. They should focus on improving journey time reliability in the transport corridors shown on the Key Diagram and in Appendix RT(a) and enhancing the accessibility of the region's gateways and interchanges, particularly the international ones, as listed in Appendix RT(b).

8.2   A sustainable approach to integrated transport requires each mode to contribute to future travel needs in an efficient and complementary way. The transport corridors essential for both external and internal connectivity are as shown on the Key Diagram, together with international gateways. These transport corridors include the public transport and highway networks for which policy frameworks are set out in Policies RT3 and RT4 respectively. Local authorities, the Highways Agency, the rail industry and other transport providers will need to work together to ensure that all of the region's transport networks are planned, managed, operated and improved in an integrated context.

8.3   It is now widely accepted that constructing new roads to accommodate future traffic growth is neither environmentally nor economically sustainable. The emphasis should therefore be on increasing the role of public transport together with making best use of existing highway infrastructure through the development of effective strategies for network and demand management. Congestion has a significant impact on journey time reliability, affecting the productivity of businesses and industry, and in urban areas reduces the reliability of road-based public transport. It can also affect access to key ports and airports, potentially undermining the region's economic competitiveness and growth potential. Although congestion on the highway network occurs mainly during peak periods, these are becoming increasingly longer.

# 8 Transport in the North West – Connecting People and Places

## Policy RT 2

### Managing Travel Demand

The Regional Planning Body, local authorities, and other highway and transport authorities should develop a coordinated approach to managing travel demand. Early consultation with the Highways Agency will be required for any proposal that may affect the trunk road network. In particular, efforts should be aimed at reducing the proportion of car-borne commuting and education trips made during peak periods and tackling the most congested parts of the motorway network including M6, M56, M60 and M62. In rural areas, the focus should be on major tourist areas where visitor pressure is threatening the local environment and quality of life. Measures to discourage car use should consider improvements to and promotion of public transport, walking and cycling.

Plans and strategies will need to be specific to the nature and scale of the problems identified, set clear objectives and specify what is being proposed, why it is necessary and what the impacts will be. They should:

- ensure that major new developments are located where there is good access to public transport, backed by effective provision for pedestrians and cyclists to minimise the need to travel by private car;
- seek to reduce private car use through the introduction of 'smarter choices' (see examples in paragraph 8.6) and other incentives to change travel behaviour which should be developed alongside public transport, cycling and pedestrian network and service improvements;
- consider the effective reallocation of road space in favour of public transport, pedestrians and cyclists alongside parking charges, enforcement and provision and other fiscal measures, including road user charging;
- make greater use of on-street parking controls and enforcement;
- incorporate maximum parking standards that are in line with, or more restrictive than, Table 8.1, and define standards for additional land use categories and areas where more restrictive standards should be applied. Parking for disabled people and for cycles and two-wheel motorised vehicles are the only situations where minimum standards will be applicable.

8.4    Road traffic is a major source of carbon dioxide emissions, with increasing car use contributing towards global warming and climate change. Policy DP5 seeks to reduce the need to travel and to assist people to meet their needs locally, whilst at the same time ensuring that all new development is genuinely accessible by public transport, walking and cycling. Travel in the North West is currently over-reliant on the private car, particularly for journeys to and from work and educational establishments. The dispersed patterns of development that have taken place in recent years have contributed to an increase in both the number and length of journeys undertaken. For journeys to work, 74% of residents travel by car [76], and it is estimated that around 20% of vehicles on the road during the morning peak period are associated with the 'School Run' [77]. In rural areas, many tourist attractions and facilities are largely dependent on access by car.

---

76    National Travel Survey, Department for Transport, 2004.
77    No More School Run: Proposal for a National Yellow Bus Scheme in the UK, The Sutton Trust, June 2005.

**8.5** Strategies need to be developed to manage the demand for travel in the most sustainable way, and a co-ordinated approach across local authority boundaries should help to prevent inefficient competition between different locations. A thorough understanding of relevant problems and issues will be essential if local authorities are to ensure that specific proposals are the most appropriate solutions to achieving desired outcomes, and are politically, socially and environmentally acceptable. The Highways Agency currently updates Stress Maps on an annual basis. These should serve to inform strategic decision making and monitoring of developments on the strategic road network.

**8.6** 'Smarter choices', including company, school and personal travel plans, safer routes to school, travel awareness campaigns such as TravelWise, car pooling, car sharing schemes, car clubs and park and ride schemes, the availability of real time travel information and integrated ticketing and the increasing popularity of home working can contribute towards changing travel behaviour and will complement enhancement of the public transport, pedestrian and cycling networks (Policies RT3 and RT9) and the exploitation of new technology to manage existing transport infrastructure more effectively. Fiscal measures such as charging for travel on congested roads or for workplace parking are also likely to be an important factor in influencing the number of people prepared to switch from private cars to public transport, and funds raised could be re-invested in public transport, pedestrian and cycle networks.

**8.7** Parking charges, enforcement and provision are all key elements of an effective strategy to manage the demand for travel by car as the availability and cost of parking is potentially a major influence on travel decisions and can promote more sustainable transport choices. To maximise effectiveness, parking policies and provision should complement wider land-use and accessibility plans and strategies.

**8.8** The North West Parking Standards as set out in Table 8.1 specify the upper limit of parking to be provided at developments. Guidance is given as to how the appropriate standards for a particular site should be determined. These standards are equally as restrictive as those contained in PPG13 and are based on current regional practice. The urban values are intended to be more restrictive than the regional ones as there are generally higher levels of public transport accessibility and development densities in the former. Standards could be even more restrictive in those areas that have the highest levels of public transport accessibility and development density and, where appropriate, in environmentally sensitive areas such as the Lake District National Park. Further advice and examples are given in Appendix RT(c).

**Table 8.1 North West Parking Standards**

| Land Use | Regional [6] | Urban [6] |
|---|---|---|
| **A1: Shops** | | |
| Food Retail | 1 space per 14 sqm | 1 space per 16 sqm |
| Non-food Retail | 1 space per 20 sqm | 1 space per 22 sqm |
| **A3: Restaurants and Cafes** | | |
| Restaurant | 1 space per 5 sqm of public floor area | 1 space per 7 sqm of public floor area |
| **A5: Hot Food Takeaways** | | |
| Fast Food & Drive Through | 1 space per 7.5 sqm of gross floor area [1] | 1 space per 8.5 sqm of gross floor area [1] |
| **B1: Business** | | |
| B1 including offices | | |
| Stand alone offices | 1 space per 30 sqm | 1 space per 35 sqm |

## 8 Transport in the North West – Connecting People and Places

| Land Use | Regional [6] | Urban [6] |
|---|---|---|
| Business Parks | 1 space per 35 sqm | 1 space per 40 sqm |
| **B2: General Industry** | | |
| General Industry | 1 space per 45 sqm | 1 space per 60 sqm |
| **B8: Storage and Distribution** | | |
| Storage and Distribution | 1 space per 100 sqm | 1 space per 100 sqm |
| **C1: Hotels** | | |
| Hotels | 1 space per bedroom including staff [3] | 1 space per bedroom including staff [3] |
| **D1: Non-Residential Institutions** | | |
| Medical and Health facilities | 1 space per 2 staff plus 4 per consulting room | 1 space per 2 staff plus 3 per consulting room |
| Higher and Further Education | 1 space per 2 staff [2,4] | 1 space per 2 staff [2,4] |
| **D2: Assembly and Leisure** | | |
| Cinemas and Conference Facilities | 1 space per 5 seats | 1 space per 8 seats |
| Other leisure facilities | 1 space per 22 sqm | 1 space per 25 sqm |
| **Miscellaneous** | | |
| Stadia | 1 space per 15 seats | 1 space per 18 seats |

Notes:

1. For predominantly drive-through/take-away establishments. For 'Drive-through' restaurants featuring significant seating then they should be considered as a conventional restaurant.
2. To be backed up with a more detailed justification including 'Travel Plans' proposals.
3. Additional facilities, such as leisure and conference facilities should be considered separately if appropriate.
4. Parking for students should be included within this figure. Separate consideration would be required for any parking related to residential facilities.

| Land Use | Regional [6] | Urban [6] |
|---|---|---|
| 5. The standard for students relates to the total number of students attending an educational establishment rather than full-time equivalent number. | | |
| 6. Local Development Frameworks should identify the areas where 'urban' and 'regional' standards will apply. | | |

## Policy RT 3

### Public Transport Framework

The Public Transport Framework set out in Appendix RT (a) defines the North West's main public transport corridors. These are also shown in Diagram 2 of Appendix RT. Appendix RT(b) defines a hierarchy of gateways and interchanges in the North West. Similar frameworks should be developed by local authorities for sub-regional and local networks and set out in Local Transport Plans.

Plans and strategies should seek to reduce existing or forecast overcrowding along the main public transport corridors by improvements to transport infrastructure in partnership with operators and delivery partners including Network Rail where appropriate. Local authorities and station operators should consider making additional provision for car parking at railway stations, so as to promote maximum use of the rail network.

Local authorities should introduce measures to enhance the accessibility by public transport, cycling and walking of the regional centres and towns / cities identified in RDF1. In rural areas, priority should be given to providing access from rural hinterlands to key service centres.

Local authorities should work in partnership with public transport providers to improve the quality and provision of public transport services. Proposals and schemes to enhance services in the corridors identified in Appendix RT(a) should include priority measures to improve journey time reliability. Interchange and service improvements should be supported by better information provision, marketing and integrated ticketing.

Local authorities should identify in Local Transport Plans where existing public transport provision is insufficient and where public, community and demand responsive transport networks should be developed which link employment, education and training opportunities with areas of need.

Regional public transport priorities for investment and management are included in policy RT10.

**8.9**    Travel by car dominates movement in the North West with the average person making 672 journeys per annum by car compared to 63 by local bus and 27 by other public transport. This is also reflected in commuter choices: 74% travel by private car; 8% by bus and only 2% by heavy rail. Nevertheless, the percentage of modal share by public transport equates to 66 million rail journeys and 470 million bus journeys across the region each year. As the regional economy has grown, the extra demand for travel generated has placed a significant strain on the public transport network.  Successful urban regeneration and economic development requires an integrated approach to public transport, walking and cycling whilst at the same time discouraging car use and improving public transport accessibility.  Development of the rail network as part of a comprehensive integrated public transport system is particularly important in the Manchester and Liverpool city regions, where the greatest potential exists to increase patronage.

8.10    Opportunities for the physical expansion of public transport, especially with regards to heavy and light rail, are restricted by the high cost of providing new infrastructure, and the limited funding available for local bus services. Furthermore, the significant improvements in public transport provision necessary to support the Regional Spatial Strategy will not be fully achieved unless the critical issues of regulation and revenue support are addressed. However, Authorities should be encouraged to explore alternative funding opportunities, for example through partnership with private funding streams. As a result, the policy concentrates on making best use of existing resources to ensure that corridors which connect city regions and those that provide links within them continue to function effectively and are improved in such a way as to make public transport a viable and attractive alternative to the private car. As overcrowding is already an issue on a number of the rail and bus routes that serve the regional centres of Manchester/Salford and Liverpool, local transport authorities should work with operators to ensure that passenger capacity is increased where required.

8.11    Sub-regional and local public transport frameworks should complement the regional framework identified in this policy and ensure access to jobs and services (especially in disadvantaged areas) in line with the Department for Transport's "Guidance on Accessibility in Local Transport Plans" [78]. This is especially pertinent in areas of deprivation which can suffer isolation and lack access to job opportunities and often have the lowest levels of car ownership.

8.12    Effective interchange both within and between modes is essential, and can be achieved through improvements to the quality and attractiveness of bus and rail interchanges, introducing measures such as through-ticketing and providing better information to make journeys easier to plan.  Local authorities should work in partnership with operators to deliver improvements to the public transport network including addressing issues of personal safety and security, and, where practicable, the promotion of solutions to reduce the impact of public transport on the environment.  If partnership working does not prove to be possible, provided the lack of engagement is not due to the restrictions of competition legislation, the local authority should seek to introduce bus quality contracts.  Local authorities and other stakeholders should engage with government and the rail industry to deliver the greatest benefit to passengers through the rail refranchising process. Targeted marketing initiatives should also be used to attract people to public transport, especially once improvements have been made. With regard to accessing public transport services, adequate consideration needs to be given to parking provision (including suitable secure facilities for cycles and two-wheel motorised vehicles).

8.13    Community and demand responsive transport has an important role to play in improving access to employment, services and facilities. This is particularly so in rural areas where traditional commercial bus services are less likely to be financially viable and revenue support opportunities are limited. Furthermore, it is essential that adequate community consultation is undertaken when changes to service provision are proposed to ensure that proposals deliver the desired benefits to likely users of services.

---

78    Guidance on Accessibility in Local Transport Plans, Department for Transport, December, 2004.

## Policy RT 4

### Management of the Highway Network

The region's road network is vital to the economy of the North West, providing the means to transport goods and people within and outside the region. However, existing and forecast traffic congestion is a constraint on economic growth and needs to be addressed if the North West is to reduce the productivity gap.

The Functional Road Hierarchy set out in Appendix RT(c) and shown on Diagram 3 of Appendix RT identifies those routes which comprise the Regional Highway Network. Local authorities should extend the concept of functional hierarchies to sub-regional and local highway networks.

The Highways Agency and Local Highway authorities should prepare Route Management Plans in accordance with Regional Planning Body guidance for all routes in the Regional Highway Network. Plans should make best use of existing infrastructure and proposals for major highway improvements should only be included following an examination of all practical alternative solutions to a particular problem.

Plans and strategies for managing traffic should focus on improving road safety, reducing traffic growth and maintaining a high quality environment through mitigating the impacts of road traffic on air quality, noise and health, with traffic encouraged to use the most appropriate routes wherever possible. In rural areas, particular emphasis should be given to maintaining the tranquillity of the countryside. Where safety is not compromised, highway engineering measures should reflect local character, including landscape and conservation.

Where a route is the responsibility of more than one highway authority, the relevant authorities should adopt a consistent approach to maintenance and management, including the adoption of appropriate speed limits by reference to the road's function, standard and environmental context. The harmonisation of speed limits across highway authority boundaries should be considered to achieve consistency on routes of similar function and standard. Maximum use should be made of secondary and recycled aggregates in road construction and maintenance schemes in line with policies EM9 and DP4.

Local authorities should work with freight, coach and parking operators to develop plans and strategies to identify sites for the provision of driver rest and parking facilities.

**8.14** Application of the Functional Road Hierarchy concept to sub-regional and local road networks should help to ensure a consistent approach to highway management and maintenance across the Region, and provide a framework through which local authorities can develop their role as a network operator. Networks of sub-regional importance should be identified in Local Transport Plans. In defining such networks, local authorities will need to take account of the environmental and social impacts of road freight transport. Routes of less than sub-regional importance should not form part of the Primary Route Network.

**8.15**    Route Management Plans should be prepared in accordance with separate guidance to be developed by the Regional Planning Body. Where a particular route is the responsibility of more than one highway authority, a single Route Management Plan should be developed and a consistent approach to management and maintenance agreed.

**8.16**    The King Review (HM Treasury, 2007) indicates that road transport has dramatically enhanced the mobility, economic prosperity and quality of life for millions of people. However, the lack of a systematic approach to highway management in the past has contributed in part to a multitude of different problems, including through traffic using residential streets in urban areas to avoid congestion at junctions on main roads and an increasing use of unsuitable local roads in rural areas to avoid congestion on strategic routes (for example, the M6 corridor through Cheshire). On the other hand, the effective operation of some sections of motorway in the Manchester City Region is undermined through extensive use by local traffic making short distance trips, particularly during peak periods (for example, the M62/M60 between Junctions 12 and 18). In addition to the problem of congestion and its impact on journey time reliability, inappropriate use of the highway network has significant health and safety implications, including road safety and the environmental and social consequences of traffic in towns, villages and the wider countryside. Road transport has a significant impact on the natural, built and historic environment.  Across the North West there is growing concern that local communities in both urban and rural areas are now suffering from the negative effects of traffic, including problems of road safety, poor air quality, noise, severance and visual intrusion. In rural areas, where traffic growth is increasing at a faster rate than elsewhere, the loss or fragmentation of tranquil areas and light pollution are also issues of concern.

**8.17**    Whilst good progress has been made in the North West towards the 2010 casualty reduction targets for killed and seriously injured (KSI) compared with the 1994 to 1998 average, road traffic collisions remain one of the principal causes of injury and loss of life in the region, affecting pedestrians and cyclists as well as drivers, passengers and motorcyclists. The majority of children killed or seriously injured on the region's roads are either pedestrians or cyclists hit by vehicles travelling at speed. Road traffic collisions have consequences for health service resources and delays arising from additional congestion and disruption can have an adverse impact on the economy. It is important, therefore, that road safety considerations are taken into account in regional transport planning, particularly those relating to issues such as the observance of speed limits and inappropriate speed, which can be of benefit for all road users.

**8.18**    EU legislation [79] obliges drivers of freight vehicles and coaches to take statutory breaks, creating a need for appropriate short stay and for lorries, in particular, overnight parking facilities. Local Authorities should work with freight, coach and parking operators to develop a comprehensive approach in providing these facilities, as increased pressure to develop land in urban areas has led to goods vehicles being forced to park in unsuitable locations. In tourist and other areas that attract large numbers of coaches, local authorities should identify short stay drop-off and pick-up points close to amenities along with nearby, secure long stay parking areas.

---

79    Road Transport Sectoral Directive 2002/15/EC.

## Policy RT 5

### Airports

Plans and strategies should support the economic activity generated and sustained by the Region's airports, in particular, the importance of Manchester Airport as a key economic driver for the North of England and Liverpool John Lennon Airport for the Liverpool City Region. Airport operators, in partnership with stakeholders, should implement surface transport initiatives which ensure that access by public transport, walking and cycling for both passengers and employees across the site is continually enhanced to reduce car dependency and ensure that all local environmental standards are met.

For Manchester, Liverpool John Lennon and Blackpool Airports, the future operational and infrastructure requirements, surface access demands and environmental impacts for each airport should be identified and measures to address and monitor them included in Airport Master Plans and other relevant plans and strategies, based on the strategic framework for the development of airport capacity set out in the White Paper 'Future of Air Transport'. For Carlisle Airport, proposals for development should be considered through the local planning process. If proposals exceed 20,000 air transport movements annually by 2030 the airport should consider developing an Airport Masterplan.

Airport boundaries, as existing or as proposed, should be shown in Local Development Documents. Development that would impede the operational requirements of an airport should not be permitted within this boundary.

In determining requirements for the expansion of an airport beyond its existing boundary, plans and strategies should take account of:

- the scope for intensification and rationalisation of activities and facilities within the existing boundary;
- the scope for relocating existing activities or facilities off-site;
- the scope for developing proposed activities or facilities off-site.

Plans and strategies for airports and adjacent areas should include measures to regulate the availability of car parking space for passengers and employees across the site.

In considering applications for development at airports, account will be taken of:

- the extent to which surface access and car parking arrangements encourage the use of public transport, walking and cycling;
- the effect of the proposed development on noise and atmospheric pollution, and the extent to which this can be mitigated;
- the effect of the proposed development on the health and wellbeing of local communities; and
- the adverse effects on sites of national and international nature conservation importance to ensure that these effects are avoided, mitigated or compensated as appropriate.

In formulating plans and strategies, account should be taken of the contribution general aviation makes to the regional and local economies, and the role smaller airfields have in providing for both business and leisure.

8.19    This policy should be read in conjunction with RDF 4 (Green Belt) and DP7 (Promote Environmental Quality) which are particularly relevant given the location of some of the regions airports. Development at Liverpool John Lennon Airport could lead to impacts upon the integrity of the sites of international importance found within the wider Liverpool Bay area and at Carlisle Airport on the sites associated with the Solway. Accordingly, proposals and plans related to airport development which would be likely to have a significant effect on the areas listed above would be subject to assessment, under the Habitats Regulations.

8.20    Airports generate employment, attract businesses to the area, open up markets and encourage tourism and visitors.  The Future of Air Transport recognises that building of local supply chain and capacity for the aviation industry could bring important benefits to the economies of regions and promotes the establishment of Centres of Excellence outside the South East of England.  However, regionally significant business development that is not required for the operation of an airport should be located in accordance with the criteria set out in Policy W2 above.  Manchester Airport is by far the largest in the UK outside of the South East of England, serving some 21 million passengers each year and offering a broad range of flights including long-haul scheduled services. More intensive use of the two runways could see the Airport increase the number of passengers it caters for up to 50 million per annum. Liverpool John Lennon Airport is the North West's second airport and has seen rapid recent growth in recent years with passenger numbers exceeding 4 million annually. Blackpool Airport has recently experienced considerable growth in scheduled routes and now caters for around 300,000 passengers per year, supporting the resort's tourism-led regeneration and serving the Central Lancashire City Region.

8.21    The Government's Air Transport White Paper [80] sets out a strategic policy framework for the development of air services in the UK to around 2030. The White Paper does not authorise or preclude any particular development, but intends to inform plans and strategies and guide decisions on future planning applications. Airport operators, in conjunction with the Highways Agency, local authorities, the rail industry and transport providers, need to address issues that restrict access to airports by road and rail for passengers, staff, freight operators and visitors, which may impede the development of the national and regional economies. It should, however, be recognised that the significant growth in aviation forecast in the White Paper will have environmental and social impacts and must be managed in such a way that these are minimised. Airport operators should also set themselves challenging targets for increasing the proportion of journeys made to airports by public transport, cycling and walking in Surface Access Strategies that will reduce dependence on the private car, and environmental targets that will reduce noise and atmospheric pollution from surface activities.  Airport development should be contingent upon adherence to such targets, and this principle should be incorporated in development plan policy.

8.22    Smaller airports can serve local business needs, especially in more remote areas, as well as accommodating recreational flying and providing training facilities. Local authorities should therefore recognise in their plans and strategies the contribution general aviation can make to the regional and local economies. As demand for commercial air transport grows, general aviation users may find that access to the larger airports becomes increasingly restricted and hence they are forced to look to smaller airfields to provide facilities.

---

80    The Future of Air Transport, Department for Transport, December 2003.

## Policy RT 6

### Ports and Waterways

The region will optimise the use of its ports and waterways assets, for trade and leisure, whilst at the same time protecting the environment and the integrity of their biodiversity. Plans and strategies should support the economic activity generated and sustained by the Region's major ports and waterways, in particular, the Port of Liverpool, as the North West's key international sea port, and the Manchester Ship Canal. Port operators in partnership with stakeholders should develop land-side surface access plans to accommodate existing and projected freight and passenger traffic. There should be a presumption in favour of making best use of existing infrastructure where possible, and opportunities to secure the transfer of port-related freight from road to rail or water should be explored.

It is recommended that for the Port of Liverpool, the Manchester Ship Canal, Port of Heysham and Fleetwood, the future operational and infrastructure requirements, surface access demands and environmental impacts for each port should be identified and measures to address and monitor them included in Port Masterplans and relevant plans and strategies. For navigations and waterways, Local Authorities and operators should work in partnership with appropriate navigation authorities to investigate and identify bottlenecks and develop solutions.

Port boundaries, as existing or as proposed, should be shown in Local Development Documents. Development that would impede the operational requirements of a port should not be permitted within this boundary. There should be a strong presumption in favour of safeguarding land close to ports for logistics, transport and port-related development where there is at least a reasonable likelihood of restitution to significant operational use within fifteen years and where the alternative use in contemplation is one, such as residential development, which will be difficult to reverse. Land with wharfside frontages should also be protected for future uses that require a water connection where there is a likelihood of such re-use in the short term.

In determining requirements for the expansion of a port beyond its existing boundary, plans and strategies should take account of:

- the scope for intensification and rationalisation of activities and facilities within the existing boundary;
- the scope for relocating existing activities or facilities off-site;
- the scope for developing proposed activities or facilities off-site.

Plans and strategies for ports and adjacent areas should include measures to regulate the availability of car parking spaces to accommodate existing and projected passengers and employees across the site.

In considering applications for development at ports, account will be taken of:

- the extent to which land-side surface access can assist the transfer of port traffic from road to rail and/or water;
- the extent to which it reduces unsustainable use of ports in other UK regions;

- the effect of the proposed development on the health and wellbeing of local communities; and
- the adverse effects on sites of national and international nature conservation importance to ensure that these effects are avoided, mitigated or compensated as appropriate.

**8.23**    This policy should be read in conjunction with policies RDF3 (The Coast) and EM6 (Managing the North West's Coastline) and DP7 (Promote Environmental Quality). The proximity of potential port developments at Liverpool, Birkenhead and the Manchester Ship Canal and the 'in-combination' impacts of such development on the integrity and conservation objectives of the sites of international importance found within the wider Liverpool Bay area will need to assessed and mitigated against. Similarly such assessment and mitigation may be necessary at Heysham and Fleetwood, where there may also be 'in combination' disturbance impacts of development on the integrity of the sites of International Importance associated with Morecambe Bay and Liverpool Bay. The impacts from development include (but are not limited to) construction and shipping related disturbance and pollution and land take leading to a potential risk of "coastal squeeze". "Coastal squeeze" occurs when rises in sea levels along with coastal development reduce the available coastal strip between the land and sea.

**8.24**    The North West ports and waterways are important gateways for trade and travel and provide opportunities to promote the cultural diversity and history of the region.  In 2005, 47.5 million tonnes of cargo was moved through the region's ports.  In addition to handling freight, the ports provide major leisure and tourism opportunities for the region. 984,000 passengers (2005 based figures) used the roll-on, roll-off (Ro-Ro) ferry services which operate from Liverpool, Birkenhead, Heysham and Fleetwood, which are of major importance to the economies of Northern Ireland and the Republic of Ireland.  There are also opportunities to develop cruise liner facilities, particularly at the Port of Liverpool.  The North West Ports Economic Trends and Land Use Study [81] has informed policy development. National policy is set out in 'Modern Ports: A UK Policy' [82] which is being reviewed. In the North West, Liverpool, Manchester (Manchester Ship Canal), Heysham and Fleetwood are categorised as major ports by the Department for Transport in that they handle at least one million tonnes of cargo per annum. Other ports are located at Barrow-in-Furness, Silloth and Workington in Cumbria, Glasson Dock near Lancaster and Garston Dock on the River Mersey.

**8.25**    Liverpool is by far the most dominant port in the Region and in 2005 handled 33.7 million tonnes of cargo, an all time record.  It operates the UK's largest Freeport zone with extensive facilities on both sides of the River Mersey, acting as a hub connecting world-wide deep-sea services with an extensive network of Continental, UK and Irish Sea short-sea services. Birkenhead in particular and Seaforth Container Terminal have the potential for significant further development. Ports in the North West also have a role to play in supporting EC initiatives to encourage the transfer of freight from land to water transport (see Policy RT7 and RT8).

**8.26**    North West ports benefit the regional economy by helping to attract investment and new employment opportunities, assisted by their capacity to act as multi-modal interchanges and to provide logistical services and manufacturing on-site. The availability of suitable land to accommodate these facilities is essential, as are good road, rail and inland waterway connections. Port estates often have land available where industry could locate, reducing the need for onward distribution of goods by road and delivering environmental benefits. The development of rail

81    North West Ports Economic Trends and Land Use Study, NWDA, December 2005.
82    Modern Ports: A UK Policy, DETR, November 2000.

facilities at ports will generally require support from the Government's Sustainable Distribution Fund to make investment viable, but once such facilities are in place, the potential exists to increase the volume of port-related traffic moved by rail.

8.27    Port-related road traffic, particularly bulk and unitised freight, can contribute to congestion and damage environmental quality on approach routes to ports. Road and rail access to the region's main ports is an important issue, particularly in terms of the potential to reduce unnecessary and unsustainable use of ports in other UK regions such as east and south-east of England. Improvements that include measures to assist the transfer of port traffic from road to rail and/or water will be necessary to maintain the region's continued economic competitiveness. Land-side surface access strategies should include proposals that maximise opportunities for shifting traffic away from road and onto rail and water, and to minimise the adverse impact of heavy goods vehicles on local communities and the natural environment.

## Policy RT 7

### Freight Transport

Plans and strategies should take account of the aims and objectives of the Regional Freight Strategy. Local authorities should develop sub-regional freight strategies, including the establishment of Freight Quality Partnerships to promote constructive solutions to local distribution problems and issues.

The Regional Highway Network, as detailed in Appendix RT(c), forms the North West's strategic network for the movement of freight by road, supplemented by sub-regional highway networks defined in Local Transport Plans. Heavy Goods Vehicles should not be restricted from any routes in these networks.

Local authorities should work with distribution companies and their customers to develop a consistent approach to lorry management, including access restrictions and curfews. Signing strategies should be developed and introduced for key freight routes and local destinations.

Local authorities should work with rail, port and inland waterway operators, Network Rail, the freight transport industry and business to capitalise on the opportunities available in the North West for increasing the proportion of freight moved by short-sea, coastal shipping and inland waterways. This will encourage a shift from road based transport.

Local authorities should work with airport operators to facilitate the development of air freight at the region's airports, in line with the White Paper 'The Future of Air Transport', having particular regard to the need to minimise and mitigate environmental impacts (including night noise).

8.28    The Regional Freight Strategy [83] has informed policy development and also provides guidance to local authorities on developing sub-regional and local freight strategies. Road haulage accounts for the majority of all goods moved in the North West, and will continue to be the dominant mode in the foreseeable future.  Local authorities, distribution companies and

---

83    Regional Freight Strategy, North West Freight Advisory Group, November 2003.

customers all influence the choice of route taken by road freight vehicles, and there are benefits to be gained from interested parties working together to develop strategies and to gain a mutual understanding of distribution problems and issues.

8.29    Freight Quality Partnerships (FQPs) can be instrumental in finding constructive solutions to a wide range of challenges, including balancing the needs of local businesses with local environmental and social concerns, identifying the need for and location of lorry parks, and understanding the contribution that sustainable distribution practices can make towards improving air quality and reducing noise pollution. It will be essential for adjacent FQPs to liaise with each other to ensure a consistent approach is applied across local authority boundaries. Concerns about issues such as the incidence of bridge strikes by road vehicles, which may result in significant disruption to both road and rail networks, can be addressed through, for example, partnerships between highway authorities and Network Rail.

8.30    Increasing opportunities exist for ports and inland waterways in the North West to benefit from the potential to transport cargoes such as containers and bulk freight by water. This is particularly encouraged by the EC in its White Paper on transport, published in 2002 [84], and funding is available through, for example, the Marco Polo Programme [85]. Short-sea and coastal shipping, operating between ports within the UK, is a substantially under-utilised mode, and can contribute towards reducing the volume of freight moved on the region's road and rail networks. More stringent drivers' hours regulations arising from EC legislation [86] are likely to place upward pressure on road freight costs and may make the case for sea transport more compelling. Ports closest to the origin or destination of the freight could provide transfer facilities, thereby reducing the requirement for lengthy journeys by road. This may be of benefit to the Cumbrian ports of Barrow-in-Furness, Silloth and Workington in particular.

8.31    The growth in container volumes, combined with the trend for container lines to use feeder services to distribute containers from hub ports by sea offers significant potential for the River Mersey ports and Port Manchester (Manchester Ship Canal) in particular. The Ship Canal also has the capability to play a greater role in the internal transportation of freight as, to a lesser degree, do small waterways such as the Weaver Navigation and navigable rivers. However, this cannot be achieved without the necessary wharves, warehousing and facilities to enable interchange between road, rail and water. This in turn requires land to be identified, allocated and safeguarded in Local Development Frameworks for such developments. The Government's Sustainable Distribution Fund [87] can provide useful financial contributions towards the capital investment associated with the transfer of freight from road to water.

---

84    European Transport Policy for 2010: Time to Decide, European Commission, 2002.
85    The MARCO POLO Programme (2003-2010), http://europa.eu.int/comm/transport/marcopolo/index_en.htm
86    Road Transport Sectoral Directive EC/2002/15.
87    Sustainable Distribution Fund: A Single Pot for Investments in England, February 2005

## Policy RT 8

### Inter-Modal Freight Terminals

Plans and strategies should facilitate the transfer of freight from road to rail and/or water by the identification of sites for inter-modal freight terminals, and by encouraging greater use of existing terminals and private sidings. Consideration should be given to the allocation of land for inter-modal freight terminals in the following broad locations:

- South West Greater Manchester (with access to rail and the Manchester Ship Canal);
- Widnes (with access to the West Coast Main Line (Liverpool Branch));
- Newton-le-Willows (with access to the West Coast Main Line and Chat Moss rail route);
- Birkenhead Waterfront and Eastham Docks (Wirral Waterfront SIA).

Proposals for inter-modal freight terminals should satisfy the following criteria:

- be accessible from the Regional Highway Network and Regional Rail Network as listed in Appendix RT(c) and consistent with its operation and management;
- conform with rail industry strategies for freight and network and capacity utilisation and the Regional Planning Assessment;
- be compatible with the local environment and adjacent land uses;
- be capable of accommodating, as required,
    - an appropriate road and / or rail layout;
    - facilities for water-borne freight;
    - provision for the development of activities that add value; and
    - scope for further growth;
- develop a site Travel Plan prior to approval that sets out measures for providing genuine access to the site for potential employees other than by private car;
- address potential community, health, and quality of life impacts, including air and light pollution, visual intrusion and noise.
- the effect of the proposed development on the health and wellbeing of local communities; and
- the adverse effects on sites of national and international nature conservation importance to ensure that these effects are avoided, mitigated or compensated as appropriate.

Local authorities should satisfy themselves that the prime purpose is to facilitate the movement of freight by rail and/or water and that rail access and associated facilities are available before the site is occupied.

A review of the Green Belt boundary in the local development framework would be justified in order to accommodate an inter-modal freight terminal in accordance with this policy. If land is removed from the Green Belt in accordance with this policy, the relevant development plan document should include a presumption against its development for purposes other than an inter-modal freight terminal.

8.32    The transfer of movement of freight from the highway network to rail or water could potentially yield substantial benefits in reducing carbon emissions, and easing road congestion. Attempts to increase the volume of freight moved by rail or water in the region could be constrained by a shortage of inter-modal freight terminals close to the major origins and destinations of freight in the North West. Delivery will, however, be through the private sector, and the fact that significant capital investment is required before such facilities become operational means that investment is only likely when there is a clear market opportunity and the rail network operator is able to provide the necessary train paths. Although financial constraints make any significant improvement to loading gauge a long term aspiration, advances in wagon technology offer potential for development of the inter-modal freight business in the short to medium term, as will incremental capacity enhancements through small-scale measures such as improvements to terminal and port infrastructure and access. Existing terminals and private sidings across the region also have a role to play, and greater use could be made of these to encourage modal shift.

## Policy RT 9

### Walking and Cycling

Local Authorities should work with partners to develop integrated networks of continuous, attractive and safe routes for walking and cycling to widen accessibility and capitalise on their potential environmental, social and health benefits. A high priority should be given to routes linking residential areas with employment areas, transport interchanges, schools, hospitals and other community services.

Local authorities should ensure that proposals and schemes for new developments incorporate high quality pedestrian and cycle facilities, including secure cycle parking. Routes should connect with those in nearby developments, and provision of all facilities should take into consideration integration with likely future development.

When considering improvements to the region's transport networks, scheme promoters should take the opportunity to enhance walking and cycling provision, including crossings, signage, lane markings, allocation or re-allocation of road space, and off-road routes wherever possible.

8.33    Better provision for pedestrians and cyclists can contribute towards reducing car dependency and assist with the achievement of wider regional objectives, including the development of sustainable communities, enhancing accessibility for all to a range of facilities, improving community health and supporting tourism. The introduction of measures such as pedestrianisation, Home Zones, Quiet Lanes and segregated cycleways, together with more effective demand management (Policy RT2) and highway management (Policy RT4), can have a significant impact on the walking and cycling experience.

8.34    Local Authorities should produce action plans for the development of walking and cycling networks in line with the DfT publication 'Walking and Cycling: Action Plan' [88]; these should be combined with 'Rights of Way Improvement Plans'. Integrated networks of regional and

---

88    Walking and Cycling: An Action Plan, Department for Transport, June 2004.

sub-regional footpaths, bridleways, cycleways, quiet lanes and greenways should also be developed, linked to each other and to National Trails and the National Cycle Network. Walking and cycling networks can provide important elements of 'Green Infrastructure' (Policy EM3) and/or contribute towards the objectives of Regional Parks (Policy EM4). Canal towpaths and disused railway lines should be incorporated if practical.

---

## Policy RT 10

### Priorities for Transport Management and Investment

The general priorities for transport investment and management will be determined in accordance with the Regional Economic Strategy, RSS transport objectives, spatial principles (DP 1 – 9) and the regional and sub-regional spatial frameworks in RDF1 and sub regional policies (chapters 10-13). The region's principles for investment are set out in the Implementation Plan. The Plan includes schemes for which funding has been provisionally allocated, subject to Department for Transport approval, and those under development.

---

8.35    The Eddington report [89] recommended that in carrying out long-term transport planning it is important to consider the full range of policy options in order to identify those which offer the best value for money, alongside other advantages, such as long-term flexibility.  This consideration should include (but need not be restricted to) the following types of actions [90]:

- behavioural change;
- getting better use out of existing infrastructure;
- technology and innovation;
- pricing signals;
- regulation and enforcement;
- changes to public transport services;
- small infrastructure schemes which address a specific need;
- major infrastructure schemes.

8.36    The region's transport networks are a valuable resource, but scope for their improvement is limited by financial, physical, environmental or social constraints. It is therefore imperative that these assets are adequately maintained and in particular, deterioration in the condition of local roads halted. There is, however, still the need for further targeted investment in infrastructure if the Vision for the North West is to be achieved.

8.37    The implementation plan includes the region's priorities for major transport investment, based on work undertaken for the Regional Planning Body by JMP Consulting [91].  It includes those schemes which have been given full approval by the Department for Transport and for which funding has been allocated. It also sets out the investment programme up to 2015/16, depending on the availability of resources, which emerged from the Regional Funding Allocation (RFA) work [92]. Contingency schemes should additional funding become available or if schemes within the investment programme receive funding from other sources such as the Transport

---

89    The Eddington Transport Study The case for action:Sir Rod Eddington's advice to Government, 2006.
90    Towards a sustainable transport system
91    A Methodology for Determining Regional Transport Priorities in the North West, Final Report, JMP Consulting, January 2006.
92    Regional Prioritisation of Major Transport Schemes Study Report, Atkins, January 2006.

Innovation Fund are also included. Given that all schemes are subject to detailed appraisal and relevant statutory processes, it is possible that delivery of some schemes within the programme may be deferred or withdrawn. The region may need to revisit the list of RFA priorities if requested to do so by Government, if scheme costs increase or the overall funding envelope reduces. The implementation plan also lists those schemes and broad interventions currently under development for delivery by 2021. Delivery will however depend on the availability of resources within the relevant funding mechanism. The progress of schemes will be kept under review as part of the RSS Implementation, Monitoring and Review process.

8.38    Decisions about transport investment priorities beyond 2014 may be influenced and informed by the Government's strategic transport planning framework which it will be seeking to produce in 2012 in line with its response to the Eddington and Stern reports. The intended framework will comprise a strategy document and output specification covering all modes.

# 9 Environment, Minerals, Waste and Energy

**9.1**  Whilst conserving and enhancing the North West's valued environmental and cultural assets is of utmost importance, plans and strategies should also recognise the role of the environment when seeking to achieve social and economic objectives and addressing the issue of climate change. The environmental economy makes a significant contribution towards the North West's GVA.  This chapter seeks to address these issues in an integrated way, through policies covering:

- Land management (including heritage, biodiversity, woodlands, contaminated land, green infrastructure and regional parks);
- Water management;
- Waste management;
- Minerals;
- Energy.

**Objectives**

**9.2**  The RSS is committed to using our natural and man-made resources actively, prudently and efficiently, as well as protecting and enhancing the Region's historic, built and natural environmental assets, and unique culture and heritage.

**9.3**  It seeks to:

- promote a more integrated approach to delivering a better environment through land and water management, including better relationship of new development to water resources, flood risk and adaptation to the impacts of climate change;
- create multi-functional networks of green spaces;
- produce a concise waste strategy that:
    - breaks the link between economic growth and the environmental impact of waste;
    - increases recycling rates in the Region;
    - provides a framework in which communities take responsibility for their own waste;
    - delivers a pattern of facilities of national regional and sub-regional importance including supporting policies.
- reduce energy demand and break the link between energy demand and economic growth;
- promote and exploit low carbon and renewable energy technologies and increase the amount of electricity and energy for heating from renewable sources supplied and consumed within the Region.

**9.4**  Significant opportunities exist through multi-purpose policy frameworks such as green infrastructure to significantly improve access to greenspace, contributing towards social objectives such as creating sustainable communities and making attractive places to live.  Access to greenspace has a central role to play in securing successful and sustainable economic regeneration.  The adoption of sustainable design and construction methods are needed to contribute towards the effort to increase energy efficiency and reduce climate change.  We need to make better use of the region's derelict land, and employ sustainable remediation technologies to tackle our considerable legacy of contaminated land.  Making the most of what we have, and improving on, the natural assets of the region, is fundamentally important as the region will not move forward to a new, modern economy without addressing the environmental legacy of the past.

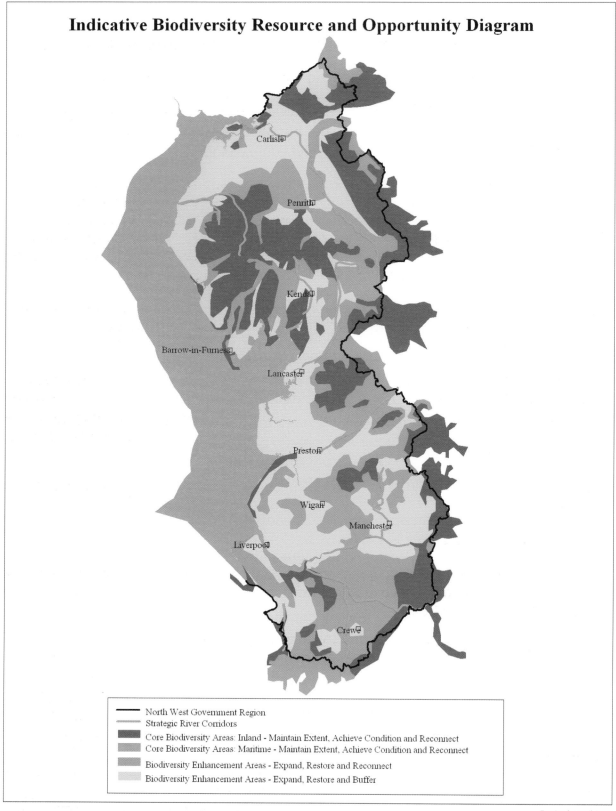

Indicative Biodiversity Resource and Opportunity Diagram

North West Government Region
Strategic River Corridors
Core Biodiversity Areas: Inland - Maintain Extent, Achieve Condition and Reconnect
Core Biodiversity Areas: Maritime - Maintain Extent, Achieve Condition and Reconnect
Biodiversity Enhancement Areas - Expand, Restore and Reconnect
Biodiversity Enhancement Areas - Expand, Restore and Buffer

Revised, April 2008

**Diagram 9.1: Indicative Biodiversity Resource and Opportunity Diagram**

## Policy EM 1

**Integrated Enhancement and Protection of the Region's Environmental Assets**

The Region's environmental assets should be identified, protected, enhanced and managed.

Plans, strategies, proposals and schemes should deliver an integrated approach to conserving and enhancing the landscape, natural environment, historic environment and woodlands of the region.

Plans and strategies should define spatial objectives and priorities for conservation, restoration and enhancement as appropriate, and provide area-based guidelines to direct decisions and target resources. These will be founded on a sound understanding of the diversity, distinctiveness, significance and sensitivity of the region's environmental assets, and informed by sub-regional environmental frameworks. Special consideration will be given to the impacts of climate change and adaptation measures.

Priority should be given to conserving and enhancing areas, sites, features and species of international, national, regional and local landscape, natural environment and historic environment importance.

Where proposals and schemes affect the region's landscape, natural or historic environment or woodland assets, prospective developers and/or local authorities should first avoid loss of or damage to the assets, then mitigate any unavoidable damage and compensate for loss or damage through offsetting actions with a foundation of no net loss in resources as a minimum requirement.

With regard to specific elements of this integrated approach, the following should be taken into account:

**Policy EM1 (A): Landscape**

Plans, strategies, proposals and schemes should identify, protect, maintain and enhance natural, historic and other distinctive features that contribute to the character of landscapes and places within the North West.

They should be informed by and recognise the importance of:

- detailed landscape character assessments and strategies, which local authorities should produce, set in the context of the North West Joint Character Area Map [93]. These will be used to identify priority areas for the maintenance, enhancement and/or restoration of that character and will under-pin and act as key components of criteria-based policies in LDFs;
- the special qualities of the environment associated with the nationally designated areas of the Lake District National Park, the Yorkshire Dales National Park, the Peak District National Park, the Forest of Bowland Area of Outstanding Natural Beauty (AONB), the Arnside and Silverdale AONB, the North Pennines AONB and Solway Coast AONB and their settings;
- the characteristics and setting of World Heritage Sites.

## Policy EM1 (B):  Natural Environment

Plans, strategies, proposals and schemes should secure a 'step-change' increase in the region's biodiversity resources by contributing to the delivery of national, regional and local biodiversity objectives and targets for maintaining extent, achieving condition, restoring and expanding habitats and species populations [94].  This should be done through protecting, enhancing, expanding and linking areas for wildlife within and between the locations of highest biodiversity resources, including statutory and local wildlife sites, and encouraging the conservation and expansion of the ecological fabric elsewhere.

Broad locations where there are greatest opportunities for delivering the biodiversity targets are shown on the Indicative Biodiversity Resource and Opportunity Diagram (see Diagram 9.1).  More specific locations will be informed by sub-regional biodiversity maps and frameworks of statutory and local wildlife sites.

Local authorities should:

- develop a more detailed representation of this spatial information for use in their Local Development Frameworks; and
- develop functional ecological frameworks that will address habitat fragmentation and species isolation, identifying and targeting opportunities for habitat expansion and re-connection.  Active arrangements will be needed to address ecological cross-boundary issues within areas such as the Pennines, Solway Firth, the Mersey Estuary, the Lune Estuary, the River Dee Estuary and the Cheshire Meres and Mosses, as well as including biodiversity policies in any developing Marine Spatial Planning System in the Irish Sea.

Plans, strategies, proposals and schemes should protect and enhance the region's geological and geomorphological resources including statutory and local sites by contributing to the delivery of national, regional and local geodiversity objectives and targets.

## Policy EM1 (C):  Historic Environment

Plans, strategies, proposals and schemes should protect, conserve and enhance the historic environment supporting conservation-led regeneration in areas rich in historic interest, and in particular exploiting the regeneration potential of:

- the maritime heritage of the North West coast including docks and waterspaces, and coastal resorts and piers;
- the Pennine textile mill-town heritage that exists in East Lancashire and Greater Manchester; and the textile mill-town heritage of East Cheshire;
- Victorian and Edwardian commercial developments in Liverpool and Manchester city centres;
- the traditional architecture of rural villages and market towns of Cumbria, Cheshire and Lancashire;
- the historic Cities of Carlisle, Chester and Lancaster; and
- the Lake District Cultural Landscape.

---

94    Revised regional biodiversity targets (30 April 2008) and further information can be found on the NW Biodiversity Forum website (www.biodiversitynw.org.uk)

**Policy EM1 (D): Trees, Woodlands and Forests**

Plans, strategies, proposals and schemes should:

- support the aims and priorities of the North West Regional Forestry Framework and sub-regional forestry strategies;
- encourage a steady targeted expansion of tree and woodland cover and promote sustainable management of existing woodland resources to enable the delivery of multiple benefits to society;
- support the continued role of community forestry;
- identify and protect ancient semi-natural woodland and veteran trees.

9.5    The Government has set out detailed national guidance on biodiversity, landscape and heritage within this context.  This policy outlines the priorities for the management of the North West environmental land assets, adding further interpretation where appropriate to national planning policy guidance.  Traditionally, the policy approach to these environmental issues has been to address them separately.  This policy aims to encourage a more integrated approach to the management of the landscape and the natural environment, within both rural and urban areas.  In order to provide for environmental improvements in the North West, plans and strategies need to foster a joined-up approach to deliver built and natural environment policy objectives.  This integrated form of management will be important in securing other benefits including improved health through access to recreation and economic benefits associated with providing a quality environment in which to live and boosting the Region's image.

**Policy EM 2**

**Remediating Contaminated Land**

Plans, strategies, proposals and schemes should encourage the adoption of sustainable remediation technologies.  Where soft end uses (including green infrastructure, natural habitat or landscape creation) are to be provided on previously developed sites, appropriate remediation technologies should be considered which reduce or render harmless any contamination that may be present.

9.6    The North West was at the forefront of the industrial revolution and to this day remains one of the UK's major manufacturing centres.  This past industrial activity has left a legacy of land contamination, which needs to be managed.  Successful remediation of contaminated land is fundamental to improving the image of the region. The contaminated land regime [95] was introduced 7 years ago to identify this legacy, where it posed an unacceptable risk, and ensure it's remediation to appropriate standards.  The regime favours voluntary remediation and in many cases is being brought about as a consequence of proposed development.  In the North West, the Environment Agency and others are developing best practice guidelines based on a hierarchy of remediation methods.

95    Part IIA of the Environmental Protection Act 1990, introduced in England on 1st April 2000.

## 9 Environment, Minerals, Waste and Energy

### Policy EM 3

**Green Infrastructure**

Plans, strategies, proposals and schemes should aim to deliver wider spatial outcomes that incorporate environmental and socio-economic benefits by:

- conserving and managing existing green infrastructure;
- creating new green infrastructure;
- enhancing its functionality, quality, connectivity and accessibility.

Local authorities should work with partners to:

- identify partnerships at an appropriate scale to take forward green infrastructure planning, in the context of relevant environmental and socio-economic objectives. Green infrastructure should include the identification, development and management of new areas of open space. This should be complemented by the retention, enhancement and adaptation of existing sites;
- ensure that a key aim of green infrastructure is the maintenance and improvement of biodiversity;
- protect the integrity of sites of national and international importance including the historic environment;
- use existing strategies and frameworks to develop consensus on green infrastructure priorities and associated data needs;
- promote physical and mental health benefits through access to and usage of open spaces by disadvantaged groups and communities;
- set out the significant green infrastructure needs across the spectrum of economic, environmental and social objectives;
- identify and secure opportunities for delivery and put in place implementation plans;
- integrate proposals to improve green infrastructure in the delivery of new developments, particularly through area based regeneration initiatives and major proposals and schemes;
- maximize the role of green infrastructure in mitigating and adapting to climate change;
- provide new areas of appropriate greenspace where development would otherwise cause unacceptable recreational pressure on sites of international ecological importance, for example where new housing is proposed close to such sites.

Local Delivery of Green Infrastructure Plans should seek first to make use of existing delivery mechanisms supplemented by bespoke delivery mechanisms where necessary.

A Green Infrastructure Guide for the North West has been produced which provides more detailed guidance and will assist the way this policy is put into practice.

9.7    Green infrastructure is the region's life support system – the network of green and blue spaces that lies within and between the North West's cities, towns and villages which provides multiple social, economic and environmental benefits. Green infrastructure can contribute to a high quality natural and built environment and can enhance that quality of life for present and future residents and visitors and delivers "liveability" for sustainable communities.  The green infrastructure approach calls for networks of green space to be managed in an integrated way that allows for the provision of wider socio-economic and public health benefits e.g. increased opportunities for physical activity, while at the same time contributing to the delivery of regional biodiversity targets. Other benefits of green infrastructure include the adaptation and mitigation of climate change. Local authorities should adopt a cross disciplinary approach to the identification, management and creation of green infrastructure. There is a need for the planning system to work in tandem with bodies responsible for leisure, countryside and environmental management in order to deliver wider benefits. LDF policy should identify and protect existing green infrastructure and seek to deliver improvements where possible. Regional Parks will be complementary to this policy, incorporating several elements of green infrastructure provision (see Policy EM4). This policy should be read in conjunction with RT9 which promotes a regional framework for walking and cycling applicable to green infrastructure.

9.8     Provision of alternative recreational space can help to attract recreational users away from sensitive sites, particularly those of international significance for nature conservation, and reduce additional pressure on them. The location and type of alternative space must be carefully designed to be effective. A strategic approach to the provision of alternative recreational space is likely to be particularly effective, rather than small piecemeal provision of open space in association with individual developments.

# 9 Environment, Minerals, Waste and Energy

## Policy EM 4

### Regional Parks

Three Areas of Search for Regional Parks have been identified as shown on Diagram 9.2 and within Table 9.1.

- the North West Coast;
- the Mersey Basin; and
- east Lancashire.

The Regional Planning Body will work with partners to prepare a Strategic Framework for each area of search. The Strategic Framework will provide the context for the delivery of regional parks in the area of search by setting out:

- an assessment of assets, opportunities, functions and potential to meet overall objectives of regional parks set out in Figure 9.1, including target populations;
- a broad vision and objectives; and
- guiding principles for projects being promoted within its area of search.

The protection of European sites and the enhancement of biodiversity should form guiding principles for the Strategic Frameworks. In particular, Strategic Frameworks should include an assessment of potential impacts on sites of international nature conservation importance.

Plans and strategies should have regard to the Strategic Frameworks and for each specific regional park should:

- identify the locations and boundaries;
- secure successful delivery and management arrangements;
- ensure that access provision is only delivered where access for recreation will not result in adverse impact on the integrity of any site of international nature conservation importance. Where this cannot be ensured, access restrictions must be put in place to prevent the occurrence of any adverse effect;
- as part of this process, systems should be in place to ensure effective monitoring of and appropriate response to any impact of recreational pressure on sites of international nature conservation importance that lie within or close to Regional Parks;
- access to the Regional Parks by walking, cycling and public transport should be promoted, and car transport to the Regional Parks should be managed in order to ensure that air pollution at sensitive European sites is not affected by the development of Regional Parks.

9.9    The parts of the region identified as likely locations for designated Regional Parks, referred to as 'areas of search' and listed in Policy EM4, are all expansive areas linked by various aspects of their natural landscape and/or cultural heritage, and which lend themselves to the coordinated promotion of opportunities for informal outdoor recreation, leisure and sporting activities. They are, in addition, areas where positive planning and management in line with the principles of RSS will assist urban and rural renaissance in the North West as a whole. The development of Regional Parks will be a key component in the implementation of the concept of Green Infrastructure (see Policy EM3).

## Figure 9.1 - Overall Objectives of Regional Parks

To deliver:

- major improvement in the provision of high quality, easily accessible recreation, leisure and sporting opportunities, sustainable tourism, appropriate to the character and environmental sensitivity of the area;
- major environmental quality improvement to aid regeneration and image and contribute towards mitigating the impacts of climate change;
- significant increases in employment and business activity in leisure, sport and recreation; and
- a mechanism for the conservation of the landscape close to where people live, its character, biodiversity and heritage assets.

9.10    Existing or potential proposals have been identified for the location of Regional Parks in every area of search (Table 9.1), each containing varying landscape quality, cultural heritage and protected areas.  Regional Parks do not supersede or compromise national designations and their statutory protection \ policy frameworks.  Policies relating to statutory designations in the area, for example Areas of Outstanding Natural Beauty, will be taken into account within the Strategic Framework prepared to govern the management of the Regional Park.

## Table 9.1 Regional Parks Areas of Search and Potential Projects

| Regional Parks Areas of Search | Existing or Potential Projects |
|---|---|
| The North West Coast | The North West Coastal Trail<br>River Dee<br>Mersey Waterfront Regional Park<br>Ribble Estuary<br>Morecambe Bay<br>Cumbria and Furness Coastal Beacons |
| The Mersey Basin | Wigan / Salford Greenheart Regional Park<br>Weaver Valley<br>Croal-Irwell River Valley<br>Mersey Valley |
| East Lancashire | East Lancashire Regional Park |

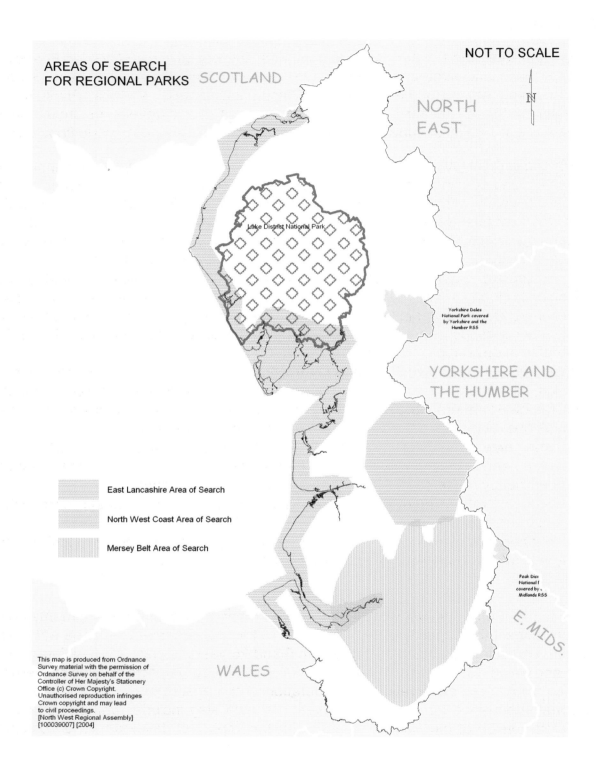

**Diagram 9.2: Areas of Search for Regional Parks**

## Policy EM 5

### Integrated Water Management

In achieving integrated water management and delivery of the EU Water Framework Directive, plans and strategies should have regard to River Basin Management Plans, Water Company Asset Management Plans, Catchment Flood Management Plans, and the Regional Flood Risk Appraisal. Local planning authorities and developers should protect the quantity and quality of surface, ground and coastal waters, and manage flood risk, by:

- working with the Water Companies and the Environment Agency when planning the location and phasing of development. Development should be located where there is spare capacity in the existing water supply and waste water treatment, sewer and strategic surface water mains capacity, insofar as this would be consistent with other planning objectives. Where this is not possible development must be phased so that new infrastructure capacity can be provided without environmental harm;
- producing sub-regional or district level strategic flood risk assessments, guided by the Regional Flood Risk Appraisal. Allocations of land for development should comply with the sequential test in PPS25. Departures from this should only be proposed in exceptional cases where suitable land at lower risk of flooding is not available and the benefits of development outweigh the risks from flooding;
- designing appropriate mitigation measures into the scheme, for any development which, exceptionally, must take place in current or future flood risk areas, to ensure it is protected to appropriate standards, provides suitable emergency access under flood conditions, and does not increase the risk of flooding elsewhere;
- requiring new development, including residential, commercial and transport development, to incorporate sustainable drainage systems and water conservation and efficiency measures to the highest contemporary standard;
- encouraging retrofitting of sustainable drainage systems and water efficiency within existing developments;
- raising people's awareness of flood risks (particularly for vulnerable groups) and the impacts of their behaviours and lifestyles on water consumption.

9.11    In its bid to achieve integrated water management, growth and development, the North West must respect the capacity of the water and wetland environments to cope with changes in land use, particularly as it can take between 5 and 25 years to plan and develop new water resource and waste water disposal schemes, and avoid adverse impacts on sites of international importance for nature conservation. Consideration of the effects of development on sites of international importance for nature conservation should also include, where relevant, those sites located outside of the Region, in particular the impact of development on coastal and inland waters in Wales.

9.12    Climate change creates an additional, major challenge to the bid to achieve integrated water management [96]. It is expected that excesses of water in winter, shortages in summer and increasingly intense rainfall will occur, which will affect the assessment and management of future risks associated with water resources, water quality and flooding. This will affect the additional issues of urban and rural diffuse pollution – that is, pollution arising from a number of dispersed sources – and the region's ageing water supply and disposal infrastructure, that are of particular concern in the North West. It should be recognised that more subtle effects caused by climate change, such as changes in water table levels are important and need to be considered.

9.13    There is an imperative need to manage the demand for water in the region and address the detrimental effect of urban and agricultural run off on water quality. The region's current and future flood risks must also be managed in a sustainable way to avoid potential damage to property and even loss of life.

9.14    Sustainable Drainage Systems, including multi-benefit water treatment solutions such as artificial wetlands, represent one key mechanism for addressing these issues as they reduce the rate, quantity and improve the quality of surface water run off during rainfall events, minimising flooding and environmental damage as a result of uncontrolled surface run-off. Further guidance is provided in the North West Best Practice Design Guide.

## Policy EM 6

### Managing the North West's Coastline

Plans, strategies, proposals and schemes (including Shoreline Management Plans) should take a strategic and integrated approach to the long term management of flood and coastal erosion risk by:

- taking account of natural coastal change and the likely impacts of climate change, to ensure that development is sited or re-sited carefully to avoid:
  - the risk of future loss from coastal erosion, land instability and flooding;
  - unsustainable coastal defence costs;
  - damaging existing defences and the capacity of the coast to form natural defences or to adjust to future changes without endangering life or property;
- making provision for mitigation of and adaptation to natural coastal change and the predicted effects of climate change over the medium to long-term (100 years) and supporting a 'whole shoreline approach' [97] being taken to coastal risk management;
- minimizing the loss of coastal habitats and avoiding damage to coastal processes; and avoiding adverse impacts now and in the future on coastal sites of international nature conservation importance;
- promoting managed realignment as a tool for managing flood and coastal erosion risk and delivering biodiversity targets and compensatory habitat requirements under the Habitats Directive.

9.15    This policy should be read in conjunction with Policy RDF3 which provides further guidance on sustainable development and use of the coast and EM3 and EM4.

9.16    The majority of the region's coastal zone is low lying (below the 10m contour), comprised of soft sediments and therefore vulnerable to coastal erosion and flooding. Historically development, construction of coastal defences and other development such as ports on the

---

97    Making space for water. Taking forward a new Government strategy for flood and coastal erosion risk management in England." First government response to the autumn 2004. Making space for water consultation exercise. March 2005.

estuaries and open coast have resulted in significant impacts on the extent and distribution of coastal habitats and disruption of coastal processes. Rises in sea level and extreme weather conditions like sudden, heavy storms, which can cause storm surges and which are becoming more frequent due to climate change have major implications for the North West Coast and on the way in which it is planned and managed.

9.17    The government is committed to a more holistic approach [98] to secure sustainable and cost effective management of flood and coastal erosion, whilst at the same time securing a greater overall contribution to sustainable development. Shoreline Management Plans and Catchment Flood Management Plans will provide a strategic approach to the assessment of options within a broader planning matrix [99] which will include River Basin Management Plans and Integrated Coastal Zone Management strategies. These should ensure that more flood and coastal erosion solutions work with natural processes and natural coastal defence features such as sand dunes and salt marshes. Changes to Shoreline Management Planning policy [100], reflecting the need to adapt to the likely effects of climate change, such as flooding and coastal erosion, will require the careful siting of new economic assets and infrastructure, including new port development, so as to avoid any risk of future loss or of excessive coastal defence costs. They will also create opportunities for managed realignment and the associated identification and creation of new wildlife habitats.

---

98    Paper FMS/SF 08: Management of Flood Risk and Coastal Erosion, Development of Revised Vision, Aims and Objectives, DEFRA, 2003.

99    Where issues \ scope of strategies cross national and regional boundaries, it will be necessary to involve government agencies, local authorities and other stakeholders in Isle of Man, Northern Ireland, Republic of Ireland, Scotland and Wales.

100    The development of the 2nd generation of Shoreline Management Plans started in 2007, with target completion by March, 2010. These will develop a 100-year forward look at natural changes to the coast and the likely effects of climate change. They will identify shoreline management policies for the coast over 0-20, 20-50 and 50-100 year periods. The plans should provide clear guidance to promote and ensure sustainable planning and management of the shoreline and coast.

## 9 Environment, Minerals, Waste and Energy

### Policy EM 7

**Minerals Extraction**

Plans and strategies should make provision for a steady and adequate supply of a range of minerals to meet the region's apportionments of land-won aggregates and requirements of national planning guidance. This will take into account:

- the national significance of the Region's reserves of salt, silica sand, gypsum, peat and clay (including fireclay);
- the need to maintain land banks of permitted reserves of certain minerals as identified in relevant government guidance [101] including silica sand and materials for the cement industry;
- the contribution that substitute, secondary or recycled sources, or imports from outside the Region, should make;
- the potential supply of marine dredged aggregate in contributing towards overall regional aggregate needs, applying the principles of sustainable development alluded to in relevant government guidance [102] and reflect any future Marine Spatial Planning arrangements.

Minerals extraction forms an exception to the sequential approach set out in the Core Development Principles.

Plans and strategies should:

- include criteria-based policies to indicate the circumstances under which extraction might or might not be permitted;
- include opportunities for the transportation of minerals by pipeline, rail or water, including the maintenance of existing wharves and railhead facilities, the provision of new ones, and of facilities for on-shore processing and distribution of hydrocarbons;
- safeguard mineral resources from other forms of development and, where appropriate, reserve highest quality minerals for applications that require such grades;
- identify and protect sources of building stone for use in repairing and maintaining historic buildings and public realm improvements; and
- ensure sensitive environmental restoration and aftercare of sites including improved public access where they are of amenity value.

9.18    Government policy promotes the general conservation of minerals while at the same time ensuring an adequate supply is available to meet needs. Mineral resources are not distributed evenly across the country and some areas are able to provide greater amounts of certain minerals than they actually use. The North West is an important national source of salt, silica sand, gypsum, peat and clay and has significant reserves of building stone, clay, shale

101    Revisions to MPG6 "National & Regional Guidelines for Aggregates Provision in England 2001-2016", ODPM, June 2003.
MPG10 "Provision of Raw Material for the Cement Industry", DoE, 1991.
MPG13, "Guidelines on Peat Provision in England including the Place of Alternative Materials" DoE, 1995.
MPG15, "Provision of Silica Sand in England" ODPM.
102    Consultation Paper on Annexes to Minerals Policy Statement 1, Annex 1 – Aggregates Provision in England. "Marine Mineral Guidance1: Extraction by dredging from the English seabed", ODPM, 2005.

and coal, as well as aggregates, for which guidance is given in Policy EM8 below. The region has important reserves of minerals in offshore, coastal and estuary locations, notably hydrocarbons but also marine sand.

9.19 Whilst extraction is dependent upon the location of workable mineral resources, it is important that it is carried out where there is access to sustainable modes of transport as far as is possible. It is also essential to assess the likely generation of traffic and its impact upon the surrounding highway network before drafting plans for mineral extraction.

## Policy EM 8

### Land-won Aggregates

Mineral planning authorities should continue to work together to make provision for the agreed regional apportionment of land-won aggregate requirements to 2016 on the basis of the revision to Minerals Planning Guidance Note 6 (MPG6) [103], and the sub-regional apportionment set out in Table 9.2.

9.20 As a large-scale user of aggregates, the North West relies heavily on imports from other regions. MPG6 sets out the current government advice on planning for the necessary level of aggregate supplies between 2001 and 2016, which is based on technical advice from the Regional Aggregates Working Parties (RAWP) and studies into long-term demand. This amounts to 55 million tonnes of sand and gravel and 167 million tonnes of crushed rock from primary land won sources in the North West and an additional 155 million tonnes from elsewhere, including imports from outside the region, marine-dredged sources and the use of secondary or recycled materials. The Regional Planning Body will work together with RAWP to identify the level of aggregates that should be provided for the period until 2021 based on the advice of the ODPM.

## Policy EM 9

### Secondary and Recycled Aggregates

The Regional Planning Body will work with the Regional Aggregates Working Party, mineral and waste planning authorities, and others to maximise the role played by secondary and recycled sources of aggregates in meeting the Region's requirements by:

* working with the construction industry to achieve a target of 20% of construction aggregates to be from secondary or recycled sources by 2010 and 25% by 2021;
* encouraging local authorities and developers to incorporate temporary materials-recycling facilities on the sites of major demolition or construction projects; and
* plans and strategies identifying, sites or criteria for the provision of permanent recycling plants for construction and demolition waste in appropriate locations.

## 9 Environment, Minerals, Waste and Energy

9.21    Revisions to MPG6 assume that 101 million tonnes – that is, 26% – of the 377 million tonnes of aggregates required in the North West between 2001 and 2016 will come from secondary and recycled sources.  The figures currently available are believed to underestimate the use of recycled materials, which varies across the Region therefore improved data will be necessary to assist strategic monitoring activity.  This Policy sets an aspirational target for the Region as a whole, which will need to be reviewed in the light of improved information.  Working together with the minerals planning authorities, and the industry itself, the Regional Aggregates Working Party should play a leading role in ensuring that data collected is both robust and consistent.

**Table 9.2 Sub-regional Apportionment of Aggregates in the North West 2001-2016 (million tonnes)**

|  | Sand and Gravel | Crushed Rock |
|---|---|---|
| Cheshire | 31.5 | 2 |
| Cumbria | 11.2 | 66 |
| Lancashire | 8.2 | 73 |
| Merseyside / Greater Manchester / Halton / Warrington | 4.1 | 26 |
| Total | 55 | 167 |

## Policy EM 10

### A Regional Approach to Waste Management

Plans, strategies, proposals and schemes should promote and require the provision of sustainable new waste management infrastructure, facilities and systems that contribute to the development of the North West by reducing harm to the environment (including reducing impacts on climate change), improving the efficiency of resources, stimulating investment and maximising economic opportunities.

Plans and strategies should reflect the principles set out in the Waste Strategy for England 2007 and PPS10. They should seek to achieve the following regional waste targets, and to exceed them where practicable:

- growth in municipal waste to be reduced to zero by 2014;
- 40% of household waste to be reused, recycled or composted by 2010; 45% by 2015; and 55% by 2020;
- value to be recovered from 53% of municipal solid waste by 2010 (including recycling/composting); and 67% by 2015 and 75% by 2020;
- zero future growth in commercial and industrial wastes;
- recycle 35% of all commercial and industrial wastes by 2020;
- value to be recovered from at least 70% of commercial and industrial wastes by 2020 (including recycling/composting).

9.22    European legislation, Government targets, increasing waste generation, the need for improved environmental protection and rising public expectations drive the need for rapid changes in our approach to managing waste. In particular, we need to reduce our reliance on landfill by providing alternative facilities for reprocessing, treatment and disposal. The regional strategy for waste sets out targets for waste minimisation, recycling and recovery (energy) from both commercial and industrial waste and municipal waste. The targets have been set to promote the management of waste up the waste hierarchy and to follow the Government's policy of decoupling waste growth from economic growth. The nature of waste management and geographic variation is such that targets for individual local authority will vary with locally determined circumstances. The Regional Waste Annual Monitoring Report will include update performance assessments on a regional basis.

9.23    An important contribution to sustainable development can be made by recycling and the use of recycled materials. In preparing plans and strategies and considering applications for development, local planning authorities should promote the minimisation of waste and the maximised use of recycled materials.

## Policy EM 11

### Waste Management Principles

Every effort should be made to minimise waste, maximise re-use, and maximise opportunities for the use of recycled material. Such residual waste as does arise should be managed at the highest practicable level in the Government's waste hierarchy. The following sequence of initiatives should be followed, and appropriate facilities provided:

- first, waste minimisation; then
- maximise the re-use of waste for the same or a different purpose; then
- composting or recycling (for instance through streamed "kerbside" collections, "bring" banks, civic amenity sites, and centralised recycling facilities); then
- intermediate treatment of wastes that cannot readily be composted or recycled (through anaerobic digestion or mechanical biological treatment (MBT)); or
- treatment to deal with hazardous materials; then
- production of refuse derived fuels from waste; then
- recovery of energy from residual waste and refuse derived fuels (by a range of thermal treatments); and finally
- disposal of residual wastes by land-filling (or land-raising), including the recovery of energy from landfill gas where practicable.

9.24    Every type of development, redevelopment and regeneration project, including town centres, retail parks and leisure facilities as well as industrial and commercial business parks, should:

- promote the minimisation of waste in site development such as the separation of different waste materials for recycling and reuse;
- maximise the use of recycled materials in construction and encourage developers and contractors to specify these materials wherever possible;

9 Environment, Minerals, Waste and Energy

- provide infrastructure that facilitates and meet the needs of local residents, business and industry for segregated storage, collection and recycling of waste materials;
- incorporate sufficient space to separate and store segregated waste streams waste and enable kerbside collection of materials;
- adopt best practice techniques to prevent and minimise waste during the design and construction phases of development; and
- promote the use of site waste management plans.

9.25    Commercial and industrial planning proposals should be encouraged to exploit significant opportunities that are likely to exist to increase the extent of on-site recovery of commercial and industrial wastes and construction and demolition waste.

9.26    Waste Disposal Authorities (WDAs) should undertake detailed assessment of the need for intermediate treatment and energy recovery facilities in their areas during the life of their Municipal Waste Management Strategy (MWMS).  This will mean the early assessment of progress in waste minimisation, raising recycling rates and reducing residual waste arisings in order to provide sufficient time to plan and construct facilities to assist in achieving later, more stringent targets.

9.27    It is also recognised that new waste treatment technologies and innovations, may become available which provide for increased sustainability and financial viability. The introduction of new waste treatment technologies to serve all waste streams is supported subject to proven success in terms technical development, financial viability and sustainability appraisal.

---

### Policy EM 12

**Locational Principles**

Waste planning and disposal authorities should provide for communities to take more responsibility for their own waste.  The final residue, following treatment, of municipal, commercial and industrial waste should be disposed of in one of the nearest appropriate installations.  Local authorities should ensure that waste management facilities are sited in such a way as to avoid the unnecessary carriage of waste over long distances.  In considering the location of new waste management facilities, they should take account of the availability of transport infrastructure that will support the sustainable movement of waste, seeking when practicable to use rail or water transport.  They should also take account of the environmental impact of the proposed development.

---

9.28    Local planning authorities should have regard to the integration that is required within the waste management industries.  They should ensure that there is an adequate range and capacity of facilities to support the collection, handling, sorting and separation of wastes and recyclates, pre-treatment of wastes, composting and bulk handling. The benefits of co-locating waste handling, re-processing and disposal facilities should be recognised. Local Authorities will ensure that there are convenient and accessible 'Bring' systems / facilities for the public to deposit waste.

## Policy EM 13

**Provision of Nationally, Regionally and Sub-Regionally Significant Waste Management Facilities**

Plans, strategies, proposals and schemes should provide for an appropriate type, size and mix of development opportunities to support, bring forward and safeguard sites for waste management facilities that will deliver the capacity to deal with the indicative volumes of non-hazardous commercial and industrial waste, hazardous waste and municipal waste in each sub-region, as set out in Tables 9.3, 9.4 and 9.5 respectively.

Plans and Strategies should identify locations for waste management facilities and allocate suitable sites for the provision of facilities up to 2020. When identifying these sites, account should be taken of the scope for co-location of complementary activities, such as resource recovery parks, to support the provision of adequate reprocessing and re-manufacturing capacity.

In considering proposals for waste management facilities (including additional landfill capacity) the ability of existing established sites to meet the needs of the region / sub region should be fully explored. Wherever possible, such sites should be used in preference to other sites where waste management activities have not previously been located, provided proposals for the development of waste management facilities satisfy general planning and licensing conditions, including the likely cumulative impact on the environment, landscape, cultural heritage, groundwater, the amenity and health of the neighbourhood and residents, the traffic impact; available transport links; the prevention and control of pollution and any specific technical issues.

For both the municipal, and the commercial and industrial waste streams, primary reception, treatment and transfer facilities should be located near to the sources of arisings. Secondary treatment and disposal facilities may be located on a sub-regional strategic basis, to serve a wider catchment area. Regionally significant facilities may be needed to serve the Mersey Belt, which includes the Manchester and Liverpool conurbations. The provision of nationally significant waste management facilities may be appropriate where the region offers a particular waste management advantage on a national scale.

Where it is appropriate at the sub-regional level, waste planning, disposal and collection authorities should work together to produce joint waste management strategies in partnership with the Environment Agency, the waste management industry, Regional Planning Body and other stakeholders.

## Pattern of Facilities

9.29     With respect to municipal waste it is generally expected that new primary residual waste treatment capacity will be located within the Waste Planning Authority area in which the waste arises. The capacity gap is clear, as almost all of the treatment capacity will be new. However, secondary treatments such as energy recovery from RDF and specific material reprocessors for recyclate are more likely to be located on a regional strategic basis. Energy recovery through substitution of RDF for fossil fuels in existing power generation or process industries may also be developed to meet strategic needs.

9.30    Waste arisings and suitable locations for economically viable waste management facilities are not determined by administrative boundaries. Strategic facilities will be required where viability is dependent on economies of scale and logistics for supply of inputs and treatment products. Every effort should be made to minimise the need to export waste outside the region, apart from in the case of specific hazardous wastes or in exceptional sub regional circumstances. Co-ordinated approaches and joint working is encouraged between sub regions, in partnership with the waste management industry. The inter-regional movement of waste may be appropriate where this is assessed to be the most sustainable option.

9.31    The North West currently provides commercial and industrial waste management facilities that are important on a national scale (UK). Additional development of such strategic facilities should be assessed in the national (UK) context of sustainability.

9.32    Producer responsibility legislation in particular through EU Directives and rising costs of landfill disposal (including the increasing landfill tax burden) is placing pressures on commerce and industry to minimise its waste production and to treat, recycle and reuse its waste materials. These pressures are also driving requirements for new waste treatment and processing capacity. Increasing sorting and segregation of waste into specific materials will result in a requirement for specialised treatment and processing which can only be developed through economies of scale at a regional or national (UK) level. The logistics of waste collection transport and process will increase the demand for strategic regional and national sites and facilities. Strategic facilities will include:

- hazardous waste treatment;
- recovery of energy from refuse derived fuels;
- re-processing capacity for source segregated recyclate including construction & demolition waste;
- new landfill development.

Further research by local authorities, the North West Development Agency, private landowners and other regional partners into the development of the integrated waste / reprocessing park concept is encouraged.

9.33    Landowners, waste management companies, local planning authorities, waste planning authorities (WPAs), waste disposal authorities (WDAs), waste collection authorities (WCAs) and the Environment Agency should work together to identify suitable landfill disposal sites, for hazardous, non-hazardous wastes including municipal waste residues that can be brought forward through the planning and licensing regimes over the life of this Strategy.

9.34    Some facilities may need to be located outside the main urban areas in order to ensure an adequate buffer between local communities and minimise any adverse impacts from waste management activities. Local authorities should safeguard existing, proposed and allocated waste management facilities from encroachment by other forms of development, which would inhibit their operation and contribution to achieving the region's waste targets.

9.35    The large urban areas, as the biggest producers of waste, are unlikely to meet planning and other requirements for the development of landfill facilities. They will need to provide opportunities for developing waste management treatments higher up the waste hierarchy. Largely urban WPAs with little or no opportunities for landfill should contribute to the overall strategy by accommodating more treatment capacity than otherwise might be planned for, where consistent with RSS and the Key Planning Objectives in PPS10. Waste arisings in rural areas demand different considerations for collection and treatment; small scale community projects may be particularly suitable for such locations.

9.36    Economies of scale may see capacity being shared between the waste streams and any resulting investment may also help to achieve greater recovery from the industrial and commercial sectors.

9.37    The regional strategy for waste recognises the importance of new environmental technologies in fulfilling the above and WDAs \ WCAs should seek to encourage links between the waste management sector and re-processing/manufacturing sectors at a strategic level.

## Apportionments

### a) Commercial and Industrial Waste

9.38    Commercial and industrial waste (estimated at 8.3 million tonnes per annum) together with construction and demolition waste (estimated at 11 million tonnes per annum) account for 80% of the total waste produced in the North West (excluding agricultural and mining waste). About 7.8 million tonnes of this waste is sent to landfill [105] and a large proportion is mixed unsorted wastes. With segregation at source, resource efficiency measures and the use of 'Site Waste Management Plans', this waste could be diverted from landfill and be sent for reuse, recycling, composting or energy recovery.   The available baseline data and information on waste management capacity and waste arisings and projected capacity requirements is inadequate to provide indicative projections of the gap between existing and planned capacity and medium and long term requirements.   There will be a need to provide waste management capacity for commercial and industrial waste streams across the region in particular for new recycling, processing and treatment capacity which will be increasing driven by legislative requirements and increasing costs of landfill disposal.   This matter will be addressed through publication of updated information in annual monitoring reports.

**Table 9.3 Indicative Annual Capacity of Non-Hazardous Commercial and Industrial Waste Arisings to 2020**

| Sub Regional Area | Indicative total waste treatment capacity *(000's Tonnes) Composting/Recycling/ Treatment/Thermal* | Landfill requirement *(000's Tonnes)* |
|---|---|---|
| Cheshire | 403 | 346 |
| Cumbria | 297 | 223 |
| Lancashire (including Blackburn with Darwen and Blackpool) | 900 | 649 |

---

105    RTAB Monitoring Report 2005 - Environment Agency 2004 site licence returns.

9 Environment, Minerals, Waste and Energy

| Greater Manchester | 1,583 | 1228 |
|---|---|---|
| Merseyside and Halton | 677 | 788 |
| Warrington | 134 | 96 |
| **North West Total** | **3,998** | **3,333** |

**Table 9.4 Indicative Capacity of Hazardous Waste Management Per Annum to 2020 (Special waste management figures (2004) using source data from Environment Agency SWAT Database)**

| Total Hazardous Waste managed in the North West (2004) allowing for Imports & Exports (000's Tonnes) | Treatment / Recycling Capacity (000's Tonnes) | Thermal Capacity (000's Tonnes) | Landfill Requirement (000's Tonnes) |
|---|---|---|---|
| 960 | 470 | 125 | 400 |

9.39    The implications of the Government's Landfill Directive make arrangements for the future management of hazardous waste uncertain.  Key issues will be the classification and treatment of waste and the need to stop the co-disposal of hazardous and non-hazardous waste. The requirements of the EC Hazardous Waste Directive have led to more types of waste being classified as hazardous, for example motor vehicles that are no longer useable, and the vast majority of this will now have to be pre-treated to reduce its hazard or volume: factors which indicate an increased demand for new waste treatment facilities and capacity. Recent figures for the management of special waste within the region are shown in Table 9.4 above, but do not take into account either the increase in levels of hazardous waste that reclassification will create or potential changes in the way it is imported and exported to and from the region.

**b) Municipal Waste Management Facilities**

9.40    Despite recent increases in the rate of recycling and composting, local authorities still rely heavily on landfill facilities for the disposal of municipal waste.  The Landfill Allowance Trading Scheme (LATS) [107] and introduction of severe penalties for authorities that exceed their allowance should lead to a reduction in this form of disposal. New facilities will be required to divert waste that is not recycled or composted away from landfill by intermediate treatment and using it as end products in processes such as energy recovery from Refuse Derived Fuel / Solid Recovered Fuel (RDF/SRF) or undergoing processes such as anaerobic digestion or related processes.  It is expected that new primary waste treatment capacity for materials recovery facilities, composting and residual waste will be located within the WPA in which the waste arises.

9.41    Based on information from the North West RTAB [108]. Table 9.5 forecasts the amount of municipal waste likely to arise between 2005 and 2020 and landfill capacity requirements.

---

107    Landfill Allowance and Trading Scheme (England) Regulations 2004 and the Landfill Allowances and Trading Scheme (England) (Amendment) Regulations 2005.
108    RTAB Annual Monitoring Report, 2005.

## Monitoring and updating of Baseline Data and Information

9.42    On-going monitoring will be used to update data on waste arisings and waste management capacity and projected capacity requirements. This information will be used to review and update both the pattern of waste management facilities and the apportionment. The RTAB annual monitoring framework provides for comprehensive monitoring of RSS targets and objectives and includes data and information requirements specified by PPS10. Updated information will be published in the Annual Monitoring Report produced by the RTAB.

**Table 9.5 Indicative Capacity Requirements for Municipal Waste Arisings 2005 – 2020**

| Sub Regional Area | Predicted waste arisings ('000s tonnes pa) | | | Total residual landfill capacity requirement ('000s cubic metres) | | |
|---|---|---|---|---|---|---|
| | 2005-2010 | 2010-2015 | 2015-2020 | 2005-2010 | 2010-2015 | 2015-2020 |
| Cheshire | 490 | 515 | 515 | 2,318 | 1,103 | 807 |
| Cumbria | 360 | 380 | 380 | 1,655 | 725 | 530 |
| Greater Manchester (Including Wigan) | 1,765 | 1,850 | 1,850 | 9,250 | 4,185 | 2,893 |
| Lancashire (including Blackburn with Darwen and Blackpool) | 895 | 930 | 930 | 4,634 | 2,129 | 1,556 |
| Merseyside & Halton | 1,077 | 1.136 | 1,136 | 5,024 | 2,227 | 1,627 |
| Warrington | 123 | 129 | 129 | 521 | 290 | 212 |
| North West Total | | | | 23,402 (2,979 pa in 2010) | 10,659 (1,814 pa in 2015) | 7,625 (1,327 pa from 2020) |
| Assumption made in compiling Table 9.5: | | | | | | |

9 Environment, Minerals, Waste and Energy

- Waste growth in line with regional strategy for waste targets;
- Residual landfill capacity is based on the Landfill Allowance Trading Scheme allocations (including biodegradable waste as 68% and non biodegradable waste as 32% of total) plus 25% to take into account landfill capacity required for daily cover and site engineering.

## Policy EM 14

### Radioactive Waste

Plans and strategies should continue to support the North West as a centre of national and international expertise in the fields of nuclear fuel fabrication, reprocessing, radioactive waste management and decommissioning.

National and regional partners should work together to promote an agreed solution to the safe long-term management of radioactive waste, based on consultation with all relevant interests. This should incorporate a long-term commitment to the reduction of radioactive discharges and to radioactive waste minimisation, management and safe storage techniques.

9.43    In April 2005, sites operated by British Nuclear Fuels plc (BNFL) in Cheshire, Lancashire and Cumbria including the Sellafield reprocessing facilities and the now closed Calder Hall Magnox Nuclear Power Station, became the responsibility of the Nuclear Decommissioning Authority. British Energy plc operates two Advanced Gas Cooled Reactor (AGR) power stations in Lancashire.

9.44    Arrangements for the long-term management and disposal of radioactive wastes are a national issue. The Nuclear Decommissioning Authority has published a draft consultation strategy which aims to secure, through completed contracts, the progressive decommissioning of reprocessing facilities and nuclear power stations in the region over the next ten to twenty years [109].

9.45    Enhanced focus on decommissioning is anticipated to generate growing volumes of Low Level (LLW) and Intermediate Level (ILW) waste in the Region. Small amounts of radioactive waste are also produced by local industry, universities and hospitals. The majority of the solid LLW produced in the UK is transferred to the shallow surface storage site near Drigg in Copeland. Most of the UK's ILW is conditioned and transferred into passive safe surface stores at Sellafield, pending national agreement on a long-term waste management strategy. Liquid High Level Waste, a by-product of reprocessing, is stored to cool in surface tanks at Sellafield for a period of years and then subject to a process of 'vitrification' pending policy clarification.

---

109    Assumption made in compiling Table 11.5,
    - Waste growth at in line with Regional Waste Strategy targets;
    - Recycling and composting within RWS projections (35%, 45% & 55%) with a ceiling of 15% of total municipal waste arisings for composting;
    - Composting includes all processes providing biological treatment of source segregated organic materials including windrow composting, in vessel composting and anaerobic digestion;
    - Residual waste treatments include Mechanical / Biological Treatment (MBT), Refuse Derived Fuel (RDF/Solid Recovered Fuel (SRF), Energy from Waste (EfW) (mass burn), Anaerobic Digestion together with new technologies under research and development;
    - Residual waste treatment provided for waste above the landfill allowance limits 2010 and subsequently for all residual waste;
    - Products of residual waste treatment require addition treatment capacity 2020.

## Policy EM 15

### A Framework For Sustainable Energy In The North West

Plans and strategies should promote sustainable energy production and consumption in accordance with the principles of the Energy Hierarchy set out in Figure 9.2 and within the Sustainable Energy Strategy. In line with the North West Sustainable Energy Strategy the North West aims to double its installed Combined Heat and Power (CHP) capacity by 2010 from 866 MWe to 1.5 GW, if economic conditions are feasible.

All public authorities should in their own proposals and schemes (including refurbishment) lead by example to emphasise their commitment to reducing the annual consumption of energy and the potential for sustainable energy generation, and facilitate the adoption of good practice by the widest range of local stakeholders.

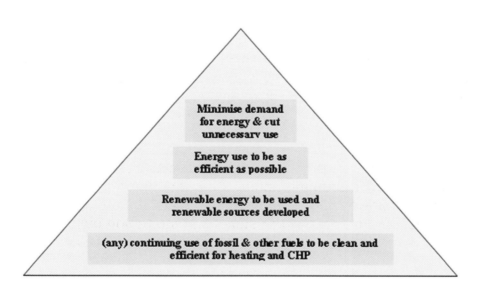

9.46    The production, security of supply and efficient use of energy is essential to 21st Century society and the increase in global demand will have an impact on life in the North West. The Government's 2003 Energy White Paper recognised the scale of the challenge faced and set out strategic priorities for UK energy policy [110]. The Energy Review in 2006 [111] assessed progress against these objectives, and the subsequent Energy White Paper 2007 [112] contains a range of proposals designed to address the climate change and energy challenge by reducing the demand for energy, by securing a mix of clean, low carbon energy sources and by streamlining the planning process for energy projects. The legislative aspects of the Energy White Paper 2007

110    The Energy White Paper, Our energy future - creating a low carbon economy, CM5761, February 2003 set out four key goals:
      - To put ourselves on a path to cut the UK's carbon dioxide emissions by some 60% by about 2050 with real progress by 2020;
      - To maintain the reliability of energy supplies;
      - To promote competitive markets in the UK and beyond, helping to raise the rate of sustainable economic growth and to improve our productivity; and
      - To ensure that every home is adequately and affordably heated.
111    The Energy Challenge, Energy Review Report 2006, CM6887.
112    Meeting the Energy Challenge, A White Paper on Energy, May 2007, CM7124.

will be implemented by the Energy Bill 2007-8. These themes have also been developed in the North West Sustainable Energy Strategy [113], which supports national targets to reduce CO2 emissions through a combination of approaches pursued as parallel initiatives.

9.47    In July 2007, the Government published Building a Greener Future, a policy statement outlining a timetable for tightening national Building Regulations to achieve a 25% reduction in carbon emissions from new homes in 2010, and 44% in 2013, before reaching zero carbon in 2016. The Government also announced in the Budget 2008 an ambition for all new non-domestic buildings to be zero carbon from 2019 with consultation on the timeline and its feasibility.

9.48    The Planning and Climate Change PPS (PPS1 Supplement) confirms that there will be situations where it could be appropriate for local planning authorities to expect higher levels of building sustainability than the prevailing standards set nationally through building regulations. Local requirements should be brought forward through Development Plan Documents and focus on known opportunities. Local planning authorities are expected to demonstrate clearly the local circumstances that warrant and allow the local requirement.

9.49    When proposing any local requirements for sustainable buildings, local planning authorities should, in line with the PPS on climate change, focus on development area or site-specific opportunities. They should fulfil the tests set out in paragraph 33 of the supplement including ensuring that any requirements are evidence-based and viable, and consistent with securing the expected supply and pace of housing development [114]. Any local requirements should be specified in terms of the achievement of nationally described sustainable buildings standards, for example, in the case of housing, by expecting identified proposals to be delivered at a specific level of the Code for Sustainable Homes.

## Policy EM 16

### Energy Conservation & Efficiency

Local authorities, energy suppliers, construction companies, developers, transport providers and other organisations should ensure that their approach to energy is based on minimising consumption and demand, promoting maximum efficiency and minimum waste in all aspects of local planning, development and energy consumption. To support this, Distribution Network Operators [115] and local planning authorities should make effective provision for required energy network upgrades in terms of distribution connections and substations.

Plans and strategies should actively facilitate reductions in energy requirements and improvements in energy efficiency by incorporating robust policies which support the delivery of the national timetable for reducing emissions from domestic and non-domestic buildings.

---

113    North West Sustainable Energy Strategy", North West Regional Assembly (published July 2006).

114    Planning Policy Statement 12 – Local Spatial Planning. Paragraph 4.52. Department of Communities and Local Government, June 2008.

115    There are currently 2 licensed Distribution Network Operators for the North West – United Utilities Electricity and Scottish Power.

9.50    The Government recommends that the move towards a sustainable energy system should concentrate on reducing demand and increasing energy efficiency, which it believes play a bigger role in reducing $CO_2$ emissions than renewable energy and carbon emissions trading combined. Organisations across the North West can make a significant contribution to this bid.  Efforts to improve energy efficiency include:

- eliminating unnecessary energy use;
- reducing demand, for example, by positioning buildings to take advantage of solar heat and improving their thermal insulation;
- ensuring that processes, systems and equipment are working at optimum level to deliver the maximum output per unit of energy consumed;
- using combined heat and power (CHP) where possible, for example within institutional or mixed use schemes; and
- recognising the benefits of and making effective provision for sustainable travel and access via public transport, walking and cycling, in line with policies RT1 and RT9.

9.51    In July 2007, the Government published Building a Greener Future, a policy statement outlining a timetable for tightening national Building Regulations to achieve a 25% reduction in carbon emissions from new homes in 2010, and 44% in 2013, before reaching zero carbon in 2016.  The Government also announced in the Budget 2008 an ambition for all new non-domestic buildings to be zero carbon from 2019 with consultation on the timeline and its feasibility.

9.52    The Planning and Climate Change PPS (PPS1 Supplement) confirms that there will be situations where it could be appropriate for local planning authorities to expect higher levels of building sustainability than the prevailing standards set nationally through building regulations. Local requirements should be brought forward through development plan documents and focus on known opportunities.  Local planning authorities are expected to demonstrate clearly the local circumstances that warrant and allow the local requirement.

9.53    When proposing any local requirements for sustainable buildings, local planning authorities should, in line with the PPS on climate change, focus on development area or site-specific opportunities.  They should fulfil the tests set out in paragraph 33 of the supplement including ensuring that any requirements are evidence-based and viable, and consistent with securing the expected supply and pace of housing development [116].  Any local requirements should be specified in terms of the achievement of nationally described sustainable buildings standards, for example, in the case of housing, by expecting identified proposals to be delivered at a specific level of the Code for Sustainable Homes.

9.54    The Climate Change Action Plan for England's Northwest [117], the mechanism through which the North West Sustainable Energy Strategy will be implemented, initiated research to develop a regional inventory of greenhouse gas emissions and consider targets for emissions reductions and generation of renewable heat.  It is also anticipated that the forthcoming Climate Change Bill [118] will propose national emissions targets. Therefore, work to develop targets for reduced energy consumption will be considered in a future review of RSS.

---

116    Planning Policy Statement 12 – Local Spatial Planning. Paragraph 4.52. Department of Communities and Local Government, June 2008.

117    Rising to the Challenge, A Climate Change Action Plan for England's Northwest 2007-09, Northwest Climate Change Partnership, November 2006.

118    Climate Change Bill March 2007, Defra, CM7040.

## Policy EM 17

### Renewable Energy

In line with the North West Sustainable Energy Strategy, by 2010 at least 10% (rising to at least 15% by 2015 and at least 20% by 2020) of the electricity which is supplied within the Region should be provided from renewable energy sources. To achieve this new renewable energy capacity should be developed which will contribute towards the delivery of the indicative capacity targets set out in Tables 9.6 and 9.7a-c. In accordance with PPS22, meeting these targets is not a reason to refuse otherwise acceptable development proposals.

Local authorities should work with stakeholders in the preparation of sub regional studies of renewable energy resources so as to gain a thorough understanding of the supplies available and network improvements, and how they can best be used to meet national, regional and local targets. These studies should form the basis for:

- informing a future review of RSS to identify broad locations where development of particular types of renewable energy may be considered appropriate [119]; and
- establishing local strategies for dealing with renewable resources, setting targets for their use which can replace existing sub regional targets for the relevant authorities.

Plans and strategies should seek to promote and encourage, rather than restrict, the use of renewable energy resources. Local planning authorities should give significant weight to the wider environmental, community and economic benefits of proposals for renewable energy schemes to:

- contribute towards the capacities set out in tables 9.6 and 9.7 a-c; and
- mitigate the causes of climate change and minimise the need to consume finite natural resources.

Opportunities should be sought to identify proposals and schemes for renewable energy. The following criteria should be taken into account but should not be used to rule out or place constraints on the development of all, or specific types of, renewable energy technologies:

- anticipated effects on local amenity resulting from development, construction and operation of schemes (e.g. air quality, atmospheric emissions, noise, odour, water pollution and disposal of waste). Measures to mitigate these impacts should be employed where possible and necessary to make them acceptable;
- acceptability of the location/scale of the proposal and its visual impact in relation to the character and sensitivity of the surrounding landscape, including cumulative impact. Stringent requirements for minimising impact on landscape and townscape would not be appropriate if these effectively preclude the supply of certain types of renewable energy, other than in the most exceptional circumstances such as within nationally recognised designations as set out in PPS22 paragraph 11;
- effect on the region's World Heritage Sites and other national and internationally designated sites or areas, and their settings but avoiding the creation of buffer zones

---

119     Requirement of Paragraph 6, Planning Policy Statement (PPS22) "Renewable Energy", ODPM 2004.

and noting that small scale developments may be permitted in such areas provided there is no significant environmental detriment;

- effect of development on nature conservation features, biodiversity and geodiversity, including sites, habitats and species, and which avoid significant adverse effects on sites of international nature conservation importance by assessment under the Habitats Regulations;
- maintenance of the openness of the Region's Green Belt;
- potential benefits of development to the local economy and the local community;
- accessibility (where necessary) by the local transport network;
- effect on agriculture and other land based industries;
- ability to make connections to the electricity distribution network which takes account of visual impact (as qualified above);
- integration of the proposal with existing or new development where appropriate;
- proximity to the renewable fuel source where relevant – e.g. wood-fuel biomass processing plants within or in close proximity to the region's major woodlands and forests;
- encourage the integration of combined heat and power (CHP), including micro CHP into development.

Developers must engage with local communities at an early stage of the development process prior to submission of any proposals and schemes for approval under the appropriate legislation.

9.55    In the short to medium term, the majority of the power generated in the North West will continue to come from the large-scale nuclear, coal and gas-fired power stations that supplied around 80% of the region's electricity in 2001 [120]. However, as fossil fuel resources are in serious decline and nuclear stations are scheduled to close, the UK is likely to become a major importer of energy during the next two decades. Much of the Region's existing capacity for generating power is from long term unsustainable non renewable sources, although there may still be a role for cleaner coal production. Renewable energy technologies must now be developed to support an increasing proportion of the Region's capacity for generating electricity.  Tables 9.6 and 9.7 a-c provide indicative regional and sub regional targets.  These are flexible and will change.  However they provide an important indication of the way in which regional and sub regional targets might be met and new renewable energy capacity should be developed with the aim of meeting or exceeding these targets. It is proposed that the targets should be subject to bi-annual review, allowing them to be revised periodically through an active process of monitoring of renewable energy deployment against proposed targets and regional energy consumption.  The replacement of non-renewable capacity by improved energy efficiency and Combined Heat & Power (CHP) will bring new economic opportunities to the region, as part of a strategic and sustainable approach to energy.

9.56    The Energy and Greenhouse Gas Emissions Study published by NWRA in 2007 [121] examined the potential for installation of renewable heat technologies, and proposed regional targets for their uptake.  Work to agree such targets for renewable heat will be considered in a future review of the RSS.

---

120    Energy in England's Northwest - Achieving Sustainable Growth" Northwest Regional Development Agency, July 2003.
121    www.nwra.gov.uk

## 9 Environment, Minerals, Waste and Energy

9.57    Each renewable technology has its own locational characteristics and requirements and different areas will be better suited to different technologies. The international importance of much of the coastline and all of the major estuaries of the Region for nature conservation is likely to inform choice of location for marine schemes.

9.58    In line with PPS22, developers must consult and engage with local communities at an early stage of the development process prior to submission of any proposals and schemes for approval under the appropriate legislation.

### Policy EM 18

**Decentralised Energy Supply**

Plans and strategies should encourage the use of decentralised and renewable or low-carbon energy in new development in order to contribute to the achievement of the targets set out in Table 9.6 and 9.7a-c. In particular, local authorities should, in their Development Plan Documents, set out:

* targets for the energy to be used in new development to come from decentralised and renewable or low-carbon energy sources, based on appropriate evidence and viability assessments; and
* the type and size of development to which the target will be applied.

In advance of local targets being set, new non residential developments above a threshold of 1,000m² and all residential developments comprising 10 or more units should secure at least 10% of their predicted energy requirements from decentralised and renewable or low-carbon sources, unless it can be demonstrated by the applicant, having regard to the type of development involved and its design, that this is not feasible or viable.

9.59    PPS1 supplement on Climate Change expects local planning authorities to provide a framework that promotes and encourages renewable and low carbon energy development. Local planning authorities should have an evidence-based understanding of the local feasibility and potential for renewable and low-carbon technologies, including microgeneration, to supply new development in their area. Targets for the percentage of energy to be use in new development to come from decentralised and renewable or low-carbon energy sources should be set out and tested in Development Plan Documents to ensure they are evidence-based, viable and consistent with ensuring housing and affordable housing supply is not inhibited.

9.60    Microgeneration has the potential to play a significant role in moving towards the Government's objective of sustainable, reliable and affordable energy for all, delivered through competitive markets. The Microgeneration Strategy, published in 2006, aims to create conditions in which microgeneration is a realistic alternative, or supplementary energy generation source, for individual householders, the wider community and small businesses [122].

---

**9.61** Government policy, as re-stated in the Energy White Paper 2007 [123] and Energy Bill 2007-8, is quite clear that diversity in the provision of energy is fundamental and that it is essential to maintain electricity supply system security. Therefore, whilst renewable energy and microgeneration have an important role to play, there will be a continued need for other electricity generation including potentially nuclear, clean coal and gas generation technologies.

### Table 9.6 Indicative Regional Renewable Energy Generation Targets

| Renewable Energy Type / Scale | Existing Generating Capacity in 2005 | | Indicative Target for Total Generating Capacity in 2010 (including existing schemes) [Target = 3.59 TWh/ yr (3,590 GWh/yr)] | | | Indicative Target for Total Generating Capacity in 2015 (including existing schemes) [Target = 5.66 TWh /yr (5,660 GWh/yr)] | | | Indicative Target for Total Generating Capacity in 2020 (including existing schemes) [Target = 7.93 TWh/yr (7,930 GWh/yr)] | | |
|---|---|---|---|---|---|---|---|---|---|---|---|
| | No of schemes | Capacity (MW) | No of schemes | Capacity (MW) | Energy Output (GWh/yr) | No of schemes | Capacity (MW) | Energy Output (GWh/yr) | No of schemes | Capacity (MW) | Energy Output (GWh/yr) |
| Offshore wind farms | 0 | 0 | 3 | 297 | 937 | 4 | 747 | 2,356 | 5 | 1347 | 4,248 |
| On-shore wind farms | 16 | 68.9 | 35 – 51 | 600 | 1,183 | 44 – 62 | 720 | 1,561 | 44 – 62 | 720 | 1,561 |
| On-shore wind clusters | | | | | | | | | | | |
| Single large wind turbines | | | 30 | 48 | 88.7 | 50 | 75 | 162.6 | 50 | 75 | 162.6 |
| Small stand-alone wind turbines | Small | Small | 50 | 1.5 | 3.0 | 75 | 2.25 | 4.9 | 75 | 2.25 | 4.9 |
| Bldg.-mounted micro-wind turbines | 0 | 0 | 1,000 | 1 | 1.7 | 10,000 | 10 | 16.6 | 20,000 | 20 | 33.3 |
| Biomass-fuelled CHP / electricity schemes | 2 | 11.1 | 7 | 31.1 | 150.5 | 12 | 56.1 | 271.5 | 15 | 106.1 | 513.5 |
| Biomass co-firing | 2 | 103 | 2 | 103 | 498.5 | 0 | 0 | 0 | 0 | 0 | 0 |
| Anaerobic digestion of farm biogas | 0 | 0 | 5 | 10 | 48.4 | 10 | 20 | 96.8 | 15 | 30 | 145.2 |
| Hydro power | 9 | 2.7 | 12 | 3.5 | 7.1 | 12 | 3.5 | 7.1 | 12 | 3.5 | 7.1 |
| Solar photovoltaics [124] | V small | V small | 1,000 | 2 | 1.7 | 25,000 | 50 | 52 | 50,000 | 100 | 124.8 |
| Tidal energy | 0 | 0 | 0 | 0 | 0 | 2 | 30 | 67 | 2 | 30 | 67 |
| Wave energy | 0 | 0 | 0 | 0 | 0 | 0 | 0 | 0 | 1 | 30 | 39.4 |
| Energy from waste | | | | | | | | | | | |
| Landfill gas | 52 | 113.4 | 52 | 113.4 | 548.8 | 19 | 79.1 | 382.8 | 0 | 0 | 0 |
| Sewage gas | 16 | 13.4 | 16 | 13.4 | 64.9 | 16 | 13.4 | 64.9 | 16 | 13.4 | 64.9 |
| Thermal treatment of municipal / industrial waste | 1 | 10.5 | 1 | 10.5 | 50.8 | 3 | 125.5 | 607.4 | 6 | 215.5 | 1043 |
| TOTAL | 97 | 312.5 | 215 – 229 plus PV plus Micro Wind | 1,234.4 | 3,584.1 | 247 – 265 plus PV plus Micro Wind | 1932 | 5,650.6 | 241 – 259 plus PV plus Micro Wind | 2,692.8 plus Waste | 8,014.7 plus Waste |

---

123  Meeting the Energy Challenge, A White Paper on Energy, May 2007, CM7124.
124  This category is assumed to consist of a variety of different scales of domestic, commercial and "motorway" scheme with an average size of 2kW

9 Environment, Minerals, Waste and Energy

## Table 9.7a Indicative Sub-Regional Breakdown of Target for Total Generating Capacity in 2010 (including existing schemes)

| Indicative Renewable Energy Generation Type/Size | Region-Wide Targets | Cheshire | Cumbria | Greater Manchester | Lancashire | Merseyside | Warrington & Halton | TOTAL |
|---|---|---|---|---|---|---|---|---|
| Offshore wind farms | 3 (297) | - | - | - | - | - | - | 3 (297) |
| On-shore wind farms On-shore wind clusters | - | 5-7 (82.5) | 13-18 (210) | 5-7 (90) | 11-16 (195) | 2 (15) | 1 (7.5) | 37-51 (600) |
| Single large wind turbines | - | 3 (4.5) | 4 (9) | 8 (12) | 7 (10.5) | 6 (9) | 2 (3) | 30 (48) |
| Small stand-alone wind turbines | - | 8 (0.24) | 10 (0.3) | 12 (0.36) | 10 (0.3) | 8 (0.24) | 2 (0.06) | 50 (1.5) |
| Bldg.-mounted micro-wind turbines | - | 95 (0.095) | 75 (0.075) | 370 (0.37) | 205 (0.205) | 190 (0.19) | 65 (0.065) | 1,000 (1) |
| Biomass-fuelled CHP / electricity schemes | - | 1 (4) | 2 (8) | 1 (4) | 1 (9) | 1 (4) | 1 (2.1) | 7 (31.1) |
| Biomass co-firing | 2 (103) | - | - | - | - | - | - | 2 (103) |
| Anaerobic digestion of farm biogas | - | 1 (2) | 1 (2) | 1 (2) | 1 (2) | 1 (2) | 0 | 5 (10) |
| Hydro power | - | 0 | 8 (2.4) | 2 (1) | 2 (0.1) | 0 | 0 | 12 (3.5) |
| Solar photovoltaics [126] | - | 95 (0.19) | 75 (0.15) | 370 (0.74) | 205 (0.41) | 190 (0.38) | 65 (0.13) | 1,000 (2) |
| Tidal energy | 0 | - | - | - | - | - | - | 0 |
| Wave energy | 0 | - | - | - | - | - | - | 0 |
| Energy from waste | | | | | | | | |
| Landfill gas | - | 7 (16.2) | 6 (5.4) | 13 (23.7) | 14 (20.2) | 7 (13.5) | 5 (34.4) | 52 (113.4) |
| Sewage gas | - | 3 (0.7) | 0 | 5 (8.5) | 4 (1.2) | 2 (2.0) | 2 (1.0) | 16 (13.4) |
| Thermal treatment of municipal / industrial waste | - | 0 | 0 | 1 (10.5) | 0 | 0 | 0 | 1 (10.5) |
| Total [127] | 5 (400) | 28-30 (110.4) | 44-49 (237.3) | 48-50 (153.2) | 50-55 (239) | 27 (46.3) | 13 (48.2) | 215-229 (1,231.4) [1234.4?] |

---

126   This category is assumed to consist of a variety of different scales of domestic, commercial and "motorway" scheme.

127   All totals are exclusive of micro wind and photovoltaics installations

## Table 9.7b Indicative Sub-Regional Breakdown of Target for Total Generating Capacity in 2015 (including existing schemes)

| Indicative Renewable Energy Generation Type/Size | Region-Wide Targets | Cheshire | Cumbria | Greater Manchester | Lancashire | Merseyside | Warrington & Halton | TOTAL |
|---|---|---|---|---|---|---|---|---|
| Offshore wind farms | 4 (747) | - | - | - | - | - | - | 4 (747) |
| On-shore wind farms | - | 7-10 (120) | 15-21 (247.5) | 6-8 (97.5) | 13-20 (232.5) | 2 (15) | 1 (7.5) | 44-62 (720) |
| On-shore wind clusters | | | | | | | | |
| Single large wind turbines | - | 6 (9) | 6 (9) | 14 (21) | 11 (16.5) | 10 (15) | 3 (4.5) | 50 (75) |
| Small stand-alone wind turbines | - | 12 (0.36) | 15 (0.45) | 18 (0.54) | 15 (0.45) | 12 (0.36) | 3 (0.09) | 75 (2.3) |
| Bldg.-mounted micro-wind turbines | - | 950 (0.95) | 750 (0.75) | 3,700 (3.7) | 2,050 (2.05) | 1,900 (1.9) | 650 (0.65) | 10,000 (10) |
| Biomass-fuelled CHP / electricity schemes | - | 2 (9) | 3 (13) | 2 (9) | 2 (14) | 2 (9) | 1 (2.1) | 12 (56.1) |
| Biomass co-firing | 0 | - | - | - | - | - | - | 0 |
| Anaerobic digestion of farm biogas | - | 2 (4) | 2 (4) | 2 (4) | 3 (6) | 1 (2) | 0 | 10 (20) |
| Hydro power | - | 0 | 8 (2.4) | 2 (1) | 2 (0.1) | 0 | 0 | 12 (3.5) |
| Solar photovoltaics [129] | - | 2,375 (4.75) | 1,875 (3.75) | 9,250 (18.5) | 5,125 (10.25) | 4,750 (9.5) | 1,625 (3.25) | 25,000 (50) |
| Tidal energy | 2 (30) | - | - | - | - | - | - | 2 (30) |
| Wave energy | 0 | - | - | - | - | - | - | 0 |
| Energy from waste | | | | | | | | |
| Landfill gas | - | 2 (8.7) | 3 (3.9) | 2 (12) | 7 (14.3) | 3 (9.7) | 2 (30.5) | 19 (79.1) |
| Sewage gas | - | 3 (0.7) | 0 | 5 (8.5) | 4 (1.2) | 2 (2.0) | 2 (1.0) | 16 (13.4) |
| Thermal treatment of municipal / industrial waste | - | 1 (25) | 0 | 2 (100.5) | 0 | 0 | 0 | 3 (125.5) |
| Total [130] | 6 (777) | 35-38 (182.5) | 52-58 (284.8) | 53-55 (276.2) | 57-64 (297.4) | 32 (64.5) | 12 (49.6) | 247-265 (1,932) |

129  This category is assumed to consist of a variety of different scales of domestic, commercial and "motorway" scheme. With domestic PV now encouraged via the Bldg. Regulations the number of domestic installations increases greatly.

130  All totals are exclusive of micro wind and photovoltaics installations

9 Environment, Minerals, Waste and Energy

## Table 9.7c Indicative Sub-Regional Breakdown of Target for Total Generating Capacity in 2020(including existing schemes)

| Indicative Renewable Energy Generation Type/Size | Region-Wide Targets | Cheshire | Cumbria | Greater Manchester | Lancashire | Merseyside | Warrington & Halton | TOTAL |
|---|---|---|---|---|---|---|---|---|
| Offshore wind farms | 5 (1,347) | - | - | - | - | - | - | 5 (1347) |
| On-shore wind farms On-shore wind clusters | - | 7-10 (120) | 15-21 (247.5) | 6-8 (97.5) | 13-20 (232.5) | 2 (15) | 1 (7.5) | 44-62 (720) |
| Single large wind turbines | - | 6 (9) | 6 (9) | 14 (21) | 11 (16.5) | 10 (15) | 3 (4.5) | 50 (75) |
| Small stand-alone wind turbines | - | 12 (0.36) | 15 (0.45) | 18 (0.54) | 15 (0.45) | 12 (0.36) | 3 (0.09) | 75 (2.3) |
| Bldg.-mounted micro-wind turbines | - | 1,900 (1.9) | 1,500 (1.5) | 7,400 (7.4) | 4,100 (4.1) | 3,800 (3.8) | 1,300 (1.3) | 20,000 (20) |
| Biomass-fuelled CHP / electricity schemes | - | 2 (9) | 4 (18) | 2 (9) | 3 (19) | 2 (9) | 2 (42.1) | 15 (106.1) |
| Biomass co-firing | 0 | - | - | - | - | - | - | 0 |
| Anaerobic digestion of farm biogas | - | 2 (4) | 3 (6) | 3 (6) | 5 (10) | 2 (4) | 0 | 15 (30) |
| Hydro power | - | 0 | 8 (2.4) | 2 (1) | 2 (0.1) | 0 | 0 | 12 (3.5) |
| Solar photovoltaics [132] | - | 4,700(9.5) | 3,750 (7.5) | 1,8500 (37) | 10,250 (20.5) | 9,500 (19) | 3,250 (6.5) | 50,000 (100) |
| Tidal energy | 2 (30) | - | - | - | - | - | - | 2 (30) |
| Wave energy | 1 (30) | - | - | - | - | - | - | 1 (30) |
| Energy from waste | | | | | | | | |
| Landfill gas | - | 0 | 0 | 0 | 0 | 0 | 0 | 0 |
| Sewage gas | - | 3 (0.7) | 0 | 5 (8.5) | 4 (1.2) | 2 (2.0) | 2 (1.0) | 16 (13.4) |
| Thermal treatment of municipal / industrial waste | - | 1 (25) | 0 | 2 (100.5) | 1 (40) | 1 (40) | 1 (10) | 6 (215.5) |
| Total [133] | 8 (1,407) | 33-36 (179.5) | 51-57 (292.4) | 52-54 (288.4) | 54-61 (344.4) | 31 (108.2) | 12 (73) | 241-259 (2692.8) |

132    This category is assumed to consist of a variety of different scales of domestic, commercial and "motorway" scheme. With domestic PV now encouraged via the Bldg. Regulations the number of domestic installations increases greatly.

133    All totals are exclusive of micro wind and photovoltaics installations.

# 10 Manchester City Region

## Background

**10.1**　The Manchester City Region has a wide area of influence stretching into High Peak and it has strong economic and transport links with the city regions of Central Lancashire, Liverpool, and Leeds. For the purposes of articulating RSS policy the sub region is defined as the ten Greater Manchester local authorities, East Cheshire (formerly Local Authorities of Macclesfield, Congleton and Crewe and Nantwich) and Warrington.

**10.2**　As a major centre for economic activity, the Manchester City Region contributes almost half of the North West's total Gross Value Added (GVA) [134] and offers the greatest potential for boosting its overall economic performance. Accordingly it is the focus of a significant proportion of the future development activity outlined in RSS within the North West's three city regions.

**10.3**　The vision is that by 2025 the Manchester City Region will be:

*"A world class city region at the heart of a thriving North"*

- one of Europe's premier City Regions, at the forefront of the knowledge economy, and with outstanding commercial, cultural and creative activities;
- world class, successfully competing internationally for investment, jobs and visitors;
- an area where all people have the opportunity to participate in, and benefit from, the investment in and development of their city;
- an area known for, and distinguished by, the quality of life enjoyed by its residents; and
- an area with GVA levels to match those of London and the South East.

---

134　Page 17, Manchester City Region Development Programme – Accelerating the Economic Growth of the North ( 2006) (see http://www.thenorthernway.co.uk/cityregions.html

# 10 Manchester City Region

## Policy MCR 1

**Manchester City Region Priorities**

Plans and strategies in the Manchester City Region should:

- support interventions necessary to achieve a significant improvement in the sub-region's economic performance by encouraging investment and sustainable development in the Regional Centre, surrounding inner areas, the towns/cities and accessible suburban centres as set out in RDF1 and other key locations which accord with the spatial principles policies (DP1-9) and the criteria in policies W2 and W3 in order to contribute to the growth opportunities identified in policy W1;
- secure improvements, including the enhancement of public transport links, which will enable the inner areas and the northern part of the City Region to capture growing levels of investment and reduce sub-regional disparities. Particular attention should be given to assisting with programmes to address worklessness;
- accommodate housing development in locations that are accessible by public transport to areas of economic growth. A high level of residential development will be encouraged in the inner areas to secure a significant increase in the population of these areas;
- provide high quality housing to replace obsolete stock and where appropriate refurbish existing properties, to meet the needs of existing residents, and attract and retain new population in order to support economic growth;
- improve the City Region's internal and external transport links in line with the priorities for transport investment and management set out in Policy RT10;
- maintain the role of Manchester Airport as the North of England's key international gateway in line with Policy RT5;
- develop the role of Manchester as a national public transport gateway to the region in line with policy RT3 and enhance the accessibility of the Regional Centre by public transport to support economic growth and enable the benefits of its wide range of economic, cultural and other opportunities to be shared. Investment should support policies MCR2 and MCR4 in particular;
- develop the roles of Wigan, Warrington and Crewe as regional public transport gateways in line with policy RT3;
- focus environmental improvements where they are most needed and will have the greatest benefit to facilitate the sustainable development of the Regional Centre and Inner Areas. This includes integrated flood management works, the remediation of contaminated land, and provision of high quality green infrastructure as part of comprehensive regeneration schemes;
- proposals and schemes will be directed primarily towards locations where they can contribute to these priorities.

**10.4** It will be necessary to create and sustain the conditions to realise the vision for the City Region by simultaneously exploiting its current assets and greatest opportunities to deliver accelerated economic growth; and reducing social and economic disparities within the City Region, through regeneration initiatives. Policies are based on a 'dual approach', which is to support growth in those parts of the City Region that are already performing strongly while generating additional growth in those parts which are lagging. It will be essential to monitor development to ensure that delivery in the Regional Centre and Inner Areas is at the level anticipated, and that it benefits those 'who are most in need'.

RSS aims to see the MCR deliver its full potential by ensuring that policies connect areas of economic opportunity to areas of greatest need, with a particular focus on those areas in need of economic, social and physical restructuring and regeneration.

**10.5**    The promotion of regional park and community forest resources in the context of an overall objective of "green infrastructure" provision, will help to improve the image of all parts of the City Region, maximise accessibility to facilities, greenspace and biodiversity, reduce social exclusion, promote good health, provide a high quality environment, help to attract investment in leisure, tourism and high quality employment, and support the provision of successful and sustainable neighbourhoods.

# 10 Manchester City Region

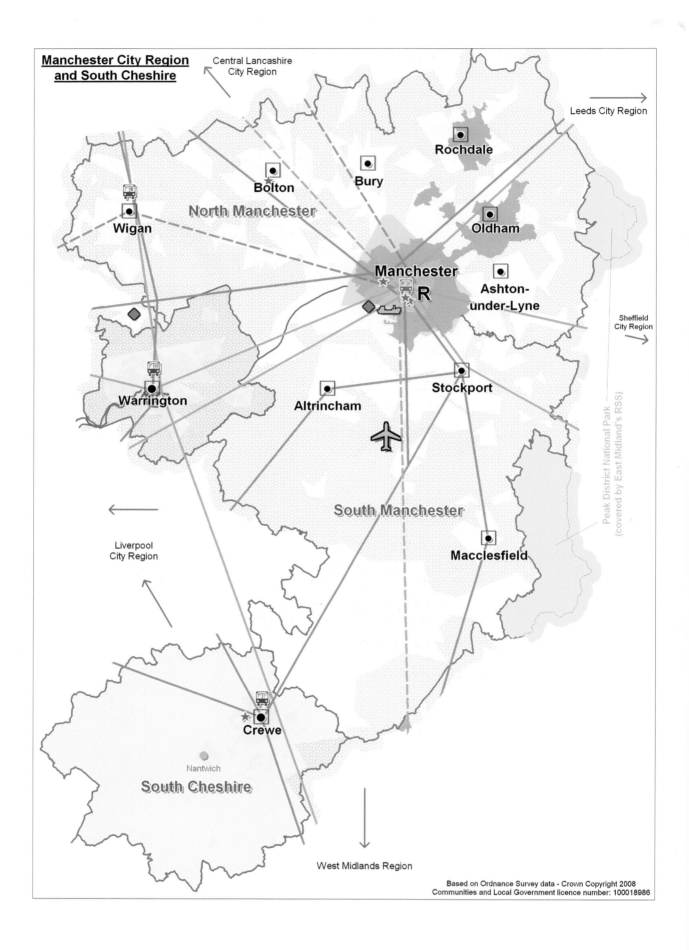

Manchester City Region and South Cheshire

# Manchester and South Cheshire Key

**R**    Regional Centre - RDF1/MCR1&2

   Inner Area - RDF1/MCR1&2

——    Sub region division - North / South Manchester

   Warrington Local Authority

   South Cheshire

●    Towns/ Cities for growth & development - RDF1/City Region Policies: MCR1-MCR6

   HMRAs - RDF1/L3

   General extent of green belt - RDF4

   Peak District National Park - EM1/W6

☐    Foci for comparison retail facilities - W5

——    National public transport corridors

- - -    Regional public transport corridors    } Appendix RT(b)/RT3

——    National road corridors

- - -    Regional road corridors    } Appendix RT(c)/RT4

✈    Airports - RT5 (RDF4/MCR1)

⛴    Ports - RT6 (MCR1)

   Public transport interchanges (Regional) - RT3/appendix RT(a&b)

   Public transport interchanges (International/National) - RT3/appendix RT(a&b)

★    Universities - W2 (MCR2)

   City Region boundaries

   Urban areas

◆    Rail Freight Locations - RT8 (RDF4)

## 10 Manchester City Region

---

### Policy MCR 2

**Regional Centre and Inner Areas of Manchester City Region**

Plans and strategies should ensure that the Regional Centre of the Manchester City Region continues to develop as the primary economic driver, providing the main focus for business, retail, leisure, cultural and tourism development in the City Region. The expansion of the knowledge economy throughout the Regional Centre, and particularly related to the Universities and Central Manchester hospitals, will be a particular priority;

- proposals and schemes for residential development in the Regional Centre will be acceptable where they are part of mixed use employment schemes that comprise a good range of housing sizes, types, tenures and affordability and where they contribute to the vitality and viability of the Regional Centre;

In the inner areas:

- residential development should be focused in the inner areas adjacent to the Regional Centre in order to secure a significant increase in their population, to support major regeneration activity including the Manchester-Salford Housing Market Renewal Pathfinder, and to secure the improvement of community facilities and the creation of sustainable communities. The emphasis will be on providing a good range of quality housing, in terms of size, type, tenure and affordability, with a high quality environment and accessible local facilities and employment opportunities;
- plans and strategies should provide for employment within the Inner Areas in accordance with policies W2 and W3 and MCR1.

---

**10.6** The Regional Centre of Manchester City Region comprises Manchester City Centre and Central Park to the East, the higher Education Precinct and Central Manchester Hospitals to the south, and Salford University, Salford Quays, Trafford Wharfside and Pomona Docks to the West. The Inner Areas surrounding the Regional Centre comprise of North Manchester, East Manchester and Central Manchester regeneration areas, Trafford Park, North Trafford and Central Salford. The expansion of the knowledge based economy will be a priority in the area which stretches from University of Salford in the West to Piccadilly Station in the east, via the Higher Education Precinct and the Central Manchester Hospitals campus. Detailed boundary definitions for these areas will need to be set out in Local Development Frameworks and will necessitate close cross authority working.

**10.7** The Regional Centre is fundamental to the success of the City Region, and will continue to be the primary economic driver in the North West. For this reason it is vital that its economy, including knowledge based industries, is encouraged to grow. Residential development as part of mixed schemes can enhance the vibrant appeal of the Regional Centre by creating attractive opportunities for people to live closer to employment and recreational facilities. Residential developments in the Regional Centre need to meet a range of needs, types and tenures and should not compromise the vitality and viability of the commercial, retail, leisure, cultural and tourism functions of the Regional Centre, or dominate any particular part of the area.

**10.8**    As the regeneration of the Inner Areas is important to the overall success of the City Region, and because these areas are identified as high priority by initiatives like the Housing Market Renewal Pathfinder project and the creation of two Urban Regeneration Companies, Central Salford and New East Manchester, they are considered to be a suitable location for significant new housing and local economic development.  It will be important to ensure the development of sustainable, mixed communities that appeal to a broad range of new and existing residents.

**10.9**    The Inner Areas have enormous potential, which, if left untapped, will limit the ability of the Regional Centre to secure investment and generate further growth.   Development within the Inner Areas will boost overall economic growth in the City Region, reduce local inequalities (such as worklessness) and deprivation and provide a clear alternative to further decentralisation and the unsustainable commuting patterns associated with it.

## Policy MCR 3

### Southern Part of the Manchester City Region

Plans and strategies in the southern part of the City Region should sustain and promote economic prosperity consistent with the environmental character of the area and the creation of attractive and sustainable communities by:

- focusing employment development in the towns as set out in RDF 1 and on brownfield sites which accord with the spatial principles (policies DP1-9) in Policies W2 and W3 and MCR1, in order to support the overall economic growth of the City Region, to meet local needs and regeneration requirements and to address worklessness. Sites should be of an appropriate scale, and accessible by public transport, walking and cycling;
- allowing residential development to support local regeneration strategies and to meet identified local needs (particularly for affordable housing), in sustainable locations which are well served by public transport;
- support and diversify the rural economy and improve access to services in the rural areas focusing development in locations which accord with RDF2.

**10.10**    The southern area of the Manchester City Region comprises of the boroughs of Stockport, Congleton, Macclesfield, and those parts of Trafford and the southern areas of Manchester City which are not in the Regional Centre or Inner Areas. The detailed boundaries particularly in relation to the Inner areas will need to be defined in Local Development Frameworks.

**10.11**    It will be essential to optimise the contribution made by the southern parts of the City Region in order to promote the growth in economic performance that The Northern Way seeks to achieve.  Residential development in these areas will be focused on meeting identified local needs particularly affordable housing, continuing the approach established in the adopted RSS( namely RPG 13).

**10.12**    The southern area of the city region has a strong inter relationship with parts of the local authority area of High Peak, which is part of the wider Manchester City Region (see City Region Diagram). High Peak falls within the East Midlands Region and is not covered by North

West RSS, however the Regional Planning Body will work with its East Midlands counterpart to develop a consistent policy for the parts of the borough that are considered to lie within the Manchester City Region.

10.13    The area of South Cheshire primarily relates to development in the town of Crewe and the surrounding rural area, including Nantwich. South Cheshire is within the Manchester City Region, but lies on its periphery and has certain economic links with both Manchester City Region and the North Staffordshire/ Potteries urban area. There are particular opportunities to build upon existing linkages with the Manchester City Region in particular the other parts of East Cheshire and Vale Royal and Chester in Liverpool City Region.

## Policy MCR 4

### South Cheshire

Plans and strategies should:

- support sustainable economic growth in Crewe and focus development on sites which accord with RDF1, the Spatial Principles ( policies DP1-9), the criteria in W2 and W3 and MCR1;
- promote the role of Crewe as a regional public transport gateway/interchange to the region;
- provide for regeneration to improve the environment, economy and image of Crewe;
- continue the protection and enhancement of the historic environment of Nantwich and its contribution to the sub-region's economy, tourism, quality of life and regeneration;
- support and diversify the rural economy and improve access to services in the rural areas focusing development in locations which accord with RDF2.

10.14    The priority for South Cheshire is to build upon the economic, educational, social, cultural and transport links with neighbouring areas in order that they can benefit from Crewe's potential for sustainable economic growth.  Future plans for Crewe will need to take account of the likely impact upon economic and regeneration activity in North Staffordshire. [135]

10.15    Crewe is set to experience significant change up to 2021 with the delivery of the economic development at Basford, the redevelopment of Crewe station and the expansion of Manchester Metropolitan University.  The Crewe South East Quadrant Masterplan has been prepared to manage these changes and to maximise the environmental and regeneration benefits for the wider area.

---

135    North Staffordshire contains the Housing Market Renewal Pathfinder based around the Potteries.

## Policy MCR 5

### Northern Part of the Manchester City Region

Plans and strategies for the northern part of the City Region should support the transformation of the local economy, regenerate communities, and enhance the environment. They should:

- secure improvements which enable the area to compete more effectively for economic investment now and in the future, helping to achieve significant improvements in productivity and creating the conditions for sustainable growth. This will require significant interventions to improve skill levels within the labour market, to deliver appropriate development sites, and to secure necessary infrastructure improvements;
- focus employment development in the town/cities as set out in RDF1 and at other locations which accord with the spatial principles (policies DP1-9), policies W2 and W3 and MCR1, to support the overall economic growth of the sub region, to encourage the 'spin-off' of functions linked to the Regional Centre and to address worklessness;
- expand the quality and choice of housing (in terms of size, type, tenure and affordability) in line with the approach set out in Policy L4;
- use the HMR Pathfinder in Oldham and Rochdale as an opportunity for wide ranging change in the economic and housing role of these areas, the renewal of communities and investment in new infrastructure;
- support and diversify the rural economy and improve access to services in the rural areas focusing development in locations which accord with RDF2.

10.16 The northern part of Manchester comprises the boroughs of Bolton, Bury, Wigan, Tameside, Oldham and Rochdale and those parts of Manchester City and Salford City which are outside the Regional Centre, Inner Areas and south Manchester areas. The detailed boundaries particularly in relation to the Inner Areas will need to be defined in Local Development Frameworks.

10.17 The local economies of the northern boroughs are still heavily dependent upon traditional manufacturing industry, and economic forecasts indicate that these will decline further over the next fifteen to twenty years. Moreover, the northern parts of the City Region suffer from being largely disconnected economically and socially from the economic drivers in the Regional Centre and the southern parts of the City Region. It is therefore essential that economic, housing and transport investments are co-ordinated both to assist in the necessary restructuring of the local economy and over time to uplift the economic performance of the north, and that future housing and transport resources are co-ordinated to make sure that improved linkages can be delivered.

10.18 Significant investment will be needed to raise the northern parts of the City Region to the same levels of economic achievement as those in the south. Considerable amounts of economic and residential development will be encouraged, but not at the expense of the regional centre and inner areas, which attract the highest priority. It will be important to ensure that residential development in the north is matched by economic development to avoid any dramatic rise in the need to travel for work.

**10.19** There is a need to develop further research and understanding of the links between Manchester and Central Lancashire City Regions. The Central Lancashire City Region Development Programme highlights the commuting links between the two city regions noting that a net outflow of 10,400 workers from the city region commuted into the Manchester City Region [136]. A future review of RSS will need to take account of emerging evidence that assists in understanding the spatial relationship between the two city regions.

---

### Policy MCR 6

**Strategic Framework for Warrington**

In Warrington plans and strategies should:

- support sustainable economic growth in Warrington and its role as a source of employment for an area including Warrington, Knowsley, Halton, St Helens and Wigan;
- focus development on sites which are accessible by public transport, walking and cycling and accord with policy RDF1, the spatial principles (policies DP1-9), policies W2 and W3 and MCR1, focusing particularly on brownfield sites to ensure no further significant expansion onto open land;
- support regeneration and restructuring of the older urban areas;
- support Warrington's role as a regional transport gateway/interchange;
- support and diversify the rural economy and improve access to services in the rural areas focusing development in locations which accord with RDF2.

---

**10.20** Warrington is dealt with as part of the Manchester City Region sub regional policies to ensure that clear and consistent policy is set out for the area. MCR5 sets out the policy for the whole of the Borough of Warrington including the rural areas of the Borough. Warrington has strong connections to both Liverpool and Manchester City Regions, the town is located midway between the two cities and is well positioned for North/South transport links (see City Region Diagram). It has evolved into a competitive location for service sector and advanced manufacturing activity and provides employment opportunities for a wide area of the North West, including parts of Halton, Knowsley, St Helens and Wigan.

---

136    Paragraph 2.41, Central Lancashire City Region Development Programme (June 2005) (see http://www.thenorthernway.co.uk/cityregions.html )

# 11 Liverpool City Region

## Background

**11.1**   The Liverpool City Region has close economic, social, cultural and transport links with Warrington [137], Manchester City Region, Central Lancashire City Region and parts of North Wales. However for the purposes of articulating RSS policy the Liverpool City subregion is defined as the City of Liverpool and local authority districts of Halton, Knowsley, Sefton, St Helens, Wirral, and extends as far as Chester, Ellesmere Port and Neston, Vale Royal and West Lancashire.

**11.2**   The local authorities of Halton, Knowsley, Liverpool, Sefton, St Helens and Wirral contributes some 17% of the North West's total GVA [138]. The City Region will play a complementary but significant role to the Manchester City Region in terms of boosting overall economic performance both at a regional and city region level.

**11.3**   The Liverpool City Region vision is to:

'*...regain our status as a premier European city region by 2025. We will secure an internationally competitive economy and cultural offer; and outstanding quality of life; and vibrant communities contributing to and sharing in sustainable wealth creation.*'

**11.4**   Liverpool City Region is already established as an important driving force in the North of England's economy and as a strategic sea and air gateway to the European Union. The potential exists to expand the City Region's strategic economic and cultural assets, the strength of its knowledge industries and its transport connections. RSS aims to see it deliver its full potential by ensuring that policies:

* maximise the City Region's economic potential and promotes urban renaissance, social inclusion and environmental sustainability;
* stabilise population;
* recognise and promote the role of Liverpool as the core city and major economic driver for its City Region, whilst also recognising and utilising the assets and potential of other locations throughout the City Region, including those in rural areas;
* connect areas of economic opportunity to areas of greatest need, with a particular focus on those areas in need of economic, social and physical restructuring and regeneration.

---

137   Policy on Warrington is included in Manchester City Region in MCR5.
138   The wider city region area including Warrington contributes an estimated 40 per cent of the Region's GVA  (Source: The Liverpool City Region – Transforming Our Economy (June 2005).

## 11 Liverpool City Region

### Policy LCR 1

**Liverpool City Region Priorities**

Plans and strategies in the Liverpool City Region should:

- support interventions necessary to achieve a significant improvement in the sub-region's economic performance by encouraging investment and sustainable development in the Regional Centre, surrounding inner areas, the towns/cities as set out in RDF1 and other key locations, including accessible suburban centres which accord with the spatial principles policies (DP1-9) and the criteria in policies W2 and W3 in order to contribute to the growth opportunities identified in policy W1;

- focus sustained and co-ordinated programmes to maximise economic potential and promote urban renaissance and social inclusion within the Regional Centre and its surrounding Inner Area (the New Heartlands Housing Market Renewal Area);

- focus a sufficient proportion of new housing development and renewal (and related social and environmental infrastructure) within the inner areas to meet the objectives of the Housing Market Renewal Initiative and, consistent with this, make provision for an increase in the supply of affordable and market housing required to address demographic needs and to support economic growth and regeneration;

- enhance the accessibility by public transport of the New Heartlands Housing Market Renewal Pathfinder Area and improve transport links between this (and other disadvantaged areas) and key employment, education and healthcare locations. Particular attention should be given to assisting with programmes to address worklessness;

- in the outer part in the Liverpool City Region, promote economic development, address worklessness, urban renaissance and social inclusion, complementary to the programmes within the Liverpool Regional Centre and the Inner Areas;

- maximise the employment potential of the Strategic Investment Areas (SIAs) and Economic Development Zones (EDZs). Detailed boundary definitions will be set out in Local Development Frameworks;

- promote the sustainable growth, local regeneration initiatives and development opportunities in West Cheshire/North East Wales sub-region and in Vale Royal. Maintain the role of the sub area and Chester in particular as an important component of the Liverpool City Region economy and promote joint working between Authorities and Agencies for its strategic planning and management;

- improve the City Region's internal and external transport links in line with the priorities for transport investment and management set out in Policy RT10;

- support and develop the roles of Liverpool John Lennon Airport and the Merseyside Ports, in line with Policies RT5 and RT6, especially the Port of Liverpool as the only Port of national significance for deep-sea trade in the North of England;

- develop the role of Liverpool as a national and regional public transport gateway and interchange to the Region in line with policy RT3 and enhance the accessibility of the Regional Centre, particularly by public transport walking and cycling to support its role as the main economic focus for the City Region;

- focus environmental improvements where they are most needed and will have the greatest benefit to facilitate the sustainable development of the Regional Centre and Inner Areas. This includes the remediation of contaminated land and provision of high quality green infrastructure as part of comprehensive regeneration schemes. Protect existing environmental assets in line with DP7 and EM1, in particular sites of international importance for nature conservation such as the Mersey Estuary.

Proposals and schemes should be directed primarily towards locations where they can contribute to these priorities.

11 Liverpool City Region

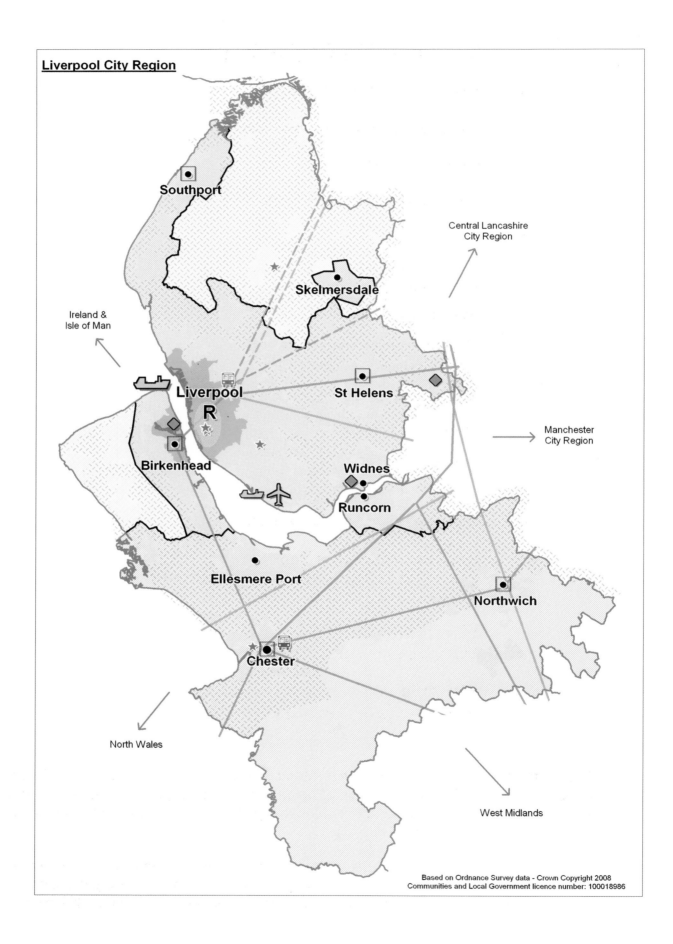

**Liverpool City Region**

Southport

Central Lancashire
City Region

Ireland &
Isle of Man

Skelmersdale

Liverpool
R

St Helens

Manchester
City Region

Birkenhead

Widnes

Runcorn

Ellesmere Port

Northwich

Chester

North Wales

West Midlands

Based on Ordnance Survey data - Crown Copyright 2008
Communities and Local Government licence number: 100018986

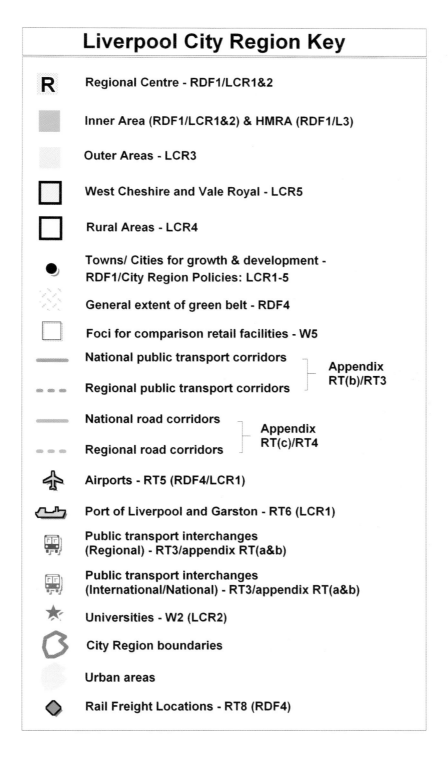

## Liverpool City Region Key

| | |
|---|---|
| **R** | Regional Centre - RDF1/LCR1&2 |
| | Inner Area (RDF1/LCR1&2) & HMRA (RDF1/L3) |
| | Outer Areas - LCR3 |
| | West Cheshire and Vale Royal - LCR5 |
| | Rural Areas - LCR4 |
| ● | Towns/ Cities for growth & development - RDF1/City Region Policies: LCR1-5 |
| | General extent of green belt - RDF4 |
| | Foci for comparison retail facilities - W5 |
| | National public transport corridors ⎤ Appendix RT(b)/RT3 |
| | Regional public transport corridors ⎦ |
| | National road corridors ⎤ Appendix RT(c)/RT4 |
| | Regional road corridors ⎦ |
| ✈ | Airports - RT5 (RDF4/LCR1) |
| 🛳 | Port of Liverpool and Garston - RT6 (LCR1) |
| | Public transport interchanges (Regional) - RT3/appendix RT(a&b) |
| | Public transport interchanges (International/National) - RT3/appendix RT(a&b) |
| ★ | Universities - W2 (LCR2) |
| | City Region boundaries |
| | Urban areas |
| ◆ | Rail Freight Locations - RT8 (RDF4) |

**11.5**    RSS policy for the Liverpool City Region is intended to secure a high level of growth and address regeneration needs. Significant levels of development should be focussed within the Regional Centre and Inner Areas in order to ensure investment and regeneration resources are directed to those areas most in need.

In the outer parts of the City Region there is a clear need for development to be focused on addressing regeneration, worklessness and housing market restructuring. The Regional Centre, Inner Areas and Outer Areas cover most of the Merseyside authorities and include the town of

# 11 Liverpool City Region

Skelmersdale. Development in West Cheshire (Ellesmere Port & Neston, Vale Royal and Chester) will be focused on harnessing opportunities for sustainable growth and local regeneration, complementary to the City Regions spatial development priorities.

11.6    Improving environmental performance is also recognized as a key part of delivering sustainable communities and underpins the Liverpool City Region policies.  Well-managed green space and a high quality local environment play an important part in the quality of life experienced by people within all of the City Regions' neighbourhoods including those which are most deprived. The protection of environmental assets will include the assessment, avoidance and mitigation of the potential effects of development on sites of international importance for nature conservation outside the region, such as coastal and inland waters in Wales.

## Policy LCR 2

### The Regional Centre  and  Inner Areas of Liverpool City Region

The Regional Centre is the primary economic driver of the Liverpool City Region and plans and strategies should support and enhance this role by:

- focusing appropriate commercial, retail, leisure, cultural and tourism development within the Regional Centre developing its role as the primary retail centre, main employment location and primary economic driver of the City Region;
- outside areas of housing market renewal, providing for proposals and schemes for residential development in the Regional Centre where they are part of mixed use employment schemes that comprise a good range of housing sizes, types tenures and affordability and where they contribute to the vitality and viability of the Regional Centre;
- expanding the knowledge economy within the regional centre particularly by maximising the research and development roles of the Universities and delivering knowledge nuclei sites and the expansion of professional services.

They should focus residential development in the Inner Areas adjacent to the Regional Centre in order to secure a significant increase in population and to support major regeneration activity.  This will entail:

- maintaining and enhancing the roles of Birkenhead and Bootle to provide community facilities, services and employment;
- the development of the New Heartlands Housing Market Renewal Pathfinder to revitalise housing in Liverpool, Sefton, and Wirral through comprehensive area based regeneration schemes;
- supporting the development of the Mersey Ports and the maritime economy;
- sustaining investment in the Mersey Waterfront Regional Park; and
- providing for employment within the inner areas in accordance with W2 and W3 and LCR1.

The emphasis will be on providing a good range of quality housing in the inner areas in terms of size, type, tenure and affordability with a high quality environment and accessible local facilities and employment opportunities.

11.7    The Regional Centre of Liverpool City Region comprises the whole of the area within the City Centre Strategic Investment Area and the Liverpool Vision Urban Regeneration Company Area, including the University Edge Knowledge Nuclei site. The Regional Centre includes the primary retail area but is more extensive than it. There are areas of Housing Market Renewal and established residential areas within the Regional Centre. In these areas the emphasis should be particularly on improvement of the quality and mix of housing including affordable housing, in order to assist with regeneration and restructuring of housing markets. The Inner Areas comprise the New Heartlands Housing market Renewal area. The detailed boundaries of the Regional Centre in particular will need to be addressed as part of Local Development Frameworks.

11.8    Liverpool's Regional Centre is fundamental to the economic growth of the Liverpool City Region. It is the major centre for the metropolitan area and forms the strategic hub in terms of its transport infrastructure; its educational establishments; its cultural, retail, business, leisure and tourism assets; and its financial and professional services. Liverpool's status as European Capital of Culture 2008 has brought significant boosts to tourism as well as providing a lasting legacy in terms of investor confidence and sustained economic growth. The fortunes of the surrounding inner area are crucial to the delivery of sustainable economic and social benefits in the City Region.  This area is one of significant challenges and opportunities for both housing and economic development, particularly in relation to the Mersey Ports and the New Heartlands Housing Market Renewal Pathfinder scheme.  It is also home to part of the Mersey Waterfront Regional Park, which provides valuable green infrastructure at the heart of the City Region.

## Policy LCR 3

### Outer part of the Liverpool City Region

In the outer part of the City Region Plans and strategies should:

- focus economic development in the town/cities as set out in RDF1 and at other locations which accord with the spatial principles (policies DP1-9), Policies W2 and W3 and LCR1. Particular attention should be given to addressing worklessness;
- support significant intervention in areas where housing market restructuring is required in line with the approach set out in Policies L3 and L4;
- expand the quality and choice of housing in line with the approach set out in Policy L4;
- maintain and enhance the roles of the regional towns, key service centres and local centres in accordance with Policy RDF2;
- identify, define and maintain the role of suburban centres in accordance with RDF1 and spatial principles DP1-9.

11.9    The outer part of Liverpool comprises those parts of Liverpool and Sefton which are outside the Regional Centre and Inner Areas, the eastern area of Wirral (to the east of the M53), the districts of Knowsley, St Helens, Halton and the town of Skelmersdale in West Lancashire. Ellesmere Port for the purposes of articulating policy is included in West Cheshire. However, it is clear that Ellesmere Port shares many of the characteristics and has strong links with the Outer area of the Liverpool City Region.

## 11 Liverpool City Region

**11.10**   It is important that the roles of suburban/urban centres, key service centres and local centres within the outer part of the City Region are recognised in relation to their regeneration needs and opportunities in terms of retail, access to local amenities, jobs and services. These centres should be supported to continue their regeneration and improvement providing a complementary function to Liverpool City Centre and the Inner Areas, reflecting their individual character and location and meeting local needs.

**11.11**   The River Mersey provides an opportunity to develop a strategic spatial approach that maximises the river frontage's commercial potential and the wider economic opportunities provided by the City Region's coastline.  The packaging together of many of the City Region's key sites and assets, to provide a critical mass of linked developments supported, where necessary, by cluster/sector development and linked with the Mersey Waterfront Regional Park, has strong marketing potential and the potential to encourage significant economic expansion and inward investment.

**11.12**   There are other locations across the City Region, particularly in the outer parts, which experience problems similar to that found in the New Heartlands Pathfinder area, such as vacancies, poor environment, poor housing stock condition and a lack of quality community facilities, although not to the same level of severity. These areas are identified in individual districts' housing strategies as being in need of regeneration. Various methods are being implemented to address these issues of low demand for example, demolitions and rebuild and stock transfer. In terms of new house building, these areas should also be a priority location, together with the provision of associated community facilities in order to secure renaissance. There are also issues of worklessness and the need to reduce health and skills inequalities these issues are illustrated in the inequalities maps 2.2-2.6.

---

### Policy LCR 4

**The remaining rural parts of Liverpool City Region**

In the remaining rural parts of the Liverpool City Region plans and strategies should:

- support and diversify the rural economy and improve access to services in the rural areas focusing development in locations which accord with RDF2;
- be consistent with other regeneration programmes and policies;
- ensure the provision of housing to address barriers to affordability and to meet identified local needs.

---

**11.13**   The remaining rural areas of the Liverpool City Region are West Wirral (that part of the Borough to the west of the M53) and within West Lancashire District (excluding Skelmersdale which is in the outer part of Liverpool City Region). The characteristics of these areas are somewhat different to the outer areas as they are predominantly rural and have issues of affordability rather than market restructuring.

## Policy LCR 5

### West Cheshire – North East Wales

Plans and strategies within West Cheshire – North East Wales sub-region covered by RSS for the NW of England should:

- focus development in the town/cities as set out in RDF1 and at other locations which accord with LCR1, the spatial principles (policies DP1-9), policies W2 and W3;
- harness the potential of Chester for sustainable growth, and as a key sub-regional centre for employment, shopping, leisure, culture and tourism, ensure development is compatible with the conservation and enhancement of the historic City and its setting and the need to improve quality of life and promote regeneration in West Chester;
- support the sustainable economic growth and regeneration opportunities of Ellesmere Port through sustained and co-ordinated programmes for development and investment, with emphasis on developing Ellesmere Ports reputation for 'high tech' manufacturing, through the diversification of the economy and the improvement of the image, quality of life and perception of Ellesmere Port;
- support sustainable economic growth, investment and regeneration opportunities in Northwich and focus on meeting local needs;
- improve the internal and external transport links, in particular with North East Wales, in line with the priorities for transport investment set out in Policy RT10;
- develop the role of Chester as a regional public transport gateway in line with Policy RT3;
- enhance links between areas of opportunity and areas of need, including those regeneration areas served by the following transport corridors:
  - Wrexham - Bidston - Liverpool rail corridor;
  - Wrexham - Chester;
  - Route leading to the Flintshire Coastal Corridor; and
  - Other corridors radiating out from Chester, in particular links to Ellesmere Port and Broughton.  The enhancement of road links does not imply the provision of additional capacity;
- ensure the strategic planning and management of the sub-region's economy, housing market, transport network and environmental and cultural assets through joint working with Authorities and Agencies across the sub-region;
- ensure the provision of housing to meet local needs and address barriers to affordability;
- further develop the skills base of the labour force and promote access to employment; and
- support and diversify the rural economy in line with policy RDF2 and improve access to services in the rural areas.

11.14    West Cheshire/North East Wales comprises the boroughs of Ellesmere Port and Neston and Chester and Vale Royal and is part of a sub region which extends into Wales (Flintshire and Wrexham).The sub region has links to wider reference areas which comprises Denbighshire, The Wirral, Warrington and Halton. Ellesmere Port has close links with the outer areas of the

## 11 Liverpool City Region

Liverpool City Region and shares many of the issues and characteristics of these areas. It is likely it will work closely with Outer Liverpool City Region local authorities and develop similar approaches to addressing the common challenges it faces.

11.15    Chester is a driving force in the sub-regional economy, with a strong national - and in some cases international role in the service employment sector, which includes financial services, and the status of an important retail, leisure and cultural destination.  There is a need for significant image and environmental enhancement along the M53 corridor and to find positive uses for derelict and underused land in Ellesmere Port.  The opportunity exists to promote the town as a world class centre of excellence for high tech manufacturing and to introduce new initiatives to support this role.

11.16    Policy LCR5 only applies to Authorities and Agencies operating in the English areas of the sub-region but joint working across boundaries for the strategic planning and management of the whole sub-region are encouraged.

11.17    The policy framework developed for Chester and Ellesmere Port has been informed by the development of a non-statutory sub-regional spatial strategy covering West Cheshire and North East Wales. [139]

11.18    Vale Royal has clear functional links to Manchester City Region and to South Cheshire, however for the purposes of the articulation of RSS policy it has been placed in the Liverpool City Region.  In common with Warrington, Vale Royal has connections and linkages with both city regions (see City Region diagram) and is influenced by both. Accordingly whilst the articulation of policy is set within the context of Liverpool City Region the development of policy in the Borough must be set with the context of the regional spatial priorities in RDF1.

---

139    West Cheshire - North East Wales Sub Regional Spatial Strategy and SEA Final report 2004.

# 12 Central Lancashire City Region

## Background

**12.1**    The main foci of the Central Lancashire City Region are the city of Preston and the towns of Blackburn, Blackpool and Burnley. Its influence, as broadly defined in The Northern Way, extends out to the local authority areas that stretch from the Irish Sea to the Pennines but for the purposes of articulating RSS policy, the sub region is defined as the County of Lancashire minus West Lancashire and Lancaster. In other words the Local Authorities of Blackpool, Wyre, Fylde, Preston, South Ribble, Chorley, Blackburn with Darwen, Hyndburn, Ribble Valley, Burnley, Rossendale and Pendle. The City Region has economic and transport links with the city regions of Manchester and Liverpool, the Leeds City Region (Yorkshire and Humber Region), North Lancashire and Cumbria.

**12.2**    It contributes around 20% of the North West's total GVA [140] and will play an important complementary role to the Manchester and Liverpool City Regions in terms of enhancing overall economic performance.

**12.3**    The vision for the Central Lancashire City Region sets out to achieve:

*'A globally competitive City Region offering a distinctive and diverse environment for prosperity.'*

**12.4**    RSS aims to support the vision to develop Central Lancashire as an area where:

- economic growth is focused on the City of Preston and the towns of Blackpool, Blackburn and Burnley, supported by high quality investment sites in sustainable locations that meet the requirements of business and industry;
- urban regeneration and growth is matched by increased prosperity in the smaller towns, villages and rural communities;
- economic growth is matched by continual improvement to quality of life and well being;
- the mix of townscapes and landscapes will continue to flourish, enhanced by high quality, energy-efficient development and quality leisure and cultural facilities;
- a range of high quality housing is available to meet the needs of the population and to support regeneration and economic growth;
- strong, vibrant town and city centres promote social inclusion and sustainable growth and compete with the best in the country.

This vision will be supported by the development of a high quality, integrated public transport network.

---

140    Central Lancashire City Region Development Programme (June 2005) (see http://www.thenorthernway.co.uk/cityregions.html)

## 12 Central Lancashire City Region

### Policy CLCR 1

**Central Lancashire City Region Priorities**

Plans and strategies for the Central Lancashire City Region should:

- focus investment and sustainable development in the City of Preston and 3 towns of Blackburn, Burnley and Blackpool, raising economic performance, particularly through:
    - tourism and housing-led regeneration in Blackpool;
    - knowledge-based development (including advanced manufacturing and aerospace) in Preston and Blackburn;
    - regeneration and restructuring of the East Lancashire economy (including actions taken under the Elevate Transformational Agenda);
    - enhanced educational opportunities which will improve the skill-base of the resident population;
    - developing new employment opportunities in accordance with policies W1 to W3 and addressing localised problems of worklessness;
- provide for a range of good quality housing, accessible to local facilities;
- improve the City Region's internal and external transport links, in line with the transport investment and management priorities set out in policy RT10;
- develop the role of Blackpool Airport, in line with policy RT5;
- develop the role of Preston as a regional transport gateway in line with policy RT3;
- improve the accessibility of employment locations by sustainable transport modes, with priority given to the Elevate Housing Renewal Pathfinder area;
- support and diversify the rural economy and improve access to services in the rural areas focusing development in locations which accord with RDF2.

Proposals and schemes will be directed primarily towards locations where they can contribute to these priorities.

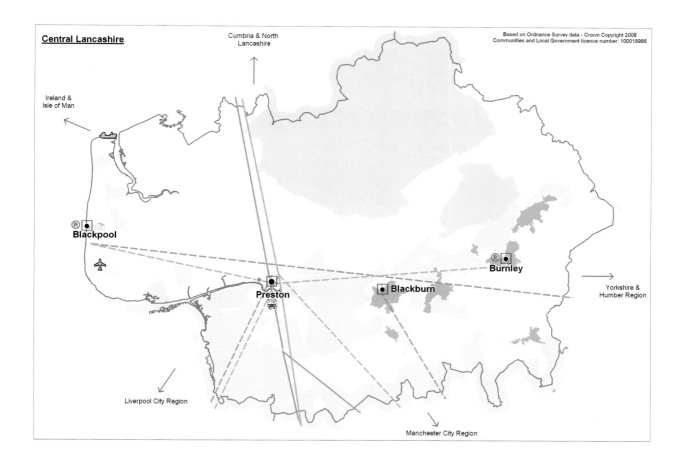

**Central Lancashire**

Cumbria & North Lancashire

Ireland & Isle of Man

Based on Ordnance Survey data - Crown Copyright 2008
Communities and Local Government licence number: 100018986

Blackpool

Burnley

Preston

Blackburn

Yorkshire & Humber Region

Liverpool City Region

Manchester City Region

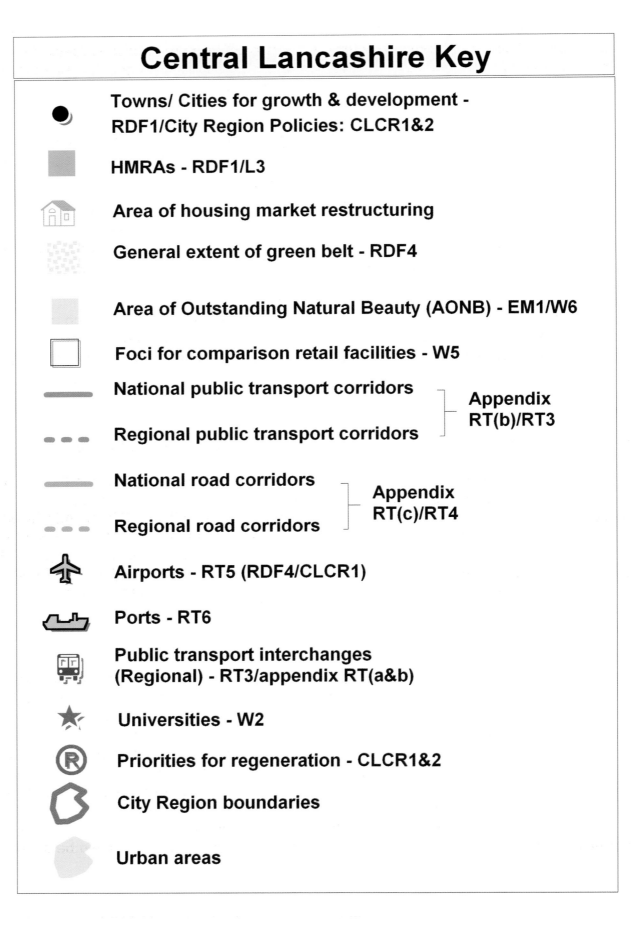

# Central Lancashire Key

● Towns/ Cities for growth & development - RDF1/City Region Policies: CLCR1&2

▪ HMRAs - RDF1/L3

Area of housing market restructuring

General extent of green belt - RDF4

Area of Outstanding Natural Beauty (AONB) - EM1/W6

□ Foci for comparison retail facilities - W5

—— National public transport corridors
- - - Regional public transport corridors
⎦ Appendix RT(b)/RT3

—— National road corridors
- - - Regional road corridors
⎦ Appendix RT(c)/RT4

✈ Airports - RT5 (RDF4/CLCR1)

⛴ Ports - RT6

Public transport interchanges (Regional) - RT3/appendix RT(a&b)

★ Universities - W2

® Priorities for regeneration - CLCR1&2

City Region boundaries

Urban areas

**12.5**    The strategy for the Central Lancashire City Region is underpinned by the need to balance improved economic growth with the regeneration of its more deprived areas. The RES identifies the need to improve skills achievement and aspirations in parts of East Lancashire and Blackpool.

**12.6**    The Greater Preston "core area" of the City Region, based on the administrative areas of Preston, South Ribble and Chorley, provides a significant economic focus for the sub-region as expressed in the Preston City Vision. Work is ongoing on a joint core strategy, a Local Development Framework document for the three authorities.

**12.7**    Elevate, East Lancashire's Housing Market Renewal Pathfinder programme, intends to transform the area's economy, housing stock and quality of life. The aerospace industries, advanced manufacturing and other knowledge-based sectors are a key source of higher quality jobs in the City Region and an established network of primary and support industries also present opportunities for growth.

**12.8**    Blackpool is a resort of national repute, but as many of its communities do not benefit from the tourist economy, it is also home to large pockets of deprivation. The Blackpool Masterplan [141] aims to redress this situation by strengthening Blackpool's tourism economy.

---

## Policy CLCR 2

### Focus for Development and Investment in Central Lancashire City Region

Development in the Central Lancashire City Region will be located primarily in the city of Preston and the three towns of Blackburn, Blackpool and Burnley, giving priority to sites in and around their centres and at other locations which accord with RDF1, DP1-9 and policies W2 and W3. Development should be pursued in a manner that addresses worklessness, enhances urban quality, and contributes to the enhancement of the natural setting of the city/towns. Outside the City and towns identified above, development in the Central Lancashire City Region will be largely confined to Key Service Centres and Local Service Centres, in line with Policy RDF2.

---

**12.9**    Preston, Blackburn, Blackpool and Burnley all have strong, functional links with smaller towns, including some in neighbouring districts. Focusing new development here reflects their existing key roles within the Central Lancashire City Region and consolidates their ability to serve their hinterlands, promoting enhanced economic growth and a better quality of life. Blackpool is the centre of a wider Fylde coast including Fleetwood, Thornton, Cleveleys and Lytham St Annes. Burnley is the principal town in an area that stretches from Padiham, through Brierfield and Nelson to Colne. Preston is strongly linked to suburbs to the south of the River Ribble consisting of Penwortham, Lostock Hall, Walton-le-Dale, Bamber Bridge, Clayton Brook and Whittle-le-Woods. Blackburn includes Whitebirk and Wilpshire. The policy boundaries of the towns and the definition of surrounding key and local service centres should be set out in Local Development Frameworks.

---

141    "Blackpool Master Plan – Executive Summary", Blackpool Borough Council 2003.
        "Blackpool Master Plan – Update Brochure", Blackpool Borough Council 2005.

# 12 Central Lancashire City Region

Policy CLCR2 builds on the identified strengths and opportunities of each centre, which are as follows:

## BLACKPOOL

- major tourist centre with potential for casino and conference development;
- need for economic growth to underpin urban restructuring;
- focal point for coastal housing market renewal;
- specialist medical services centred on Blackpool Victoria Hospital;
- centre for retailing, services, public administration and further education;
- public transport hub for the Fylde Peninsula;
- airport with potential for increased use.

## PRESTON

- focal point at the intersection of north-south and east-west transport corridors;
- centre for culture, leisure and quality city living;
- established advanced engineering and aerospace industries;
- centre of public administration, justice and financial services;
- University of Central Lancashire, with links to knowledge-based business;
- specialist medical services centred on Royal Preston Hospital;
- regional public transport gateway and interchange;
- retail and service centre.

## BLACKBURN

- focal point for economic growth and restructuring in East Lancashire;
- established advanced engineering and aerospace industries;
- focal point for Elevate Housing Market Renewal Initiative;
- specialist medical services centred on Royal Blackburn Hospital;
- centre of higher and further education, public administration, justice and legal services;
- transport hub;
- retail and service centre.

## BURNLEY

- focal point for economic restructuring;
- high value manufacturing;
- local point for Elevate Housing Market Renewal Initiative;
- heritage-based regeneration along canal corridor and in Weaver's Triangle;
- specialist medical services centred on Burnley General Hospital;
- further education centre;
- public transport hub;
- retail and service centre for Pennine Lancashire;
- centre of public administration.

12.10    Outside the four main settlements, the City Region contains a variety of smaller industrial towns, market towns and rural settlements that operate as key service centres and local service centres.   Fundamental to the concept of the zones of influence is the recognition of the inter-relationships between urban and rural areas.  The smaller settlements and rural areas will make an important contribution to the City Region, not only as a recreational resource, but also in terms of the regeneration of towns, villages and the wider rural economy. The policy framework for key service centres is contained in Policy RDF2.

## Policy CLCR 3

### Green City

The unique 'green' character of the Central Lancashire City Region, and the advantages it offers for recreation and for attracting people and investment, will be protected and further enhanced by:

a.  maintaining the general extent of the Green Belt in accordance with Policy RDF4;
b.  protecting the Forest of Bowland AONB, in accordance with Policy EM1;
c.  the further development of the City Region's three Regional Parks (East Lancashire, Ribble Estuary and Morecambe Bay) in accordance with Policy EM4, through:

- improving access to open space networks, enhancing the urban fringe, reclaiming derelict land, enhancing recreational and educational facilities, and providing public art;
- promoting the conservation, protection and enhancement of the physical and natural environment, and supporting biodiversity; and
- the inclusion of appropriate policies and projects, and the delineation of Regional Park boundaries in Local Development Frameworks in line with strategic frameworks as set out in EM4;

d.  the greening of urban areas, through measures including the renovation of existing parks; the reclamation of derelict land for 'soft' end uses; the utilisation of open space adjacent to waterways, such as the Leeds-Liverpool Canal; and the creation of green wedges extending into the countryside.

**12.11**    One of the strengths of Central Lancashire's polycentric growth is the potential to maximise the benefits offered by the close proximity of high quality countryside and environmental assets to a large proportion of the population – the 'Green City' concept. The Green Belt, the Forest of Bowland AONB and the Regional Parks will form important elements in the City Region's green infrastructure together with improved green spaces in urban areas. Such areas could offer significant opportunities for cycling and walking (RT9) and could assist in addressing health inequalities.

13 Cumbria and North Lancashire

# 13 Cumbria and North Lancashire

## Background

13.1     For the purposes of articulation of RSS policy this sub region comprises the administrative county of Cumbria – which includes the six district councils of Allerdale, Barrow, Carlisle, Copeland, Eden and South Lakeland – the Lake District National Park Authority and Lancaster City Council.  Parts of Lancaster and southern Cumbria have economic and transport links with the Central Lancashire City Region; Cumbria has similar links with Scotland and the North East Region, and to a lesser extent with the Yorkshire and Humber Region.

13.2     The challenge for Cumbria is to secure a sustainable level and pattern of development that creates balanced communities and meets needs – including that of new jobs across the county. Three spatial objectives have been identified to deliver more balanced communities and reduce inequality:

- to reduce the dependency for high level services and jobs on towns outside Cumbria;
- to increase the complementary nature of key towns;
- to develop and maintain high quality modern transport networks.

13.3     Within the Lake District National Park the relationship of the National Park with the wider area beyond its administrative boundaries needs to be addressed, whilst also developing a suitable framework that meets the locally generated needs that occur within the National Park.

13.4     North Lancashire corresponds to the local authority area administered by Lancaster City Council.  Lying between the Central Lancashire City Region and Cumbria, it has excellent communications links provided by the West Coast Mainline railway and M6 motorway.   There are close cultural links, and shared responsibility for protecting important environmental assets, with neighbouring authorities around Morecambe Bay.

## Policy CNL 1

### Overall Spatial Policy for Cumbria

Plans and strategies in Cumbria should:

- focus major developments within Barrow in Furness and Whitehaven, and Workington, and in the City of Carlisle in line with policy RDF1 and spatial principles DP1-9;
- provide for development in the key service centres and local service centres in line with RDF2;
- provide a portfolio of employment sites in accordance with RDF1 and the criteria in policies W2 and W3;
- support the restructuring of housing markets in West Cumbria and Furness;
- improve Cumbria's internal and external transport links in line with the priorities for transport investment and management set out in policy RT10;
- develop the role of Carlisle as a regional public transport gateway to the region in line with policy RT1 and harness its potential for economic growth in sustainable ways;
- ensure that network management measures are utilised to make best and most appropriate use of available highway infrastructure and to improve road safety and journey time reliability, with priority given to improving the operation of routes linking Furness and West Cumbria to the M6;
- give priority to improving access to employment, services and education/training facilities on foot and by cycle, and by public transport, in Carlisle, Workington/ Whitehaven and Barrow-in Furness, and in Key Service Centres, especially Kendal;
- support the development of sustainable tourism in Cumbria; and
- support the development of higher value knowledge based and specialist industry based employment opportunities.

Proposals and schemes will be directed primarily towards locations where they can contribute to these priorities.

13.5    As a result of its geographic, and therefore economic isolation, Cumbria is generally self contained in comparison to other parts of the North West.  This fact, together with the highly dispersed and sparsely populated nature of its settlements presents a particular challenge in securing a sustainable level of development.   Most of the development in Cumbria will be focused within Carlisle, Barrow and Workington and Whitehaven.  Elsewhere, there will be levels of moderate or small-scale development suited to the size and location of key and local service centres.  It will be particularly important to achieve a level of economic growth that sustains local needs and reduces the number of economically active people leaving the area, and to match this with appropriate housing development.   Housing must of the right type and in the right location to meet the requirements of local communities and employers and be directed to locations where it will sustain local services.

# 13 Cumbria and North Lancashire

## Policy CNL 2

### Sub-area Development Priorities for Cumbria

Within the sub-areas of Cumbria, plans and strategies should accord with CNL1 and focus on:

- supporting sustainable growth in Carlisle. Building on Carlisle city's significant potential to attract sustainable development into Cumbria. The city will enhance its role as the sub-regional centre for business, shopping, leisure, culture and tourism, serving Cumbria and the adjoining parts of Scotland and North East England. It will also develop its higher education function through the establishment of the new University of Cumbria, which should help attract investment in the knowledge – based economy. Ensure development is compatible with the conservation and enhancement of the historic city centre;

- enhancing the Regeneration Priority Area of West Cumbria, particularly through developing the roles of the existing centres of Whitehaven, Workington, and also in Cleator Moor and Maryport in a complementary manner. Efforts should be made to exploit the potential offered by a local workforce with expertise in the field of nuclear research, development and decommissioning; and the presence of the National Nuclear Laboratory. The location of part of the University of Cumbria in this area could increase its potential for the development of a knowledge-based economy. The potential of the area for tourism-based development should also be explored;

- concentrating development within the Furness Regeneration Priority Area in Barrow in Furness, to facilitate diversification of the local economy, and enable opportunities for development and regeneration to be brought forward in the wider Furness Peninsula. Efforts should be made to exploit specialist marine engineering skills and opportunities, and to develop the area's potential for tourism;

- ensuring that the needs of local people in South & East Cumbria are met with a focus on securing inward investment and improving service provision within Kendal and Penrith. High priority should be placed on the further provision of affordable housing within the sub-area.

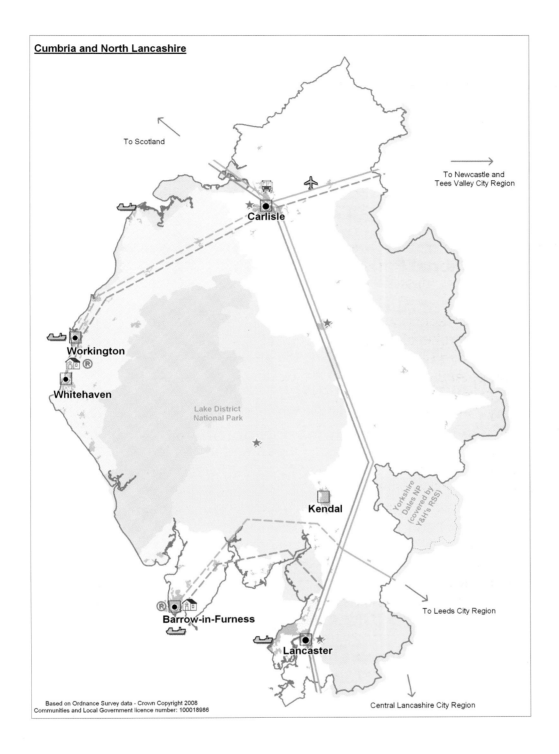

Cumbria and North Lancashire

To Scotland

To Newcastle and
Tees Valley City Region

Carlisle

Workington

Whitehaven

Lake District
National Park

Kendal

Yorkshire
Dales NP
(covered by
Y&H's RSS)

To Leeds City Region

Barrow-in-Furness

Lancaster

Central Lancashire City Region

Based on Ordnance Survey data - Crown Copyright 2008
Communities and Local Government licence number: 100018986

## 13 Cumbria and North Lancashire

# Cumbria and North Lancashire Key

West Cumbria

Towns/ Cities for growth & development -
RDF1/City Region Policies: CNL1-2

Housing Market Renewal Areas - CNL1

National Parks - EM1/CNL3/W6

Area of Outstanding Natural Beauty (AONB) - EM1/W6

Foci for comparison retail facilities - W5

National public transport corridors ⎤
                                     ⎥ Appendix
                                     ⎥ RT(b)/RT3
Regional public transport corridors ⎦

National road corridors ⎤
                        ⎥ Appendix
                        ⎥ RT(c)/RT4
Regional road corridors ⎦

Airports - RT5

Ports - RT6 (CNL4)

Public transport interchanges
(Regional) - RT3/appendix RT(a&b)

Universities - W2 (CNL2/CNL4)

Regeneration Priority Areas in West Cumbria
and Furness RDF1 CNL1&2

City Region boundaries

Urban areas

**13.6** In Carlisle, work has been commissioned under the banner of Carlisle Renaissance, to ensure the future growth and prosperity of the city. A range of employment opportunities will need to be made available in accord with employment land market sectors. Housing will need to be allocated to sustain and enhance the city's economic growth. The potential for higher education facilities linked to the economic and business expansion of Carlisle will need to be encouraged.

**13.7** Opportunities need to be taken through the development of the West Cumbria Strategic Forum's sub-regional masterplan to sustain and enhance employment, secure investment and diversify the economic base, particularly in the light of the changes being made to the nuclear industry within the area [142]. This will require investment in increased employment opportunities and the related transport infrastructure. The opportunities offered by the area's maritime and naval heritage will be developed with a view to securing a coastal renaissance. Balanced housing markets will be created through refurbishment, clearance and renewal and by enabling new houses to be built within the wider urban area. The role of Workington and Whitehaven town centres in particular will need to be supported by environmental improvements and by physical restructuring to meet the demands of modern town centre uses. The development of further education facilities will also need to be promoted focusing on nuclear issues, restoration, radiology, medical applications and engineering.

**13.8** Barrow in Furness will continue to play a significant role in providing services to the town and its catchment area. Work undertaken in the town, including the Barrow Port Masterplan, has identified the need for major investment to ensure that Barrow has a high quality environment and that the necessary infrastructure and transport networks are to modern standards. Balanced housing markets will be created through refurbishment, clearance and renewal and by building new homes that create choice and quality in the market to meet housing demand and help generate investor confidence. The role of the town centre will be supported through measures that enable refurbishment and environmental improvement and by physical restructuring.

**13.9** A high priority in South and East Cumbria will be given to meeting local affordable housing needs, in perpetuity. A range of options to meet affordable housing needs are set out in policy L5. Opportunities will be taken to secure inward investment, new businesses and services to the key service centres of Kendal and Penrith.

---

142  See Nuclear Decommissioning Authority draft strategy and website - www.nda.gov.uk

## 13 Cumbria and North Lancashire

---

### Policy CNL 3

**Spatial Policy for the Lake District**

Plans and strategies should give priority to the protection of the landscape and cultural heritage of the Lake District National Park.

In addition they should:

- promote further diversification and development of its economic base;
- redress housing imbalances through the provision of affordable and local needs housing in accordance with Policies L4 and L5;
- develop programmes for improvements to the public realm and effective traffic management in Windermere, Ambleside and Keswick, to enhance the urban fabric and support their recreational and tourism roles;
- manage recreational and sustainable tourist activities, in suitable locations;
- ensure that public transport services are improved and better integrated, and that the proportion of travel to and within the National Park by sustainable modes is increased; and
- address the relationship of the National Park with its wider area, and develop a suitable framework for meeting locally generated needs.

---

13.10    The Lake District National Park is a major regional resource and an international tourist attraction.   The relationship between the National Park and adjoining parts of Cumbria should be capitalised upon so that complementary development outside National Park boundaries can benefit communities within it, and also towns like Cockermouth, Kendal, Penrith and Ulverston. Development within the National Park itself should be focused on centres that provide key services, and allow locally generated needs to be met.

---

### Policy CNL 4

**Spatial Policy for North Lancashire**

Plans and strategies will:

- secure the regeneration of Morecambe through the development of tourism and the restructuring of the housing market;
- support sustainable growth in Lancaster in line with RDF1, the spatial principles DP1-9, W2 and W3 and CNL1, ensuring development is compatible with the conservation of the historic city;
- build on the strengths and opportunities offered by Lancaster University and the University of Cumbria;
- ensure an increase in the supply of affordable housing;
- support the role of the Port of Heysham in line with Policy RT6; and
- develop proposals for the safe and effective management of traffic in Lancaster and Morecambe to enhance the public realm and support their leisure and tourism roles.

---

**13.11** The overall aim in North Lancashire is to address the challenge of creating a model sustainable urban area, which serves and supports the needs of an extensive rural hinterland. There are significant challenges in creating highly skilled employment, regenerating areas such as Morecambe and providing affordable housing in rural areas. There is potential to marry opportunity and need in line with policy DP6 by exploring linkages with Lancaster and harnessing growth opportunities there in sustainable ways.

# 14 Implementation, Monitoring and Review

## Policy IM 1

### Implementation

In addition to the statutory requirement for Environmental Impact Analysis, economic, health, transport and other impact assessments should be carried out in appropriate cases.

The Regional Planning Body along with other partners will ensure the RSS Implementation Framework is reviewed and developed.

### Plan-Monitor-Manage

Plans and policies should be sufficiently flexible to respond to robust monitoring information which will reveal whether :

- they are having the desired impact/outcome;
- they are being implemented as intended;
- circumstances have changed and there should be appropriate mechanisms to trigger a review of policy, if necessary.

The Regional Planning Body will work with local authorities and other partners to secure, as far as possible, a common evidence base, targets and indicators, avoid duplication and improve the efficiency of monitoring activity.

They will keep the RSS monitoring framework under constant review and annually prepare a Monitoring Manual and Monitoring report.

14.1    Clear assessment of the relative benefits or likely ill-effects of development proposals are essential to planning decisions and there is growing acceptance that any tensions between development and existing environmental, social or economic 'capital' (such as road space) should be clearly stated alongside proposals for measures necessary to minimise harm, replace lost capital or provide alternative benefits. Sustainability appraisals of development plans should cover social, environmental and economic objectives. An Integrated Appraisal Toolkit (IAT) has been developed alongside Action for Sustainability and this will provide an excellent basis for such appraisals, having been used in this capacity for draft RSS and the current draft RES. Transport and environmental impact assessments are established as part of planning processes and impact assessments related to health and broader social issues are being developed both nationally and within the Region, referenced in the IAT. With regards to accessibility, planning authorities need to ensure that new developments – especially those which are anticipated to generate significant numbers of visitors – are in locations which are accessible by public transport and that measures to make walking and cycling are included from the design stage of the proposal. Furthermore, local authorities should use planning obligations such as Section 106 Agreements to ensure that these measures are delivered.

**14.2** RSS has a clear set of overarching spatial and development principles and each thematic chapter now has a set of key objectives. The RSS Implementation framework sets out a series of targets and indicators which link to the objectives and vision of RSS with their delivery and implementation being monitored through the Annual Monitoring Report. The implementation framework also indicates priorities, mechanisms, partnerships and lead agencies for delivery of RSS. The Implementation Framework is a separate document which accompanies RSS, this means it can be continually modified to reflect the emergence of new partnerships, priorities and funding sources.

**14.3** Traditionally the greatest responsibility for delivery of RSS has fallen upon Local Authorities through the preparation and delivery of Local Development Plans and Communities Strategies and now also through the delivery of Local and Multi Area Agreements. Whilst this will continue to be the case, Local Authorities and the Regional Planning Body will need to work closely with a wide range of other organisations to ensure the more spatial nature of RSS is reflected in, and delivered by, the plans and strategies of a wide range of organisations. The Implementation Plan will be useful in clearly identifying the organisations which will have the potential to deliver RSS, in addition to Local Authorities. The Regional Planning Body will need to work with potential delivery partners to raise awareness of RSS and the relevance of its objectives to their own organisations aims and objectives. In this way partnership organisations will have a clearer shared interest in delivering RSS, in order to meet their own targets and objectives. Many organisations need early involvement in RSS policy preparation in order that funding to deliver RSS objectives can be identified in their own longer term plans and strategies. Consultation has taken place with a wide range of organisations throughout the preparation of RSS, but the contacts made should be maintained and strengthened through the regular updating of the Implementation Framework and the establishment of delivery groups. It is important that awareness raising and annual feedback of key implementation themes and monitoring information continue to improve to encourage wider participation in the delivery of RSS.

**14.4** Other partners currently involved with the delivery of RSS objectives include the private sector including the utility companies; organisations such as housebuilders, transport operators, investors and landowners; public agencies like Natural England, Highways Agency, Forestry Commission, Housing Corporation, English Heritage and Environment Agency; and voluntary and community bodies and local and community groups. RSS is now a spatial rather than a land use plan and accordingly there is a clear need to forge better links in the future with new partners such as in the health, education, training and police and fire sectors.

**14.5** Along with the Local Authorities and the Regional Planning Body, the North West Development Agency (NWDA) is also a significant agent of change in the region. The need for the Regional Economic and Spatial Strategies to be complementary and aligned has been a clear priority of RSS. The July 2007 publication, the Review of Sub-National Economic Development and Regeneration - which has become known as the sub-national review - set out a number of structural reforms including the introduction of a single regional strategy in each region. This will bring together the Regional Spatial Strategy and the Regional Economic Strategy and will set out the economic, social and environmental objectives for each region.

## 14 Implementation, Monitoring and Review

### Monitoring

**14.6**    PPS11 emphasises the need to regularly monitor the effectiveness of RSS against its main objectives. In July 2008 CLG published a new set of core indicators. Therefore the RPB and LPAs will need to ensure that systems are established to monitor these and ensure that this is taken in account in future reviews. Both of these documents have been taken into account during the preparation of this strategy.

**14.7**    By the end of February each year, the Regional Planning Body will produce an Annual Monitoring Report (AMR) on RSS, the main purposes of which will be to:

- assess the impact over time of RSS against its main objectives;
- consider whether RSS is being carried out correctly, in line with its main objectives;
- offer explanations where policies are not being put into practice;
- outline the measures to be taken where RSS policies are not being put into practice;
- provide information on net and gross additions to the housing stock.

**14.8**    The AMR will comprise:

- contextual indicators relating to areas where RSS has only indirect influence. These provide information on the wider social, economic, environmental, physical and demographic background against which RSS is being implemented;
- a small number of "headline indicators" relating to the central principals of this RSS, which will be analysed on an annual basis to provide an early indication of any emerging trends that may need to be addressed;
- further indicators measured on a yearly or three yearly basis to demonstrate the overall progress made towards specific RSS policies.

**14.9**    An RSS Monitoring Manual has been published as a practical guide to data production for the agencies involved.  Developed in close conjunction with the Implementation Framework, the manual outlines the indicators that need to be monitored and the frequency with which the results should be reported.  It also sets out an annual monitoring timetable and supplies detailed definitions of the data required so as to ensure it is produced in a consistent format by the various organisations.

**14.10**    The development of a regional monitoring framework is an ongoing process.  New opportunities for acquiring and sharing information may arise as a result of work undertaken by partner organisations and new indicators may come to light as part of the monitoring process. The precise indicators to be used in monitoring RPG, together with their definitions, are therefore under constant review and will evolve over time.  Any necessary revisions to the monitoring manual will be made in the late spring of each year. There is also a need to develop the capacity to carry out sub regional monitoring, in order to measure the effectiveness of sub regional policies.

**14.11**    The success of RSS monitoring will depend upon extensive cooperation from, and coordination with a wide range of organisations in the region. The role of local planning authorities in regularly collecting data on housing, land use change and other information will be particularly important. There are clear links between the monitoring of RSS and local planning authorities' own LDF monitoring practices. The Regional Planning Body will work with local authorities to ensure, where possible, the development of a common evidence base so as to avoid duplication and achieve greater efficiency in the monitoring of both.  A regional monitoring group has been established, made up of representatives from local authorities; the three county councils and two former county councils; GONW; NWDA, and with attendees from other regional bodies such as the Environment Agency, Natural England and the ONS regional presence.

## Review

14.12    The need to review RSS can be identified as part of the monitoring process when policies are not being delivered or are having undesirable or unintended consequences, or when there is a need to address specific deficiencies. In particular, the Housing Green Paper indicated the need to undertake partial reviews of RSS to reflect Government targets to address housing affordability and other changes such as Housing Growth Points.

14.13    The scope and timetable of a partial review of RSS was consulted upon in the early 2008. The initial stage of the review is in progress with the following issues identified as the priority:

- Housing – the revision of district housing figures in line with the Housing Green Paper challenges, taking account of environmental capacity, the supply of suitable land, the housing needs in each housing market area and the likely impact of supply on affordability;
- Renewable energy –  the identification of broad areas suitable for renewable energy development; and
- Waste – the identification of the number and type of facilities required and their broad location.

14.14    Consideration is to be given to the best way to take the review of these issues forward, taking account of the current housing market conditions, the National Housing and Planning Unit's advice, proposals for new housing growth points, and the need to manage the transition to the Single Regional Strategy which will replace the RES and RSS in the near future.

14.15    Interim reviews of RSS and future single regional strategies will be informed by additional research. Ongoing research includes sub regional cross border studies for South Cheshire and North Staffordshire, and the Manchester City Region and High Peak, the revision of Parking Standards, provision for gypsies and travellers and assessment of definitions of housing market areas. The immediate priorities for future research will relate to the priorities identified in 14.13 above.

15 Replaced and Saved Structure Plan Policies

# 15 Replaced and Saved Structure Plan Policies

**15.1**   Through the Planning and Compulsory Purchase Act 2004 Structure Plan policies were 'saved' for a period of up to three years on commencement of the Act or for three years from the time or adoption of the Structure Plan, whichever is the later, unless replaced by an RSS or the Secretary of State directs to extend the 3 year period under Schedule 8 to the Act . The three Structure Plans in the North West Region are the Joint Lancashire Structure Plan (Adopted March 2005); the Joint Cumbria and Lake District Structure Plan – Modifications (September 2005); and the Cheshire Structure Plan 2016 – Alteration (December 2005).

**15.2**   The 3 year 'saved' period for the Joint Lancashire Structure Plan concluded before the publication of this plan and accordingly the Secretary of State directed that all Joint Lancashire Structure Plan policies be extended..In relation to Cheshire and Joint Cumbria and Lake District Structure Plan, the 3 year 'saved' period from adoption had not yet concluded.

**15.3**   The tables below set out those extended and saved structure plan policies replaced by the policies in the North West of England Plan. Following each of the tables there is a list of structure plan policies which have been extended because they have not been replaced by The North West of England Plan and ,which will continue to be saved until they are replaced by a future RSS revision. As set out in the Chapter on Implementation, Monitoring and Review, review of this RSS is being progressed. Local Authorities in the region are encouraged to consider whether those structure plan polices not covered by the RSS can be expressed within the appropriate Local Authorities Local Development Framework.

## JOINT CUMBRIA AND LAKE DISTRICT STRUCTURE PLAN – ADOPTED APRIL 2006

| Structure Plan Policy | RSS Proposed Changes Policy |
| --- | --- |
| ST1 | DP1, DP2 |
| ST2 | DP1, DP2 |
| ST3 | DP1 / DP4 / DP5 / DP7 / DP9 |
| ST6 | RDF2 / CNL3 |
| ST7 | RDF2 |
| ST8 | RDF1 / L4 / W1 / W2 / W6 / W5 / CNL1 / CNL2 |
| ST9 | RDF2 / CNL2 |
| ST10 | RDF1 / CNL1 / CNL2 / L3 / L4 / W1 / W2 / W5 / W6 |
| ST11 | RDF2 / L4 / L5 / CNL1 / CNL2 |
| ST12 | EM1 / L4 / L5 / CNL3 |
| EM15 | RDF2 / W3 |
| H17 | L4 |
| H18 | L4 |
| H23 | L3 / CNL1 |
| T24 | RT1 / RT2 / RT9 / CNL1 |
| T25 | RT2 / RT4 / RT10 / CNL1 / CNL3 |
| T26 | RT5 / RT6 / CNL1 |
| T27 | RT1 / RT2 / RT3 |
| T28 | RT7 / RT8 |
| T32 | RT2 |
| E34 | DP7 / EM1 |
| E36 | DP7 / EM1 |
| E39 | EM1 / EM2 / DP1 / DP7 |

| E40 | DP7/EM1 |
|-----|---------|
| C41 | RDF3 / EM6 |
| C42 | EM5 / EM6 |
| C43 | EM5 / EM6 / DP9 |
| R46 | EM7 |
| L52 | W5 / DP1 / DP2 / RDF2 |
| L53 | DP5 / RT1 / RT3 / RT9 |
| L54 | DP1 / RT2 / W3 / W5 |
| L55 | DP1 / RDF2 |
| L56 | DP1 / L1 |
| L57 | DP1 / L1 / EM1 / EM3 |
| L58 | EM4 |

The following policies have been extended but have not been replaced by this RSS:

ST4: Major Development Proposals

ST5: New Development and Key Service Centres outside the Lake District National Park

EM13: EmploymentLand Provision

EM14: Development of Employment Land for other Purposes

EM 16: Tourism

H19: Affordable Housing outside the Lake District National Park

H20: Housing in the Lake District National Park

H21: Allocation of Sites within the Lake District National Park for Social Housing

H22: Exception Sites within the Lake District National Park

T29: Safeguarding future transport schemes

T30: Transport Assessments

T31: Travel Plans

T33: Telecommunications

E35:Areas and Features of nature conservation interests other than those of national and international importance

E37: Landscape Character

E38:Historic Environment

R44: Renewable Energy outside the Lake District National Park and AONBs

R45: Renewable Energy in the Lake District National Park and AONBs

R47:Mineral Extraction outside the Lake DistrictNational Park and AONBs

## 15 Replaced and Saved Structure Plan Policies

R48:Mineral Extraction in the Lake DistrictNational Park and AONBs

R49:Waste recovery facilities

R50:Thermal treatment and energy recovery from waste plants

R51:Residual waste and landfill

### JOINT LANCASHIRE STRUCTURE PLAN

| Structure Plan Policy | RSS POLICY |
|---|---|
| Policy 1 | DP1 / RDF1 / CLCR1 |
| Policy 2 | RDF1 / RDF2 / CLCR1 / CLCR2 |
| Policy 3 | W2 |
| Policy 4 | RDF2 |
| Policy 5 | RDF2 |
| Policy 6 | RDF4 / CLCR3 |
| Policy 7 | RT2 |
| Policy 8 | RT1 / RT2 / RT10 |
| Policy 9 | RT1 / RT3 / RT10 |
| Policy 10 | RT1 / RT3 / RT10 |
| Policy 11 | RT7 / RT8 |
| Policy 12 | L4 / DP4 |
| Policy 13 | L3 |
| Policy 14 | W3 |
| Policy 15 | W2 / DP3 / CLCR2 |
| Policy 16 | W5 / L1 / RDF1 / RDF2 |
| Policy 17 | RDF1 / RDF2 / DP4 / DP5 / W3 / W5 |
| Policy 18 | W6 / W7 |
| Policy 19 | W6 / W7 |
| Policy 20 | EM1 / DP7 / CLCR3 |
| Policy 21 | EM1 |
| Policy 22 | EM5 / DP7 |
| Policy 23 | RDF3 / EM6 / W6 / W7 |
| Policy 24 | EM5 |
| Policy 25 | EM17 |
| Policy 26 | EM7 / EM8 / EM9 |
| Policy 27 | EM10 / EM11 / EM12 |
| Policy 28 | EM12 / EM13 |

The following policy  has been extended but has not been replaced by this RSS:

Policy 29 Sites for Gypsy and Traveller Families

### JOINT CHESHIRE STRUCTURE PLAN

The policies listed below are now replaced by relevant policies of the North West of England Regional Spatial Strategy.

| Structure Plan Policy | RSS POLICY |
|---|---|
| R1 | EM1 / DP7 |

| | |
|---|---|
| R2 | EM1 |
| R3 | DP4 / RDF3 |
| R4 | DP1 / DP4 |
| R5 | EM15 / EM17 / EM18 |
| R6 | DP1 / RT7 / EM1 / EM15 |
| R7 | EM7 |
| R8 | EM7 / EM10 / EM11 |
| R9 | EM7 / EM10 / EM11 |
| R10 | EM7 / EM8 |
| R11 | EM7 / EM8 |
| R12 | EM10 / EM12 |
| R13 | EM10 |
| R14 | EM11 / EM12 |
| R15 | EM12 / RDF4 |
| GEN1 | RDF1 / RDF2 / MCR3 / LCR1 / LCR5 / MCR1 / MCR4 |
| GEN2 | RDF4 |
| GEN3 | DP1, DP5, DP7, EM5, EM18 |
| GEN4 | LCR5 |
| GEN6 | EM1 |
| GEN7 | DP1 / DP7 / RT5 / EM5 |
| IND1 | DP1 / W1 / W2 / W3 / W4 |
| IND2 | W3 / W4 |
| IND3 | DP5 / W2 / W3 / RT7 / RT8 |
| IND4 | W1 / W3 / RDF2 |
| IND5 | W3 / RDF2 |
| IND6 | W1 / W2 |
| IND7 | W1 / W2 |
| IND8 | W1 / W2 |
| HOU1 | L4 |
| HOU2 | L1 / DP2 |
| HOU3 | L2 / L4 / L5 |
| HOU4 | RDF2 |
| HOU5 | RDF2 / RDF4 |
| TCR1 | W5 |
| TCR2 | DP5 / W2 / W5 |
| TCR3 | W5 / RDF2 |
| TCR4 | W5 |
| TCR5 | W5 |
| TCR6 | W5 |
| TCR7 | RDF2 |
| T1 | RT1 / RT2 / RT3 / RT9 |
| T2 | RT1 / RT2 / RT3 / RT9 |
| T3 | RT1 / RT2 / RT3 / RT9 |
| T6 | RT8 |
| T11 | RT5 |
| TR1 | DP5 / W7 / L1 / RT2 |
| TR2 | DP1 / L1 / W7 |
| TR5 | RT8 |
| TR6+TR7 | DP2 / L1 / EM3 |

# 15 Replaced and Saved Structure Plan Policies

The following policies have been extended and have not been replaced by this RSS :

GEN5: Jodrell Bank Zone

GEN8: Regional Parks

HOU6: Caravan Sites for Gypsies

T4: Strategic Improvements to Transport Network

T5: Former Railway Infrastructure

T7: Parking

T8: Improvements to rail network

T9: Motorway and truck road schemes

T10: Roadside services

TR3: Visitor Accommodation

TR4: Golf Courses and other extensive outdoor recreation

# Appendix RT

## Appendix RT(a): Regional Public Transport Framework

### Regional Public Transport Corridors and Markets

Public transport corridors defined as "regional" serve two key functions, providing links between the City Regions, sub-regions and regional towns and cities in the North West; and also between the North West and the cities and City Regions within the rest of the UK and beyond in line with the RSS Key Diagram on page 9.

| National Public Transport Corridor | Key Market(s) | Principal Provider(s) |
|---|---|---|
| London & the South East/Birmingham/South Wales/South West – Manchester City Region/Liverpool City Region/Crewe – Chester – North Wales/Central Lancashire City Region /Cumbria/Scotland | Commuter Business Leisure | Rail Express Coach Charter Coach |
| Newcastle City Region/Tees Valley City Region/Leeds City Region/Sheffield City Region – Manchester City Region/Liverpool City Region/Chester – North Wales | Commuter Business Leisure | Rail Express Coach |
| Links to/from ManchesterAirport | Business Leisure | Rail Local Bus Express Coach Airlines |
| **Regional Public Transport Corridor** | | |
| Links to/from Liverpool Airport | Business Leisure | Rail Local Bus Airlines |
| Manchester City Region - Central Lancashire City Region - Cumbria | Commuter Business Leisure | Rail Express Coach Local Bus |
| Liverpool City Region – Central Lancashire City Region | | Rail Express Coach Local Bus |
| Central Lancashire City Region – Leeds City Region | Commuter Business Leisure | Rail |
| West Cumbria – Carlisle – Newcastle City Region | Business Commuter Leisure | Rail Coach |

## Appendix RT (b): North West Hierarchy of Gateways and Interchanges [143]

### International and National Gateways and Interchanges

The North West's international gateways, through which we import and export goods and services, are vital to the region's economic productivity. Fast and reliable access to/from national and international destinations is important for North West businesses and for the tourism industry.

The international and national gateways and interchanges are the most significant, in terms of the amount of passenger and/or freight traffic to international and UK markets. They comprise:

- Manchester Airport
- The Mersey Ports
- The Manchester Ship Canal
- Liverpool John Lennon Airport
- Blackpool Airport
- Manchester Piccadilly Railway Station
- Liverpool Lime Street Railway Station

Regional Gateways and Interchanges

These are gateways and interchanges which have more than sub-regional significance. They comprise:

- Other Central Manchester Railway and Bus Stations
- Other Central Liverpool Railway and Bus Stations
- Preston Railway and Bus Stations
- Crewe Railway Station
- Chester Railway Station
- Warrington Railway and Bus Stations
- Wigan Railway and Bus Stations
- Carlisle Railway Station
- The Port of Heysham
- The Port of Fleetwood

### Criteria for Sub-Regional Interchanges

Local authorities should use the following to define sub-regional interchanges as part of their Sub-Regional and Local Public Transport Framework:

- provide connections between city-regions and sub-regions identified in RSS13 complimentary to those outlined in diagram RT1.1
- provide travel opportunities from the regional towns and cities identified in table 7.1 to the regional interchanges identified above;
- provide opportunities for interchange within or between modes and between identified sub-regional corridors within city-regions/sub regions.

---

143 Please note that interchanges will often serve multiple functions and are categorised according to the highest order services they serve (i.e. Manchester Piccadilly is a long-distance interchange but also provides regional and local travel opportunities).

Local authorities should develop similar criteria to define interchanges at the local level within towns and cities.

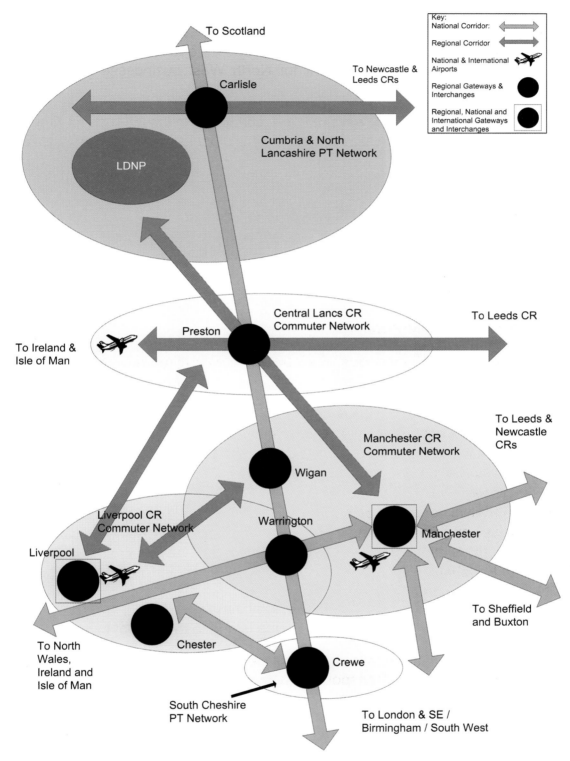

**Diagram 1: Regional Public Transport Schematic**

## Appendix RT (c): Functional Road Hierarchy and Regional Highway Network

The detailed justification for the inclusion of routes in each particular tier can be found in the RSS Technical Annex.

## Routes of Strategic National Importance

These routes have been identified as being of strategic national importance based on satisfying each of the following four criteria as defined by the Department for Transport:

- An average daily traffic flow along the length of the route of more than 60,000 vehicles;
- Link at least two of the top twenty English cities by population, or link one of these cities with an airport / seaport or Wales / Scotland;
- Carry heavy goods vehicle traffic equal to or in excess of 15% as a percentage of all traffic, as an average along the length of the route; and
- Form part of the European Union's Trans-European Road Network (TERN).

They comprise:

- M6/A74(T) North from A500(T) at Junction 16 to Scotland
- M56/A5117(T)/A550(T) West from M60 at Junction 4 to Wales
- M62/M60 East from M57 at Junction 6 to Junction 22 in Yorkshire
- M60 Manchester Outer Ring Road Clockwise from Junctions 1 to 12 & 18 to 1
- A5103(T) North from M56 at Junction 3 to M60 at Junction 5

## Other Routes of National Importance

Together with Routes of Strategic National Importance, these routes form a network the principal function of which is to connect the North West, including its two Core Cities of Liverpool and Manchester and Manchester Airport and the Port of Liverpool, with a range of destinations of UK or international significance. They are in general trunk roads of motorway or all-purpose dual carriageway standard, and include a number of routes which are part of the Trans-European Road Network (TERN). They comprise:

- M53/A55(T) South from M56 at Junction 15 to Wales (TERN)
- M57 North from M62 Tarbock Interchange to M58/A5036(T) at SwitchIsland (TERN)
- M61 North from M60 at Junction 15 to M6 at Junction 30 (TERN)
- A66(T) East from M6 at Junction 40 to the North East
- A69(T) East from M6 at Junction 43 to the North East (TERN)
- A483(T) South from A55(T) near Chester to Wales (TERN)
- A556(T) North from M6 at Junction 19 to M56 at Junctions 7/8
- A5036(T) South West from M57/M58 at Switch Island to the Port of Liverpool (TERN)

These routes are managed and maintained by the Highways Agency on behalf of the Secretary of State for Transport, although the Government intends that decisions on improvements should be taken regionally.

## Routes of Regional Importance

In general, these are key inter-urban routes whose principal function is to link the main population and employment centres as identified in the Spatial Development Framework, including Regeneration Priority Areas and coastal resort towns, major tourist destinations such as the Lake District National Park, and major ports, airports and inter-modal freight terminals, with:

i) routes of strategic national or national importance, or

ii) similar destinations in adjacent regions.

Routes of regional importance are of varying standard and include a number of motorways and all-purpose dual carriageways. Although many are trunk roads, a significant number are, or on de-trunking will become, the responsibility of local authorities. All-purpose routes are included in the Primary Route Network. They comprise:

<u>Trunk Roads</u>

- M53 North from M56 at Junction 15 to Kingsway Tunnel Approach, Wallasey
- M55 West from M6 at Junction 32 to Blackpool
- M58 West from M6 at Junction 26 to M57/A5036(T) at SwitchIsland
- M65 East from M6/A6 at BamberBridge to A56(T) at Junction 8
- M66/A56(T) North from M60/M62 at Junction 18 to M65 at Junction 8
- M67/A57(T)/A628(T) East from M60 at Junction 24 to Derbyshire
- *M602 West from A57/A5063 at Salford to M60/M62 at Junction 12*
- A41(T)/A550(T) South from M53 at Junction 5 to A5117(T) at Woodbank
- A66(T) West from M6 at Junction 40 to Workington
- A585(T) North from M55 at Junction 3 to the Port of Fleetwood
- A590(T) West from M6 at Junction 36 to Barrow-in-Furness
- A595(T) South West from A66(T) at Chapel Brow to CalderBridge
- *A627(M)/A663(T) South from Rochdale and M62 to M60 at Junction 21*

These routes are managed and maintained by the Highways Agency on behalf of the Secretary of State for Transport, although the Government intends that decisions on improvements should be taken regionally.

<u>Local Authority and Other Non-Trunk Roads</u>

- M62/A5080 West from Tarbock Interchange (J6) to A5058 Liverpool Inner Ring Road
- M65/A6068/A56 North East from A56(T) at Junction 8 to Yorkshire
- A6 South East from M60 at Stockport to Derbyshire
- A7 North from M6 at Junction 44 to Scotland
- A34 South from M60 at Junction 3 to Staffordshire
- A49 South from M56 at Junction 10 to Shropshire
- A51/A500 South East from A55(T) at Chester to M6 at Junction 16
- A54/A556 North East from A51 near Chester to M6 at Junction 19
- A65 South East from M6 at Junction 36 to Yorkshire
- A523 South from A6 in Hazel Grove to A536 in Macclesfield
- A536/A34/A534 South West from Macclesfield to M6 at Junction 17
- A537/A50/A5033 West from A523 at Macclesfield to A556 West of Knutsford
- A557 North from M56 at Junction 12 to M62 at Junction 7
- A562/A561 West from A557 in Widnes to Port of Garston
- A570 North West from M58 at Junction 3 to Meols Cop (Southport)
- A575 North from M60 at Junction 13 to A580, Worsley
- A580 East from M57 at Junctions 4/5 to M60 at Junction 14
- A591 North West from A590(T) near Levens to A5074 in Windermere
- A595/A7/A69 North East from A66(T) West of Cockermouth to M6 at Carlisle
- A596 North West from A66(T) to Northside, Workington

- A683 West from M6 at Junction 34 to the Port of Heysham
- A689 East from M6/A74(T) at Junction 44 to A69(T) at Brampton
- A5139 East from M53 at Junction 1 to A554 in Wallasey
- A5300 South from M57/M62 Tarbock Interchange to A562 West of Widnes
- Kingsway Tunnel & Approach Roads, Liverpool & Wallasey [144]

**Routes of Sub-Regional Importance**

Sub-regional highway networks, to be defined in Local Transport Plans, should comprise those routes of more than local importance which are considered to be the most appropriate for through traffic movements serving sub-regional economic and social needs, together with routes considered to function as sub-regional distributors. In defining these networks, relevant environmental factors will need to be taken into consideration. Routes of sub-regional importance should form part of the Primary Route Network and should be available for use by heavy goods vehicles.

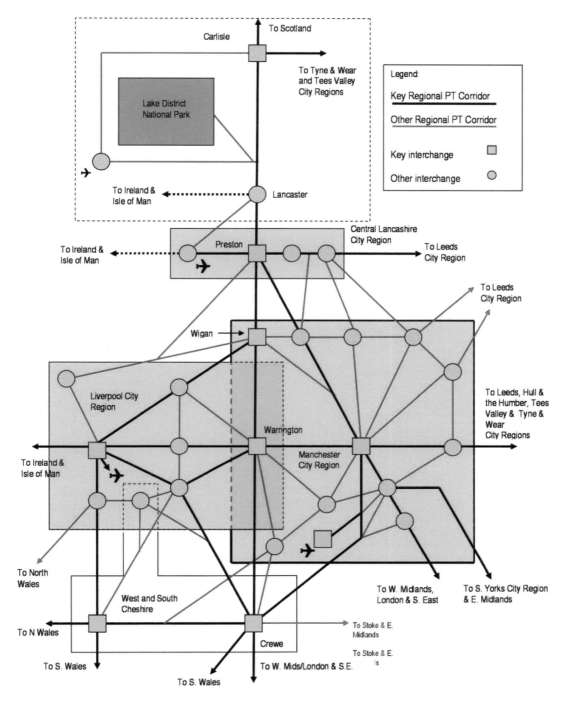

**Diagram 2: Regional Public Transport Framework**

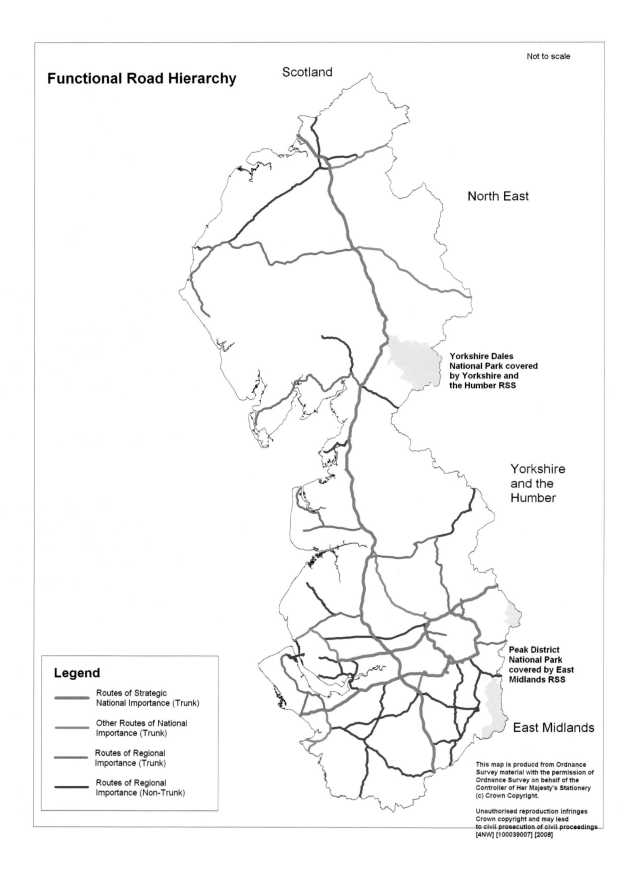

**Functional Road Hierarchy**

Not to scale

Scotland

North East

Yorkshire Dales National Park covered by Yorkshire and the Humber RSS

Yorkshire and the Humber

Peak District National Park covered by East Midlands RSS

East Midlands

**Legend**

Routes of Strategic National Importance (Trunk)

Other Routes of National Importance (Trunk)

Routes of Regional Importance (Trunk)

Routes of Regional Importance (Non-Trunk)

This map is producd from Ordnance Survey material with the permission of Ordnance Survey on behalf of the Controller of Her Majesty's Stationery (c) Crown Copyright.

Unauthorised reproduction infringes Crown copyright and may lead to civil prosecution of civil proceedings [4NW] [100039007] [2008]

**Diagram 3**

## Appendix RT (d): Advice of Developing Parking Strategies and Setting Standards

## 1. National Parking Guidance and Policy

National parking guidance and policy is currently provided in the following three documents and should form the cornerstone of local and regional parking plans and strategies. PS11 recognises that the availability of parking is a major influence on travel choice and that the RSS/RTS has an important role to play in ensuring local parking policies collectively support the wider spatial strategy. A consistent approach to parking should be set out in the RTS to avoid wasteful competition between different locations based around either the availability or cost of parking, to the detriment of sustainable development. Parking policies should be co-ordinated with parking controls and charging set out in local plans.

PPG 3 seeks to increase residential density and improve the quality of housing layouts. One way identified of achieving this objective is to limit parking spaces to an average of 1.5 per dwelling.

PPG13 requires a consistent approach to parking to be set out in RTS that will avoid wasteful competition between locations based around the relative supply or cost of parking. Parking policies should be coordinated with parking control and charging set out in LTPs. Further advice to local authorities on developing and implementing policies on parking is given in Paragraph 51 of PPG13 and advice on maximum parking standards given in Paragraphs 52 to 56 with National Parking Standards set out in Annex D. However PPG13 only provides maximum standards for 7 land uses.

## 2. Development of a Methodology for Setting Parking Standards for New Developments

Parking Standards Framework

The coarse subdivision of locations into 'City Region Urban Areas' and 'Other NW Region Areas', the latter effectively being the remainder of the region outside the city region's urban areas, should be refined to provide better guidance. This can be achieved by introducing additional land use categories whilst also recognising different levels of accessibility which take into account the availability of public transport services and cycling and walking facilities that can vary considerably within a defined location. Authorities should therefore consider developing an analytical approach with a matrix of parking standards for developments that is dependent on:

- Land use and size of development (e.g. developments with less than $500^2$m or greater than $500^2$m or number of bedrooms in house);
- Location (e.g. location in City regions, large towns outside of City Regions, key service centres and other rural centres);
- Level of accessibility (Low, medium or high).

Car parking standards should not exceed the maximum regional standards defined in Policy RT6 and example of good practice of refining land use categories is provided in Table 1 below and authorities are encouraged to establish additional categories relevant to their area.

Appendix RT

### Table 1: Examples of additional land use categories for which baseline standards should be derived.

| Land Use Categories | Sub Categories |
|---|---|
| A1 Shops | Food |
| | Non-Food |
| A2 Financial & Professional Services | |
| A3 Food & Drink | Restaurants, Pubs, Hot Food Takeaways including drive-through |
| B1 Business | B1a & B1b Office (including call centres) & R&D development |
| | B1c Light industry stand alone |
| | Business Parks |
| B2 General Industrial | |
| B8 Storage & Distribution | |
| C1 Hotels, Motels, Boarding Houses | |
| C2 Residential Institutions | Nursing Homes |
| | Training centres and colleges |
| | Halls of residences |
| | Residential schools |
| | Hospitals |
| C3 Dwelling Houses | Single bed housing |
| | Sheltered housing |
| | Family House 2 to 3 bed |
| | Family House 4+ beds |
| D1 Non-Residential Institutions | Medical/health facilities |
| | Crèche/day nurseries/ day centres |
| | Primary & secondary schools |
| | Sixth Form |
| | Further & Higher Education |
| | Training & conference centres |
| | Art galleries, museums and libraries |
| | Public halls & places of worship |
| D2 Assembly and Leisure | Cinemas & concert facilities |
| | Other D2 including leisure (buildings) |
| | Outdoor playing pitches |
| | Stadia |
| Miscellaneous Uses | Cash & Carry Wholesale |
| | Car Sales |
| | Vehicle repair & service stations |
| | Taxi booking offices |
| | Fuel filling station |

*Note : Developed for the Joint Lancashire Structure Plan (Adopted March 2005) by Blackburn with DarwenBC, BlackpoolBC and Lancashire CC.*

Though 'Baseline Standards' represent maxima, this should not automatically mean that all developments should provide parking standards to the highest level. In some circumstances such as densely developed urban core it may not be physically possible to provide the maxima. In others where there is high quality public transport and/or public parking in the vicinity then lower or 'no parking' standards would be appropriate. Where developments have mixed use there may be an opportunity to pursue shared parking arrangements. In all cases the management of retail and leisure development parking must integrate with the overall parking strategy for that centre.

## 3. Accessibility Criteria

Accessibility criteria and scoring schemes could be developed based on the accessibility assessments that authorities have undertaken to inform their LTP submission. For areas where an assessment has not been undertaken or where there is good reason for developing a different methodology, then criteria and scoring schemes could be developed that defines the accessibility to the development in terms of the provision of public transport, walking, cycling, and other facilities. Examples of good practice for commercial/business and residential development criteria and scoring, based on the Joint Lancashire Structure Plan (Adopted March 2005) by Blackburn with Darwen BC, Blackpool BC and Lancashire CC, are provided in Tables 2 and 3.

| Table 2: Examples of accessibility criteria and scoring for commercial and business development | | | |
|---|---|---|---|
| **Access Type** | **Criteria** | **Criteria Measurement** | **Score** |
| Walking | Distance to nearest bus stop from main entrance to building by a direct & safe route | < 200m | 5 |
| | | < 300m | 3 |
| | | < 500m | 1 |
| | | > 500m | 0 |
| | Distance to nearest railway station from main entrance to building by a direct & safe route | < 400m | 3 |
| | | < 1km | 2 |
| | | > 1km | 0 |
| Cycling | Proximity to defined cycle route | < 100m | 3 |
| | | < 500m | 2 |
| | | > 1km | 1 |
| Public Transport | Bus frequency of principal service from nearest bus stop | Urban & Suburban | 5 |
| | | 15 minute or less | 3 |
| | | 30 minute or less | 1 |
| | | > 30 minutes | |
| | | Villages & Rural | 5 |
| | | Hourly or less | 2 |
| | | 2 hourly or less | 1 |

| | | 1 or more per day | |
|---|---|---|---|
| | Number of bus services serving different localities stopping within 200metres of main entrance during operational hours of the site | 4 or more localities served | 5 |
| | | 3 localities served | 3 |
| | | 2 localities served | 2 |
| | | 1 locality served | 1 |
| | Train frequency from nearest station during operational hours of the site | 30 minutes or less | 3 |
| | | 1 hour or less | 2 |
| | | > 1 hour | 1 |
| Other | Travel reduction opportunities | <u>Facilities on site or within 100 metres that reduce the need to travel</u> | 1 |
| | | Food shop/café | 1 |
| | | Newsagent/general store | 1 |
| | | Crèche | 1 |
| | | Bank/ATM | 1 |
| | | Other | |

**Table 3: Example of accessibility criteria and scoring for residential development**

| Access Type | Criteria | Criteria Measurement | Score |
|---|---|---|---|
| Walking distance from centre of site to facilities using a safe direct route. | Distance to nearest bus stop | < 200m | 5 |
| | | < 400m | 3 |
| | | < 500m | 1 |
| | | > 500m | 0 |
| | Distance to nearest railway station | < 400m | 3 |
| | | < 800m | 2 |
| | | < 800m – 1000m | 1 |
| | | > 1km | 0 |

| Table 3: Example of accessibility criteria and scoring for residential development | | | |
|---|---|---|---|
| Access Type | Criteria | Criteria Measurement | Score |
| | Distance to nearest primary school | < 200m | 5 |
| | | < 400m | 3 |
| | | < 600m | 1 |
| | | > 600m | 0 |
| | Distance to nearest food shop | < 200m | 5 |
| | | < 400m | 3 |
| | | < 600m | 1 |
| | | > 600m | 0 |
| Cycling distance from centre of site | Proximity to defined cycle route | < 100m | 3 |
| | | < 500m | 2 |
| | | > 1km | 1 |
| | Distance to nearest secondary school | < 400m | 3 |
| | | < 600m | 2 |
| | | < 1km | 1 |
| | | > 1km | 0 |
| | Distance to nearest town centre | < 1km | 3 |
| | | < 3km | 2 |
| | | < 4km | 1 |
| | Distance to nearest business park or employment concentration | < 1km | 3 |
| | | < 3km | 2 |
| | | < 4km | 1 |
| Public Transport | Bus frequency from nearest stop (Mon-Sat daytime) | Urban / Suburban | 5 |
| | | 15 minutes or less | 3 |
| | | 30 minutes or less | 1 |
| | | > 30 minutes | |
| | | Rural including villages | 5 |

**Table 3: Example of accessibility criteria and scoring for residential development**

| Access Type | Criteria | Criteria Measurement | Score |
|---|---|---|---|
| | | Hourly or less | 3 |
| | | 2 hourly or less | 1 |
| | | 1 or more per day | |
| | Train Frequency from nearest station (Mon-Sat daytime) | 30 minutes or less | 3 |
| | | 30 – 59 minutes | 2 |
| | | Hourly or less frequent | 1 |
| Accessibility to other basic services | GP. Post Office, Library, Bank/ATM and pub. | At least 3 within 400m | 5 |
| | | At least 3 within 800m | 3 |
| | | At least 3 within 1.5km | 1 |
| | Play area or park | < 200m | 5 |
| | | < 400m | 3 |
| | | < 600m | 1 |
| | | > 600m | 0 |

The accessibility level could then be derived from the addition of the scores from the appropriate scheme; examples are given in the table below.

**Table 4: Examples of Accessibility Levels**

| Accessibility Level | Total Score Range | |
|---|---|---|
| | Commercial / Business | Residential |
| High | Above 23 | Above 35 |
| Medium | 16-23 | 20-35 |
| Low | 15 or less | Less than 20 |

Additional criteria could be introduced where they impact on the overall level of accessibility to the development and could include Tramway and LRT systems, guided buses and demand responsive services. Accessibility level ranges should be changed to reflect the additional criteria. The maximum baseline parking standards developed by authorities for their plans and strategies could then be reduced to reflect the 'Accessibility Level' of the development; examples are given in the following table.

**Table 5: Changes to Baseline Standards**

| Accessibility Level | Change to Baseline Standards |
|---|---|
| Low | No change to Baseline levels |
| Medium | Reduce baseline by 5 -15 % |
| High | Reduce baseline by 15 - 35% |

## 4. Parking for cycles and two wheel motorised vehicles (TWMV)

Secure parking facilities should be provided to a minimum standard of 10% of the baseline standards for each category. Where practical, new developments should include showering, changing and other facilities to meet the requirements of users and so encourage less dependence on car use.

## 5. Parking for people with disabilities

The term disability is a broad one. It includes people with physical, sensory or mental impairment and at a conservative estimate, between 12 and 13 per cent of the population have some degree of impairment. Many, though not all, face barriers to movement in the environment. As many people with disabilities rely on the car, either as a driver or passenger, to get about, parking for them must be conveniently located and well signed. The DfT Traffic Advisory Leaflet (TA 05/95) 'Parking for Disabled People' provides guidance on the provision of parking for people with all types of mobility difficulty and so should be an input to an authority's plans and strategies for parking standards. Parking for people with disabilities is the only situation where minimum standards are applicable.

For car parks associated with new employment premises, 6 bays or 3% of the baseline standards should be designated, which ever is the greater. For car parks associated with shopping areas, leisure or recreational facilities and places open to the general public, 5 bays or 5% of the baseline standards should be designated, whichever is the greater. The numbers of designated spaces may need to be greater at health centres, hospitals, hotels and sports stadia or other venues that specialise in accommodating groups of disabled people.

At railway stations where parking facilities are to be introduced or improved then the Strategic Rail Authority (SRA) recommendations should be used as a minimum as set out in Table 6 [145].

| Table 6: Additional parking spaces for disabled people | |
| --- | --- |
| Number of parking spaces | Additional parking spaces for disabled people |
| Fewer than 20 spaces | Minimum of **1** reserved space |
| 20 to 60 spaces | Minimum of **2** reserved spaces |
| 61 to 200 spaces | **6 %** of capacity, with a minimum of 3 reserved spaces |
| Over 200 spaces | **4 %** of capacity, plus **4** reserved spaces |

## 6. Strategic Park and Ride Facilities

Park and Ride (P&R) facilities can help to promote sustainable travel patterns by reducing the distance travelled by car and improving accessibility and attractiveness of the areas that they serve but should not introduce perverse incentives that encourage car use. Plans and strategies should develop P&R facilities that complement other parking and demand management measures

---

145   Further details can be found at:
      http://www.dft.gov.uk/stellent/groups/dft_control/documents/contentservertemplate/dft_index.hcst?n=12543&l=4

and are integrated with public transport provision. Though P&R is primarily for car users, facilities should be provided for disabled people, walkers, cyclists and TWPVs to access and use the services. Annex E of PPG13 and PPS2 provide advice on P&R in the Green Belt.

## 7. Design Considerations

Park and Ride and other parking facilities should be designed to the highest practical standards, reflect good practice in urban design and contribute positively to their surroundings. Large areas of unbroken road surfacing should be avoided by the introduction of high quality hard and soft landscaping. In sensitive locations such as conservation areas, local materials that complement the surroundings should be used in a sympathetic manner. In residential locations the principles of 'Places People and Movement: A Companion Guide to Design Bulletin 32 –Residential Roads and Footpaths' should be used and should be pursued in other appropriate locations. Safety and security is of paramount importance and operators should follow the principles of 'Secured by Design' in order to maximise pedestrian security and minimise vehicle theft [146].

Large vehicle parks and hard standing areas in residential locations can generate substantial volumes of surface water runoff and so the design should incorporate sustainable drainage systems (SuDS) to prevent pollution of the drainage and watercourse systems.

---

146    Details of this initiative can be found at their web site:  http://www.securedbydesign.com

# Glossary

The following glossary aims to assist understanding of this RSS, particularly where it includes technical or unfamiliar terms. It complements the Glossary available online via the Planning Portal. For a comprehensive list of Planning Terms please visit www.planningportal.gov.uk, information specifically about the RSS is available on the North West Regional Leaders Forum website at www.4nw.org.uk. Unless stated, these are not definitive or legal descriptions.

Accessible, Accessibility

The terms 'accessible' and 'accessibility', as used in this document in relation to transport and other services, refer both to proximity of services and to the ability of all sectors of the community to use those services.

Additional Dwellings

These are new or net dwellings that are built and add to or increase the region's existing dwelling stock.

Affordable Housing

Affordable housing includes social rented and intermediate housing, provided to specified eligible households whose needs are not met by the market. Affordable housing should:

Meet the needs of eligible households including availability at a cost low enough for them to afford, determined with regard to local incomes and local house prices.

Include provision for the home to remain at an affordable price for future eligible households or, if these restrictions are lifted, for the subsidy to be recycled for alternative affordable housing provision.

Aggregates

Granular or particulate material which is suitable for use in construction as concrete, mortar, roadstone, asphalt or drainage courses, or for use as constructional fill or railway ballast.

Allocation

The use assigned to a piece of land in a development plan.

Amenity

An element of a location or neighbourhood which helps to make it attractive or enjoyable for residents and visitors.

Anaerobic Digestion

Is a series of processes in which microorganisims break down biodegradable material in the absence of oxygen.

Ancient Woodlands

Areas that have had been covered by trees since at least 1600 AD and cleared only for underwood or timber production. They support species that reflect natural variations in site and soil. Some ancient woodlands are the relics of natural forest that developed after the last glaciation, some 10,000 years ago, and have never been cleared for farming while others may have developed on land last farmed or grazed before medieval times. Ancient woodland is not a statutory designation.

Annual Monitoring Report

Report to be prepared by the Regional Planning Body to cover performance against targets and indicators set out in the policies.

Apportionment (amount of minerals needed)

The splitting of regional guidelines for minerals demand between planning authorities or sub-regions.

Appropriate Assessment

In response to the EU Habitats Directive 92/43/EEC, the purpose of an Appropriate Assessment is to ensure that the protection of the integrity of European sites is a part of the planning process at a regional and local level. The assessment should be confined to the effects on the internationally important habitats and species for which the site is classified.

Areas of Outstanding Natural Beauty (AONBs)

Natural England is responsible for designating AONBs and advising Government and others on how they should be protected and managed. Areas are designated solely for their landscape qualities for the purpose of conserving and enhancing their natural beauty.

Best and Most Versatile Agricultural Land

Land identified by the Agricultural Land Classification system developed by the Ministry of Agriculture, Fisheries and Food (now the Department for Environment, Food and Rural Affairs) as falling within Grades 1, 2 or 3a. The system is based on the extent to which the land's physical or chemical characteristics impose long-term limitations on agricultural use.

Biodiversity

The whole variety of life encompassing all genetic, species and ecosystem variations.

UK Biodiversity Action Plan

The Government plan for the protection and sustainable use of biodiversity. As part of this process national action plans for individual habitats and species have been produced. These give an assessment of the current situation, 10-15 year targets and objectives for management, restoration and expansion of habitats, or maintenance or enhancement of species populations.

Biological Treatment

Any biological process that changes the properties of waste (eg anaerobic digestion, composting).

Biomass

The total mass of living matter within a given unit of environmental area, for example, plant material, vegetation, or agricultural waste used as fuel or an energy source.

Birds Directive

The EU Directive on the Conservation of Wild Birds (79/409/ EEC) which seeks to protect all wild birds and the habitats of listed species, in particular through the designation of special protection areas (SPA).

Brownfield Land

See 'Previously-developed land'.

Business Uses

This is defined by any or all of the following:

an office other than financial and professional services;

research and development of products or processes; or

any light industrial process.

Bus Priority Measures

Measures that allow buses an advantage over other traffic, e.g. bus lanes, preferential treatment at signalled junctions.

Common Agricultural Policy (CAP)

European Union policy, primarily designed to improve productivity in the agriculture sector, but currently under review to shift emphasis away from productivity subsidies.

Catchment Flood Management Plan (CFMP)

A strategic-planning tool through which the Environment Agency will seek to work with other key decision-makers within a river catchment to identify and agree policies for sustainable flood risk management.

City Region

Recognises that large towns and cities act as the focus for jobs, services and facilities for extensive hinterlands. In the North West three have been identified, based on Merseyside, Central Lancashire and Greater Manchester.

Civic Amenity Sites (CA Sites)

Sites, provided by local authorities, to which the public can bring household waste. CA Sites usually provide facilities for recycling, garden waste, and bulky items such as beds and cookers.

Climate Change

A change of climate, which is attributed directly or indirectly to human activity that alters the composition of the global atmosphere and which is in addition to natural climate variability observed over comparable time periods.

## Clusters

Geographic concentrations of interconnected companies, specialized suppliers, service providers, firms in related industries and associated institutions (for example universities, standards agencies and trade associations) in particular fields that compete but also co-operate.

## Coastal Squeeze

A result of rising sea levels, which are in turn a consequence of climate change. Coastal squeeze occurs when rises in sea level affect areas where the landward side of the coast comprises hard infrastructure such as coastal defences, and land uses which depend on these. As sea levels rise the coastal strip becomes narrower and is in effect squeezed between the sea and the land. This can be important to natural processes of erosion and deposition on the coast, and to any sites of nature conservation importance which include the coastal strip.

## Code for Sustainable Homes

A voluntary standard designed to improve the overall sustainability of new homes. It measures the sustainability of a new home against nine categories of sustainable design, rating the 'whole home' as a complete package. The Code uses a 1 to 6 star rating system to communicate the overall sustainability performance of a new home.

## Combined Heat and Power (CHP)

A highly fuel-efficient technology which produces electricity and useable heat from a single generation facility.

## Commercial Waste

Waste arising from premises used wholly or mainly from trade, sport, recreation or entertainment.

## Commitments

All land with extant planning permission or allocated in adopted development plans for development.

## Community Forest

A large area of land transformed into a wooded landscape by a partnership of local authorities, national agencies, and private and voluntary sector organisations to support employment, recreation, education and wildlife.

## Comparison Retailing

The provision of items not purchased on a frequent basis, such as clothing, footwear and household goods.

## Composting

The process that converts biodegradable material (such as garden and kitchen waste), in the presence of oxygen in the air, into stable granular material.

Conservation Areas

Areas designated by the local planning authority which are considered of special architectural or historic interest, the character of which it is desirable to preserve or enhance.

Construction and Demolition Waste

Waste produced from the construction, repair, maintenance and demolition of buildings and structures, including roads. It consists mostly of brick, hardcore and soil.

Contaminated Land

Defined in The Environment Protection Act Part IIA, Section 78A(2) as 'any land which appears to the local authority in whose area it is situated to be in such a condition, by reason of substances in, on or under the land, that:

significant harm is being caused or there is a significant possibility of such harm being caused, or;

pollution of controlled waters is being, or is likely to be, caused.'

Convenience Retailing

The provision of everyday essential items, such as food, drinks and newspapers.

Conversions

Generally means the change of use of a building from a particular use, classified in the use classes order, to another use. Can also mean the sub-division of residential properties into self-contained flats or maisonettes.

Countryside Agency

Government Agency set up on 1 April 1999 by the merger of the Countryside Commission and Rural Development Commission. Following a review, the Natural Environment and Rural Communities Act 2006 merged part of the Countryside Agency with English Nature and parts of the Rural Development Service to form Natural England. The remaining part of the Countryside Agency became the Commission for Rural Communities.

Countryside Character Areas

Areas of distinctive landscape, wildlife and natural features as defined by Natural England.

Cultural Strategy

A strategy which aims to "promote the cultural well-being" of the area it covers.

Demand Responsive Transport

## Glossary

A local transport service tailored to passenger needs with advanced booking on non-fixed routes. Can be provided where conventional bus services do not operate and with the use of GPS (Global Positioning Systems) the most sustainable interlinked routes to key services can be operated.

Derelict Land

Land damaged by industrial or other development that cannot be put to beneficial use without prior treatment.

Designated Areas

Areas which have been awarded a statutory designation because of their special features or qualities, such as National Parks, AONBs, Green Belts, SSSIs and historical and archaeological sites.

Development

Legally defined in Section 55 of the Town and Country Planning Act 1990 as, 'the carrying out of building, engineering, mining or other operations in, on, over or under land, or the making of any material change in the use of any buildings or other land'.

Development Briefs

These provide more detailed information to guide developers on the design and layout constraints and other requirements of individual sites.

Development Plans

Documents setting out a local planning authority's policies and proposals for the development and use of land and buildings in the authority's area. Development Plans consists of the RSS and Development Plan Documents prepared by district councils, unitary authorities, national park and also it include Unitary, Structure, and Local Plans prepared under transitional arrangements.

Development Plan Documents (DPDs)

Development Plan Documents are prepared by local planning authorities and outline the key development goals of the Local Development Framework.

Development Plan Documents include the Core Strategy, site-specific allocations of land and area action plans. There will also be an adopted proposals map, which illustrates the spatial extent of policies that must be prepared and maintained to accompany all DPDs.

All DPDs must be subject to rigorous procedures of community involvement, consultation and independent examination, and adopted after receipt of the inspector's binding report. Once adopted, development control decisions must be made in accordance with them unless material considerations indicate otherwise.

DPDs form an essential part of the Local Development Framework.

Edge-of-centre

For shopping purposes, this is a location within easy walking distance, i.e. 200-300 metres, of the primary shopping area. For leisure and other uses the definition would be based on how far people would be prepared to walk, but is likely to be within 300m of a town centre boundary.

## Employment Land

Land allocated in development plans for business, industrial and storage/distribution uses (B1, B2 and B8 uses).

## Employment Uses

Any undertaking or use of land that provides paid employment.

## Empty Homes Agency

Independent housing charity whose aims are to tackle the problems of empty, wasted and under-used homes.

## Environment Agency

Government agency set up with the aim of protecting or enhancing the environment, taken as a whole in order to play its part in attaining the objective of sustainable development.

## English Heritage

Government body with responsibility for all aspects of protecting and promoting the historic environment.

## Environmental Impact Assessment (EIA) and Environmental Statement

Applicants for certain types of development are required to submit an "environmental statement" accompanying a planning application. This evaluates the likely environmental impacts of the development, together with an assessment of how the severity of the impacts could be reduced.

## Estuary Management Plans

Plans which bring together a wide range of organisations involved in the development, management and use of the coast within a framework that facilitates sustainable estuarine planning.

## EU Structural Funds

The European Union provides Structural Funds for supporting social and economic restructuring across the Union. They account for over a third of the European Union budget. Structural funds are delivered through agreed operational spending programmes and strategies. These comprise the European Regional Development Fund (ERDF), the European Social Fund (ESF) and the European Agricultural Guarantee and Guidance Fund (EAGGF).

## European Spatial Development Perspective (ESDP)

ESDP is a policy framework prepared by Member States of the European Union and the European Commission which aims to achieve a balanced and sustainable development of the European territory.

# Glossary

**Examination in Public (EIP)**

Consideration of public views on a draft development plan or proposed changes to it, held before an independent inspector.

**Factory Outlet Centre**

Group of shops specialising in selling seconds and end-of-line goods at discounted prices.

**Farm Diversification**

The development of a variety of economic activities linked to working farms, designed to support farm income and use surplus land, e.g. forestry, leisure, tourism.

**Flood Plain**

Area of land adjacent to a watercourse, an estuary or the sea over which water flows in the time of flood, or would flow but for the presence of flood defences where they are in place.

**Flood Risk Assessment**

An assessment of the likelihood of flooding in a particular area so that development needs and mitigation measures can be carefully considered.

**Fossil Fuels**

Fuels derived from organic remains.  Fossil fuels result from the incomplete decomposition of organic material and are considered to be non-renewable resources as the rate at which they are consumed exceeds that of their formation.

**Freight Quality Partnerships (FQPs)**

Partnerships between local authorities and the freight industry through which benefits can be gained through working together to share responsibility for, and to understand, distribution problems and issues at both local and regional levels.

**General Conformity**

A process by which Regional Planning Bodies consider whether a Development Plan Document or a major planning application is in "general conformity" with the Regional Spatial Strategy. Also, all other DPDs must conform to a Core Strategy DPD.

**Geodiversity**

The variety of rocks, fossils, minerals, landforms and soils along with the natural processes that shape the landscape.

**Green Belt**

Areas of land where development is particularly tightly controlled.  The purposes of Green Belt are to check the unrestricted sprawl of large built-up areas; to prevent neighbouring towns from merging; to safeguard the countryside from encroachment; to preserve the setting and special character of historic towns; and to aid urban regeneration by encouraging the recycling of derelict and other urban land. The broad extent of the Green Belt is designated in structure plans, with detailed boundaries defined in UDPs/local plans.

## Greenfield Land

Land which has not previously been developed. It can include land which used to have built development on it but where little development remains; land where the development on it is limited by a planning condition which requires the land to be restored to its original pre-development condition when its useful life ends (i.e. a quarry); and land where development has been used for forestry or agriculture and that development is no longer needed for that purpose.

## Greenhouse Gases

Gases which when emitted to the atmosphere can increase the likelihood of global warming. Naturally occurring examples include water vapour, carbon dioxide, methane, nitrous oxide and ozone. Some human activities increase these gases, including fossil fuel combustion within motor vehicles and some power stations.

## Green Infrastructure

The network of green and blue spaces that lies within and between the North West's cities, towns and villages which provides multiple social, economic and environmental benefits.

## Ground Water

Water that exists beneath the earth's surface in underground streams and aquifers.

## Habitats (and Species) Directive

European Council Directive 92/43/EEC on the conservation of natural habitats and of wild flora and fauna which requires EU member states to protect scheduled species and to designate and manage special areas of conservation (SAC).

## Hazardous Waste

Waste which, because of its quantity, concentration or characteristics, poses a present or potential hazard to human health or the environment when improperly treated, stored, transported, dispersed of or otherwise managed.

## Heritage Coast

Designated by Natural England to focus attention on the management of the finest stretches of undeveloped coast where the needs of conservation, pressures of recreation and problems of pollution need to be considered in a co-ordinated way.

## Historic Environment

All aspects of the environment resulting from the interaction between people and places through time, including all surviving physical remains of past human activity, whether visible or buried, and deliberately planted or managed flora.

Homeworking

This relates to the growing practice of working from home, particularly when making use of new information technology and telecommunications, or tele-working, e.g. by freelance workers or employees using electronic links to the office.

Household Waste (or Municipal Waste)

This includes refuse from household collection rounds, waste from street sweeping and public litter bins, bulky items collected from households, waste taken to Civic Amenity sites and waste collection separately for recycling or composting or taken to recycling sites.

Housing Market Renewal Pathfinders

Nine sub-regional projects to tackle low demand and abandonment, administered by a group of local authorities working in partnership and in receipt of funding from the Housing Market Renewal Fund.

Housing Market Restructuring/Renewal

Process of arranging public sector intervention (in partnership with others) to sustain areas in which housing market failure (or low-demand housing) is evident.

Information Communication Technology (ICT)

A phrase used to describe technologies that handle information and aid communication, e.g. telephony and the development of the use of the internet for business, educational, community and domestic purposes.

Index of Multiple Deprivation (IMD)

A ward-level index made up from six indicators (income; employment; health deprivation and disability; education; skills and training; housing; and geographical access to services). IMD can help to identify areas for regeneration.

Industrial Waste

Waste from any factory or industrial process (excluding mines and quarries)

Inert Waste

Waste not undergoing significant physical, chemical or biological changes following disposal, as it does not adversely affect other matter that it may come into contact with, and does not endanger surface or groundwater.

Infilling

The filling of a small gap in an otherwise built-up frontage, e.g. a gap which could be filled by one or two houses.

Informal Open Space

Land provided for the enjoyment and amenity of residents and visitors that does not contain marked out pitches or other facilities.

Infrastructure

Services necessary to serve development, such as roads and footpaths, electricity, water, sewerage.

Integrated Coastal Zone Management (ICZM)

Integrated Coastal Zone management (ICZM) is a process which aims to establish sustainable levels of economic and social activity in our coastal areas while protecting the coastal environment. It brings together all those involved in the development, management and use of the coast within a framework that facilitates the integration of their interests and responsibilities.

Interchange

To transfer between different transport modes to complete a single journey. Transport interchanges are places where the change between modes of travel is easy, for example a bus/rail station or an airport with rail access.

Inward Investment

New business investment or expansion of an existing investment into an area from outside.

INTERREG

European Community initiative to promote trans-national cooperation in spatial planning within the context of the European Spatial Development Perspective.

Issues, Options and Preferred Options

The "pre-submission" consultation stages on Development Plan Documents with the objective of gaining public consensus over proposals ahead of submission to government for independent examination.

Kerbside Recycling

Collection of recyclable or compostable wastes usually from the pavement outside premises, most commonly from households but also from businesses.

Knowledge Based Industry

High technology industries (such as computers and office equipment, and pharmaceuticals) and knowledge based services (for example telecommunications, information technology, finance, insurance, and business services), which are important to economic development.

Land Contamination

Contamination by substances with a potential to harm the environment, from any previous use or activity but which is not considered to constitute Contaminated Land under the Environment Protection Act 1990 Part IIA.

Landfill

The permanent disposal of waste into the ground, by the filling of man-made voids or similar features, or the construction of landforms above ground level (land-raising).

Landscape Character Assessments

A tool to identify and understand the factors that give character to the landscape and to help inform policy and decisions about how the landscape may change in the future.

Listed Buildings

The Secretary of State for Culture, Media and Sport is responsible for compiling the statutory list of buildings of special architectural or historic interest. English Heritage provides expert advice on which buildings meet the criteria for listing, and administer the process. Buildings are graded to indicate their relative importance.

Local Agenda 21 (LA21)

A comprehensive programme of action prepared by local authorities and designed to achieve sustainable development.

Local Development Documents (LDD)

These include Development Plan Documents (which form part of the statutory development plan) and Supplementary Planning Documents (which do not form part of the statutory development plan). LDDs collectively deliver the spatial planning strategy for the local planning authority's area.

Local Development Framework (LDF)

The overarching term given to the collection of Local Development Documents (LDDs) prepared by a local planning authority.

Local Development Schemes

The local planning authority's time-scaled programme for the preparation of Local Development Documents that must be agreed with the Government and reviewed every year.

Local Housing Needs

These apply when employment, social and economic consequences lead people to choose or demonstrate a need to live or remain in a locality where accommodation is not available to them. Categories of need could include:

existing residents who need separate accommodation in the area, e.g. newly married couples, people leaving tied accommodation on retirement

people who need to live in proximity to the key local services they provide

people who have long-standing links with the local community such as the elderly, who need to be close to relatives people with the offer of a job in the locality.

Local Nature Reserves

Sites designated under terms of the National Parks and Access to the Countryside Act 1949 and owned, leased or managed under agreement by local authorities.

Local Planning Authority

Usually the district council, metropolitan district or unitary authority, but for some functions in the shire counties of Cheshire, Cumbria and Lancashire (e.g. structure plans, mineral control and waste disposal), the County Council. The Lake District National Park Authority is the local planning authority for the Lake District National Park.

Local Plan

An old-style development plan usually prepared by district councils, this sets out detailed policies and proposals for the development and use of land. These plans will continue to operate for a time after the commencement of the new development plan system, by virtue of specific transitional provisions, but will in time be replaced by Local Development Frameworks.

Local Strategic Partnership (LSP)

An overall partnership of people that brings together organisations from the public, private, community and voluntary sector within a local authority area, with the objective of improving people's quality of life.

Local Transport Plan (LTP)

A five-year integrated transport strategy, prepared by local authorities in partnership with the community, seeking funding to help provide local transport projects. The plan sets out the resources predicted for delivery of the targets identified in the strategy.

Materials Recycling Facilities (MRF)

A facility for sorting and packing recyclable waste.

Mechanical Biological Treatment (MBT)

A form of waste processing facility that combines a sorting facility with a form of biological treatment such as composting or anaerobic digestion

Minerals Development

The acquisition and working of minerals by surface or underground methods and associated ancillary business, like secondary mineral industries and aggregate handling depots.

Mineral Planning Authority (MPA)

The Planning Authority with responsibility for planning control of minerals development.

Minerals Planning Guidance Note (MPG) / Mineral Planning Statement (MPS)

Prepared and issued by central Government as advice to minerals planning authorities and the minerals industry.

Municipal Solid Waste

Household waste and any other waste collected by a waste collection authority such as municipal parks and gardens waste, beach cleansing waste and waste resulting from the clearance of fly-tipped materials.

Natura 2000

A network of internationally significant wildlife sites within the EU, comprising Special Areas of Conservation (SACs) and Special Protection Areas (SPAs).

National Nature Reserves (NNR)

Areas of land, all SSSIs, of national and sometimes international importance in terms of nature conservation, managed by or for Natural England.

National Parks

National Parks were created by the National Parks and Access to the Countryside Act 1949 for the purpose of:

conserving and enhancing the natural beauty, wildlife and cultural heritage of their area; and

promoting opportunities for the understanding and enjoyment, by the public, of the special qualities of those areas.

National Park Authorities also have the duty to foster the economic and social well-being of communities within the Park. They additionally act as the local planning authority and joint structure plan authority for the areas they administer.

The North West contains the Lake District National Park in its entirety and a part of two others, the Yorkshire Dales and Peak District (these are, for strategic planning purposes, covered respectively by the Regional Spatial Strategy for Yorkshire and the Humber and the East Midlands.)

Natural England

Government advisors on nature conservation, Natural England's objectives are to seek conservation and enhancement of the natural environment, for its intrinsic value, the wellbeing and enjoyment of people and the economic prosperity that it brings.

Nature Conservation

The protection, management and promotion of wildlife habitat for the benefit of wild species, as well as the communities that use and enjoy them.

Neighbourhood Renewal Strategy

A national strategy setting out the Government's vision for narrowing the gap between deprived neighbourhoods and the rest of the country so that within 10 to 20 years, no-one should be seriously disadvantaged by where they live.

New Approach to Appraisal (NATA)

Methodology introduced in the Government White Paper A New Deal for Transport, used in appraising major transport improvements. Details of the methodology are set out in "Guidance on the Methodology for Multi-Modal Studies".

Non-Fossil Fuels

Sources of energy not derived from the combustion of fossil fuels. Examples include renewable energy resources such as wind or hydroelectric (water) power.

North European Trade Axis (NETA)

Transnational spatial planning across Ireland, Northern England, Netherlands and Germany.

Northern Way

A cross-regional strategy created by the three Northern Regional Development Agencies (RDAs); North East, North West and Yorkshire and Humberside and their partners in response to the ODPM's 'Sustainable Communities Plan' progress report 'Making it Happen: the Northern Way', the purpose of which is to create a step-change in economic growth across the North of England.

North West Sustainable Energy Strategy

The North West Sustainable Energy Strategy sets out clearly the energy challenge that faces the North West.It demonstrates how different sectors across the region can act to address this challenge head on, whilst achieving wider economic, social and environmental objectives. Specific guidance is offered to local authorities, the private sector, and the construction industry. It also shows clearly the simple but important steps that individuals living and working in the region can take to use energy more efficiently, whilst at the same time saving money through lower energy bills.

Network Rail

Company responsible for the management of the rail network including stations.

Objectives 1 & 2

The European Union has a number of major policies in place with a strong regional perspective. These objectives form part of its Structural Funds programme, which is directed at areas affected by industrial decline. Merseyside is eligible for Objective 1 funding and other parts of the North West are included under Objective 2.

Open Countryside

That part of the Region outside towns and villages.

Open Space

All space of public value, including not just land, but also areas of water such as rivers, canals, lakes and reservoirs, which can offer opportunities for sport and recreation. They can also act as a visual amenity and a haven for wildlife.

Out-of-centre

A location that is clearly separate from a town centre but not necessarily outside the urban area.

Park-and-Ride

Long stay parking areas at the edge of built-up areas linked to the city or town centre by frequent bus or other public transport services.

Participatory Budgeting

A set of tools to empower people in their communities. Participatory budgeting engages people in taking decisions on the spending priorities for a defined public budget in their local area. This means engaging residents and community groups to discuss spending priorities, make spending proposals, and voting on them, as well giving local people a role in the scrutiny and monitoring of the process.

Passenger Transport Authority

An independent joint board, responsible for overseeing the coordination of public transport through the formulation of passenger transport policies. Established under the Local Government Act 1985. PTAs obtain the majority of funding through a levy on each of their constituent metropolitan district councils.

Phasing or Phased Development

The phasing of development into manageable parts. For example, an annual rate of housing release for large development that may need to be controlled so as to avoid destabilising housing markets and causing low demand.

Plan, Monitor and Manage (PMM)

Approach to housing provision involving: Plan for an overall annual rate and distribution of housing, Monitor the proposed provision against targets and indicators, Manage the process.

Plan-led System

The principle that decisions upon planning applications should be made in accordance with adopted development plans (and DPDs), unless there are other material considerations that may indicate otherwise.

Planning and Compulsory Purchase Act 2004

Government legislation bringing a new approach to development planning, control, compulsory purchase and procedure. The Act updates elements of the 1990 Town & Country Planning Act.

Planning Obligations

Legal agreements which ensure certain planning issues related to the development are undertaken.  Also known as Section 106 agreements.

Planning Policy Guidance Notes (PPG) / Planning Policy Statements (PPS)

Documents issued by the CLG setting out the Government's policies on different aspects of planning.  They should be taken into account by regional planning bodies and local planning authorities in preparing Regional Spatial Strategy and Local Development Frameworks and may also be material to decisions on individual planning applications and appeals.

Previously-developed Land

Defined in Annex B of PPS3 as:

'Previously-developed land is that which is or was occupied by a permanent structure, including the curtilage of the developed land and any associated fixed surface infrastructure."

The definition includes defence buildings, but excludes:

Land that is or has been occupied by agricultural or forestry buildings.

Land that has been developed for minerals extraction or waste disposal by landfill purposes where provision for restoration has been made through development control procedures.

Land in built up areas such as parks, recreation grounds and allotments, which, although it may feature paths, pavilions and other buildings, has not been previously developed.

Land that was previously-developed but where the remains of the permanent structure or fixed surface structure have blended into the landscape in the process of time (to the extent that it can reasonably be considered as part of  the natural surroundings).

There is no presumption that land that is previously developed is necessarily suitable for housing development nor that the whole of the curtilage should be developed.

Primary Aggregates

Naturally occurring sand, gravel and crushed rock used for construction purposes.

Primary Route Network (PRN)

The PRN was first established in the mid 1960s, and in conjunction with motorways, provides a national network for long distance traffic movements throughout Great Britain.  It consists of all-purpose trunk roads together with the more important principal ('A' Class) roads for which local highway authorities are responsible.  Although not a road classification as such, Primary Routes are designated by the Secretary of State and are required to be open to all classes of traffic without restriction.  The PRN is identifiable by green background direction signs.

Public Open Space

Space, designated by a Council, where public access may or may not be formally established, but which fulfils or can fulfil a recreational or non-recreational role (for example, amenity, ecological, educational, social or cultural usages).

Ramsar Sites

Designated by the UK Government under the Ramsar Convention to protect wetlands that are of international importance, particularly as waterfowl habitats. All Ramsar sites are also SSSIs.

Recycling

The reprocessing of wastes, either into the same material or a different one.

Regional Aggregates Working Party (RAWP)

Partnership of members of Mineral Planning Authorities, Aggregates Industry and Government, set up to prepare guidelines on the provision of aggregates in the region.

Regional Economic Strategy (RES)

The North West Development Agency's (NWDA) Regional Strategy is referred to in the text of this RSS as the 'Regional Economic Strategy' to avoid confusion with other regional strategies which may be relevant to development plan preparation.

Regional Flood Risk Appraisal (RFRA)

A technical document that accompanies the RSS to provide a broad regional understanding of flood risk. The content of the RFRA is based on guidance set out in Planning Policy Statement 25 (PPS25).

Regional Funding Allocations

The process through which the Government announces how much funding it intends making available to each of the English regions for certain types of projects over several years, including on housing and transport. Under this process each region advises Government as to which particular projects in their region should be given priority for receiving this funding.

Regional Housing Strategy

Prioritising the needs of the region (by location and/or types of expenditure) to allow decisions to be taken on how housing resources should be allocated within the region.

Regional Planning Body (RPB)

The institution responsible for monitoring and preparing draft revisions to the RSS. In the North West of England the Regional Planning Body is the North West Regional Leaders Forum (4NW).

Regional Transport Strategy

Produced by the RPB, informing local transport plans, and providing a strategic overview of transport strategies and investment priorities. The RTS is an integral part of the RSS.

Regionally Important Geological/Geomorphological Sites (RIGS)

Non-statutory sites recognised by Natural England and local authorities as of regional importance.

Regional Technical Advisory Body (RTAB)

Advise the Regional Planning Body on waste management and disposal issues.

Renewable Energy

The generation of electricity from sources that occur naturally and repeatedly in the environment, i.e. from the sun, wind, oceans and the fall of water. Plant material is an important source of renewable energy and combustible or digestible industrial, agricultural and domestic waste materials are also normally categorised as renewable sources.

Residual Waste

Waste remaining after materials for reuse recycling and composting have been removed.

Retail Uses

Defined as Shops (A1), Professional and Financial Services (A2), Restaurants and Cafes (A3), Drinking Establishments (A4) and Hot Food Takeaways (A5).

River Corridor

Land which has visual, physical or ecological links to a watercourse and which is dependent on the quality or level of the water it contains.

Rural area

An area containing open countryside and villages.

Rural Diversification

The expansion, enlargement or variation of the range of products or fields of operation of a rural business (branching out from traditional farming activities, for example new income generating enterprise like renewable energy, tourism and food processing).

Saved Policies/Saved Plans

Policies within Unitary Development Plans, Local Plans and Structure Plans that are saved for a time period during the production of replacement Local Development Documents.

Scheduled Ancient Monuments

Archaeological sites, monuments or buried remains of national importance, designated by the Secretary of State for Culture, Media and Sport.

Secondary Aggregates

Includes by-product waste, synthetic materials and soft rock used with or without processing as a secondary aggregate.

Semi-natural Habitats

Habitats modified by human activity but containing native wildlife species.

Semi-natural Woodlands

Areas of woodland that do not obviously originate from planting.

Settlements

Towns and villages where basic services are provided. This definition does not include isolated groups of buildings.

Shoreline Management Plans

Non-statutory plans prepared by coastal defence authorities (the Environment Agency and maritime local authorities) which set out a strategy for sustainable coastal defence within coastal sediment cells.

Single Regional Strategy

Subject to legislation, under the sub-national review and planning reform a new Single Regional Strategy will be prepared by the Regional Development Agency integrating previous coverage of the Regional Spatial Strategy and Regional Economic Strategy.

Sites of Special Scientific Interest (SSSI)

A site notified under the Wildlife and Countryside Act (1981) and designated by English Nature as being of special value for nature conservation or geological or physiographic interest and represents the best examples of the nation's heritage of wildlife habitats, geological features and landforms.

Social Inclusion

Positive action taken to include all sectors of society in planning and other decision-making.

Spatial Planning

Spatial planning goes beyond traditional land use planning to bring together and integrate policies for the development and use of land with other policies and programmes which influence the nature of places and how they function.

This will include policies which can impact on land use by influencing the demands on, or needs for, development, but which are not capable of being delivered solely or mainly through the granting or refusal of planning permission and which may be implemented by other means.

Special Area of Conservation (SAC)

Designated by the UK Government under the European Community Directive on the Conservation of Natural Habitats and of Wild Fauna and Flora. SACs are designated to protect internationally important natural habitats and species listed in Annex 1 and 2 of the Directive. All SACs are SSSIs and, in combination with special protection areas (SPA), these sites contribute to the Natura 2000 network.

Special Protection Area (SPA)

Areas designated by the UK Government under the European Community Directive on the Conservation of Wild Birds to safeguard the habitats of birds, particulary migrating species. All SPAs are also SSSIs. In combination with special areas of conservation (SAC), these sites contribute to the Natura 2000 network.

Statutory Undertakers/Statutory Utilities

These provide essential services such as gas, electricity, water or telecommunications.

Strategic Housing Land Availability Assessment (SHLAA)

Assessments carried out by local authorities which support the delivery of sufficient land for housing to meet the community's need for more homes. These assessments are required by national planning policy, set out in Planning Policy Statement 3: Housing (PPS3).

Strategic Housing Market Assessment (SHMA)

Assessments of housing need and demand carried out by local authorities and regional bodies which inform the housing mix and requirement policies of local development documents and regional strategies, as set out in Planning Policy Statement 3: Housing (PPS3).

Structural Funds

European Union funding allocated to reduce economic disparities within the EU and address the impact of structural change.

Structure Plan

Development plan which sets out strategic planning polices for a particular shire county and forms the basis for detailed policies in local plans.

Sub-regional Partnership

A sub-regional strategic body directing, influencing and co-ordinating a range of economic development and regeneration activities often made up of key private, public and other interests.

Sustainability Appraisal/Strategic Environmental Appraisal

Appraisal of plans, strategies and proposals to test them against the four broad objectives set out in the Government's sustainable development strategy "Securing the Future" published in 2005 and the aims of the Regional Sustainable Development Framework- Action for Sustainability (AFS).

Sustainable Development

The most commonly used definition is that of the 1987 World Commission on Environment and Development, the Brundtland Commission: 'development which meets the needs of the present without compromising the ability of future generations to meet their own needs'.

Sustainable Drainage Systems (SuDS)

# Glossary

A range of techniques used to control surface water run-off as close as possible to its origin before it enters a watercourse. They are designed to improve the rate and manner of absorption by water of hard and soft surfaces, in order to reduce the total amount, flow and rate of surface water that runs directly to rivers through stormwater systems.

## Traffic Management

Measures to control the volume and speed of traffic and assist road safety.

## Tranquil Areas

Areas sufficiently remote from visual or audible intrusion from development or traffic to be considered unspoilt by urban influences.

## Travel Plan

Help people to assess and simplify their travel patterns and behaviours and then provide a package.

## Trunk Road

A road for which the Secretary of State for Transport is legally responsible. The Highways Agency is responsible for discharging the Secretary of State's duties, including the planning, funding and execution of maintenance and other works.

## Unfit Housing

Housing which does not meet legislative standards for human habitation.

## Unitary Development Plan (UDP)

A plan prepared by a metropolitan district and some unitary local authorities which contains policies equivalent to those in both a structure plan and local plan. In the North West the districts of Bolton, Bury, Halton, Knowsley, Liverpool, Manchester, Oldham, Rochdale, St Helens, Salford, Sefton, Stockport, Tameside, Trafford, Warrington, Wigan and Wirral are all responsible for preparing a UDP for their area. UDPs will continue to operate for a time after the commencement of the new development plan system, by virtue of specific transitional provisions, but will in time be replaced by Local Development Frameworks.

## Urban Open Spaces

Parks, play areas, sports fields, commons, allotments, green corridors alongside rivers, canals and railway lines and other open areas that are vital to the cultural, aesthetic, and historic heritage of urban life.

## Urban Potential Study (UPS)

A study produced for a local planning authority area examining the potential capacity of urban areas to accommodate extra housing on new or redeveloped sites at various densities, or by the conversion of existing buildings.

## Urban Regeneration

Making an urban area develop or grow strong again through means such as job creation and environmental renewal.

Village

A group of houses in a predominantly rural area with some community facilities and employment activity, but smaller than a town.

Vitality and Viability

The factors by which the economic health of a town centre can be measured.

Waste Developments

The disposal and treatment of refuse or waste material by landfilling or other methods; the disposal of mineral waste; the development of buildings, engineering processes or other operations to deal with waste; and plants and facilities for waste water treatment and disposal are all classified as waste developments.

Waste Hierarchy

A framework for securing a sustainable approach to waste management as defined in Annex C of PPS 10.

Waste Planning Authority (WPA)

The local authority responsible for waste development planning and control. They are unitary authorities, including National Park Authorities, and county councils in non-unitary areas.

Water Framework Directive

EC legislation which requires all inland coastal water to reach 'good status' by 2015. It establishes a river basin district structure within which demanding environmental objectives will be set, including ecological targets for surface waters.

Wind Farms

A group of wind turbines located in areas exposed to wind. A wind farm may vary in terms of the number and size of turbines.

Windfall Site

A site not specifically allocated for development in a local plan, UDP or DPD but which becomes available for development or is granted planning permission during the lifetime of a plan.

World Heritage Site

A site of cultural or natural heritage considered to be of outstanding universal value and worthy of special protection, designated by UNESCO.